E
Rap

Eminem and Rap, Poetry, Race

Essays

Edited by SCOTT F. PARKER

Foreword by TALIB KWELI

McFarland & Company, Inc., Publishers

Jefferson, North Carolina

"Race ... and Other Four Letter Words: Eminem and the Cultural Politics of Authenticity" by Gilbert B. Rodman, © 2006, from *Popular Communication* vol. 4, issue 2, pp. 95–121. Reproduced by permission of Taylor & Francis Group LLC (http://tandfonline.com).

LIBRARY OF CONGRESS CATALOGUING-IN-PUBLICATION DATA

Eminem and rap, poetry, race: essays / edited by Scott F. Parker ; foreword by Talib Kweli.
    p.   cm.
    Includes bibliographical references and index.

    ISBN 978-0-7864-7675-6 (softcover : acid free paper) ∞
    ISBN 978-1-4766-1864-7 (ebook)

    1. Eminem, 1972–   —Criticism and interpretation.   2. Rap (Music)—History and criticism.   3. Music and race.   I. Parker, Scott F., editor
    ML420.E56E45 2014
    782.421649092—dc23   2014037552

BRITISH LIBRARY CATALOGUING DATA ARE AVAILABLE

On the cover: Eminem in the 2002 film *8 Mile* (Universal Pictures/Photofest)

Printed in the United States of America

McFarland & Company, Inc., Publishers
  Box 611, Jefferson, North Carolina 28640
   www.mcfarlandpub.com

Acknowledgments

In addition to the contributors, who gave generously of their time and energy to this volume, I'd like to thank Nicole Hodges Persley, Henry Louis Gates, Jr., Andrew DuBois, and Dennis Dennehy for their suggestions regarding the project. And finally big thanks to Wizard S. Newton and SiMiMiN for their important feedback on the introduction.

Table of Contents

Foreword

Talib Kweli

I was on a dollar van on Flatbush Avenue the first time I heard Eminem spit a bar. There was a cassette with the words "The Slim Shady EP" written on it that I received at some music industry function floating around the bottom of my book bag. It was the only thing I had to listen to on my ride home. I was immediately shocked and awed by the casual way in which he referenced drugs and violence. Songs like "Murder, Murder" and "Just Don't Give a Fuck" went against my sensibilities. I literally could not believe what I was hearing. Shock rap had been done before, but something about this felt more … honest.

When I got to the crib I immediately called my good friend JuJu over to play him *The Slim Shady EP*. As we rewound the punchlines over and over again in disbelief, we discovered something unexpected; this white boy could spit, and he was spitting it better than most of the MCs we were listening to. At the time I was fully immersed in underground battle-rap culture. My crew and I were among a group of MCs who would challenge rappers in the street and pray for the day we would be able to do the same on the national stage. Little did I know Slim Shady would soon be a part of this group.

There were many respected white rappers before Eminem: The Beastie Boys, Everlast, Serch and Pete Nice of 3rd Bass, to name a few. But none of them possessed Em's lyrical prowess, and that is why the white rapper was never truly taken seriously until Eminem arrived. Serch and Everlast were battle ready, lyrical MCs, and the Beastie Boys, hip hop's first platinum act, were certified down-by-law superstars, but Em entered during hip hop's first internet era. Thanks to chat rooms and early online communities like 88hiphop.com, street battles and their accompanying legends were being shared across the globe as soon as they went down. All of a sudden hip hop fans in London and Capetown could listen to the *Stretch Armstrong and*

Bobbito Show online rather than wait months for tapes to make it across the ocean. New York–based Fat Beats Records could now open stores in Los Angeles, Amsterdam, and Tokyo. All of this meant you no longer needed to be signed to a label to achieve global fame as an MC. The stakes were higher, and the battles became more vicious.

The film *8 Mile* attempted to document Eminem's early days in Detroit, learning how to MC. I witnessed Em battle, mostly impromptu, all over New York City. By this time he had made a name for himself in the D, and was now set on conquering hip hop's birthplace. I saw Eminem get dissed badly over and over again, mostly for being white, and then come back and obliterate his competition with the next rhyme. He did it every time. There were a few on his level, but nobody better. From Wetlands to Tramps to SOB's, showcase after showcase, New York City was watching Eminem come into his own. This was also around the time the difference between Eminem and Slim Shady was becoming less apparent.

By the time Eminem was booked to do a show with my group, Black Star, in Vermont in the winter of 1999, he had signed to Dr. Dre's Aftermath Records. The month of the concert, *Rolling Stone* put him on the cover— with a new blonde 'do. To be honest, my first thought was that *Rolling Stone* would've never put a brand-new hip hop artist who had never released an album on their cover if that artist was black, regardless of buzz. I still feel like that, but that is not Eminem's fault. Eminem worked hard for his recognition. However when Em took the stage that night in Vermont and all those white boys went crazy, I got it. White America had its first authentic spitter. THAT was the story.

If I ever doubted that Eminem fully understood white privilege and the role he plays in it, those doubts were erased when he compares himself to Elvis Presley when he spits in the song "Without Me" that both of them used "black music so selfishly" to make piles of money. That bar was brilliant; he was critiquing his criticizers and acknowledging the validity of their critique in the same breath. It was the same tactic he used when he brought Elton John on stage with him to perform "Stan" with him at the Grammys during the height of the "Eminem is a gay basher" fury. Em has never apologized for who he is, who he was, or where he comes from, but he has always exhibited growth and creativity when it comes to dealing with these issues. "White America" is one of his most honest songs, and it actually can be considered conscious hip hop. Macklemore, who had to have been inspired by Em's success, took this idea a step further in his song "White Privilege."

There is an elite group of technical rhymers that I look at as the master class of flow and rhyme. It contains superstars like Jay-Z and Nas, and lesser-known but no less incredible artists like Jean Grae and Pharaohe

Monch. Eminem is the heart of this group of spitters. In order for him to be accepted and respected when he got in the game, he had to be better than damn near everybody. As he grows, his subject matter and interest will undoubtedly change, as it should. But his dedication to technique will remain the same regardless of what he raps about. I knew this to be true when I took my daughter to the BET Awards a few years ago. She was eleven at the time and she really knew nothing about Em as an artist. But when he took that stage and rocked "Not Afraid" with a gospel choir, she turned to me and said, "Daddy, he rapped better than everybody." I responded, "Yes, babe. That's Eminem."

Talib Kweli is the acclaimed rapper whose work includes *Mos Def and Talib Kweli Are Black Star* and (with Hi-Tek as Reflection Eternal) *Train of Thought* and *Revolutions per Minute*. Among his solo albums are *Gravitas*, *Prisoner of Conscious*, *The Beautiful Struggle*, and *Quality*.

Introduction

Scott F. Parker

God sent me to piss the world off.
—Slim Shady

It is easy to mark the start of Eminem as cultural phenomenon and social boogeyman with the MTV debut of "My Name Is" and harder to identify exactly when his threat was neutralized as he transitioned via familiarity fully into Eminem as seemingly harmless consumer product and cultural given.[1] By the Elton John Grammy performance (February 2001) it was under way; and by the *8 Mile* premiere (November 2002), driven by unprecedented sales figures, it had occurred; but appreciate if you can't recall that from approximately 1999 to 2001 the turmoil and upheaval surrounding Eminem sounded louder than anything Kanye West has said since.

And harder still than isolating historical moments is discerning the quickly changing present, to say nothing of presuming a singular future. At the time of this writing, a new Eminem album is anticipated within the year. Any attempt to grab hold of the catalogue and make the work stand still long enough for claims to be made and books to be bound is to confront head-on the rapid turnover of hip-hop's vibrant culture (corporate-backed or otherwise). The essays in this book—Gilbert B. Rodman's 2006 "Race ... and Other Four Letter Words" most explicitly—are portraits of their moments as much as of their subjects.[2]

The same can be said of Norman Mailer's 1957 essay "White Negro: Superficial Reflections on the Hipster," which when editing a book on Eminem one feels duty-bound to read. In it, Mailer writes, "It is impossible to conceive a new philosophy until one creates a new language, but a new popular language (while it must implicitly contain a new philosophy) does not necessarily present its philosophy overtly."[3] Rap music (and hip-hop

5

culture more broadly) has been erasing and rewriting language for thirty-plus years, and for the latter half of that era Eminem has been one of its most creative philosophers.

And with that humble claim I submit this volume's only working assumption, the implied consequence of which (and the only unifying motivation for the book) being that Eminem's body of work is therefore worthy of thoughtful and impassioned criticism.

As a reader of introductions I'm not overly interested in previews of the book's essays—they're right there waiting for me to get to them.[4] Rather, I'm concerned with a book's editorial stance or agenda. As the author of this introduction the same goes, so a note on how these particular essays came to compose this book: I solicited writers and academics who I knew have written well about Eminem and/or hip hop, hoping for a wide range of approaches, including philosophy, sociology, musicology, linguistics, and so on. Receiving a number of recommendations, I was able to attract the variety of voices I sought and am happy to include here. What I'm attempting to describe for you here is a democratic approach to editing, but of course I have my own assessments of Eminem, some of which you'll encounter below. One of my goals has been to contain my own biases as much as possible to the introduction and to let contributors' conflicting positions stand for themselves. But while there is no cohesive take on Eminem herein, several consistent patterns do emerge, among them: admiration for the rapper's complication of racial stereotypes; consternation over the racialized response to him; appreciation for the sophisticated use of persona, complexity of raps, and overall attention to craft. These common themes hold the core of the book together such that the divergent angles of approach and response can essay freely.

With the remainder of this introduction I'd like to set the context in which the essays occur and along the way explicate from my own reading of Eminem.

To start, what even is rap? Davey D defines rap today as simply "saying rhymes to the beat of music."[5] While we could argue that raps needn't rhyme and may be said sometimes *over* or *against* the beat, this definition's Venn diagram overlaps the majority of rap and successfully describes its necessary components: beats and voice, both of which Eminem is a devoted student and practitioner of. Ben Hoerster traces the increasingly prominent place production has taken in Eminem's career in his essay, "Beats by Em." But as accomplished as Eminem is as a producer, it's for his voice that he's best known, *voice* here including all aspects of performative speech, and it's his voice, in its many facets, that is the focus of most of the essays gathered here. Aaron Apps, for example, considers Eminem as poet; Darin Flynn examines

Eminem's language in socio- and psycholinguistic terms; and E Martin Nolan explores some of the many ambiguities opened up by Eminem's texts.

If beat and voice are the necessary components for rap, an afternoon spent browsing YouTube will demonstrate that they're not sufficient. What makes rap *music* is the rapper's flow, which penetrates the listener long before the poetry does. In *Book of Rhymes* Adam Bradley defines flow as "the song the rapper's speech sings,"[6] which suggests where we might begin to assess rapper as musician.

Chuck Klosterman makes the point in *Sex, Drugs, and Cocoa Puffs* that Eminem "enunciates better than any rapper who ever lived."[7] If the speech is so clear, it would seem to follow that the song is too. But Eminem's clarity (and relative lack of coding) have prevented mainstream audiences from hearing what his songs, like most rap songs, are primarily about: themselves. Similar to Wittgenstein's claim that "the meaning of a word is its use in the language," the meaning of *a* rap is *the* rap itself (one's own *rap*). Tricia Rose writes in her seminal *Black Noise* that "it is not just what you say, it is where you say it, how others react to it, and whether you have the power to command access to public space."[8] It's foremost a performance produced by and contained in flow, which simultaneously produces through performance the speaking subject. The appeal of an artist—and a rapper especially—is his way of being in the world: the style his flow represents. In Eminem's case, the style's had traction.

"If effects like these had causes," Greil Marcus once wrote about Bob Dylan's genius, "then there would be people doing the same on every corner." While the same could be said of Eminem, the circumstances from which he emerged were nevertheless crucial forces in shaping the possibility of his particular becoming. Genius is never *sui generis.* It depends on a confluence of forces, some environmental (proximity to black culture and hip hop, listening to rap under his uncle's influence), some natural (ear for sound, playful sense of rhythm, dexterous tongue, etc.), some volitional (dedication, passion), and then some accidental. *The Slim Shady EP* finding its way to Dr. Dre is a prime example of opportunity following hard work, but Eminem is just as lucky he didn't become known for *Infinite* in 1996 when he was aspiring to Nas's style rather than his own. It was after *Infinite* that at the behest of Proof, Eminem conceived the Slim Shady alter-ego (and is said to have written the EP in two weeks) that would allow for his creative leap toward more urgent and compelling music. Before "My Name Is" and worldwide fame, Eminem reflected on his career: "I've been doing this for 10 years. I'm not making any money. I'm making pizzas."[9] The desperation and fed-up-ness of that statement is manifest on *The Slim Shady LP,* which gives us an MC with nothing to lose. In a review of *Detroit: An American*

Autopsy for the *New York Times*, Paul Clemens writes, "What's the point of being from Detroit if you don't know the world's going to break your heart?"[10] Eminem would at least appreciate the sentiment.

The broad strokes of Eminem biography relate to luck and success in at least one other respect. After growing through the influence of Nas, Tupac, and others, after hitting artistic rock bottom, after eventually developing a unique approach to rap—Eminem didn't just "make it," he became the best-selling artist of the twenty-first century. And if it took a confluence of forces to beget talent, what confluence begat success? One does not necessarily follow from the other. The version of events Eminem offers on "White America" is mostly right: with Dre's endorsement Eminem gained the credibility he needed to be accepted by a mainstream white audience that had learned to love hip hop. And if money talks it swears that whether they knew it or not the white audience was waiting for one of "their own" to be worthy of their fanaticism. The timing of his ascendency is important, too, coming as it did in the late '90s just before the internet decentralized media distribution. CD sales peaked in those years; MTV still played videos at least part of the day. Without any of these factors we wouldn't have Eminem as we've come to know him.

Another factor in Eminem's unprecedented success might be his function as a confessional poet. Traditionally, much of the best rap has taken the form of real or imagined witness narratives that speak *of* and *for* but no longer just *to* groups of people the speaker encounters in daily life. When Eminem blew up, though, especially on *The Marshall Mathers LP* and *The Eminem Show*, he turned his attention to autobiographical (and often psychic) detail, making "Eminem" the show. Through the specificity of his emoting, his audience came to feel like it knew the "real" Eminem and offered sympathetic ears to his complaints. Endearing as that aspect of his work has proven, he was aware of how tiresome the tough childhood story could get when he parodied it on *Encore*'s "Evil Deeds" and again years later on *Relapse*'s "My Mom." Condensing significantly here, if Eminem's confessions were important factors in the success of his first three major-label albums but the confessions have grown stale, then he faces a material challenge. Without regular infusions of new content, the autobiographer who writes himself into existence risks writing himself right back out of it. The recovery angle of *Recovery* gives Eminem another supply of archetypally American autobiographical material, but it's not toward confession that the heart of his recent work seems to be leading but toward straight virtuosity.

If you listen to Eminem's later work you can't not notice how much attention has gone into crafting his raps. He tells Ice-T in *Something from Nothing: The Art of Rap* that "words are like puzzles to me" and that one of the things he loves about rap is "trying to figure out what word could go here." As Eminem relies less on persona and humor in his later work (as well as less on confession), his language, his words—the sine qua non of rap—carry the weight of his songs. "[H]e seems to revel in the ways that he can break and reshape the laws of the language,"[11] says Adam Bradley. The challenge of craft is not merely complexity, though, but the method of conveying that complexity as well. As Bradley later adds, "the brilliance of Eminem's wordplay is that we experience it as effortless lyricism rather than complex poetic negotiation."[12]

The effortlessness, we know, is only *merely* apparent, an effect of his well-honed craft. This is why even when rappers aren't boasting explicitly they're doing so implicitly, and why the *aboutness* of Eminem's virtuoso raps on *Recovery* and with Royce Da 5'9" on Bad Meets Evil's *Hell: The Sequel* are more meta than ever, regardless of their nominal content. It's impossible to rap that well without communicating: "I'm really fucking good at this." Ask Jay-Z, who knows: "It's like a metaphor for itself; if you can say how dope you are in a completely original, clever, powerful way, the rhyme itself becomes proof of the boast's truth."[13]

With respect to Eminem, we might leave off here with a final speculation about the necessity of self-referentiality in rap. It's been argued that a rapper is obligated to the beat beneath his lyrics before the content in them. Bradley puts this nicely when he writes, "the MC's most pressing lyrical challenge is in patterning sound rather than making meaning."[14] As Eminem enters the next phase of his career it will be interesting to see whether he continues to press on the technical side of his craft and if so whether doing so pushes him in a direction analogous to painting's abstract expressionism, the raps not even posturing to represent anything but themselves.

While raps are built from sounds, they nevertheless comprise words, which contain and compose meanings, and the meanings of Eminem's lyrics are the most debated aspect of his music. His use of explicitly autobiographical material can be troubling in this regard, as it invites the very mistake it seeks to expose: the conflation of expression and action. Zadie Smith offered a corrective on this point back in 2002 when she wrote, "Eminem's life and opinions are not his art. His art is his art." The argument works as well in reverse: *Eminem's art is not his life. His art is his art.* But because listeners regularly fail to appreciate this distinction we still get, for example, in 2010, long after the Slim Shady hysteria of the early '00s, Sady Doyle's outrage over the song "Love the Way You Lie," which she takes as mere reportage even as, watching the song's music video, she does not think that Dominic Monaghan actually beat up Megan Fox. It should be equally apparent that Eminem and Rihanna are performing.

Doyle's misreading is bolstered, though, by the fact that rap has not successfully differentiated the role of speaker from that of author. In fact, the form has gathered some of its intrigue from the proximity and confusion of these two constructs, the persona (the "realness") of the speaker becoming that of the author and thereby reinforcing that of the speaker. It occurs in the artist's mind as well: Marshall Mathers nearly goes to jail for a Slim Shady-style assault; Tupac and Biggie are the (sort of) innocent victims in the crossfire of real bullets aimed at fictional characters.

Eminem asks (literally) for a pass to say whatever he likes, but sometimes he seems to want to mean what he says. While he expects his audience to be able to distinguish between the literal and the ironic in his work, the use of straight autobiography in the ironic mode invites real-life trouble. Kim is forced to live in the confusing gap between literal and actual, while fans heap real scorn and wish real harm upon her. Kim, the human being behind the character "Kim," has really suffered for Eminem's indiscriminate ironizing and our listening pleasure. Eminem belies his own claims of artistic license when he raps on "Like Toy Soldiers" that he lost it after hearing Ja Rule say Hailie's name. And Kim? It's at moments like these that critiques of an entitled Eminem bullying the relatively voiceless and powerless (the misogyny, the homophobia, even the racism everyone's always waiting for) have their strongest claims. But Eminem's mistakes do not excuse ours: as rap listeners we need to ask more sophistication of ourselves than simple-minded literal interpretation, even when—*especially when*—that's what the song seems to ask for.

Rap "complicates or even rejects literal interpretation," says Henry Louis Gates, Jr.[15] "You don't have to have a degree in semiotics to recognize that an album with three multilayered, untrustworthy narrators—Eminem, Marshall Mathers and Slim Shady—can hardly be charged with the straight-up advocacy of *anything*," says Whet Moser.[16] Eminem's mentor Dr. Dre, speaking about his vision for N.W.A.: "I wanted to make people go: 'Oh shit, I can't believe he's saying that shit.' I wanted to go all the way left. Everybody trying to do this Black power and shit, so I was like, let's give 'em an alternative. Nigger niggernigger niggernigger fuck this fuck that bitch bitch bitch suck my dick, all this kind of shit, you know what I'm saying?"[17] Eminem's friend and partner Proof about his suggestion of an alter ego for Eminem and the other members of D12: "The whole thing in D12 was to have a personality where you would just say anything. You just didn't give a fuck. Your persona was almost like a mask to hide behind, know what I'm sayin?' We all took our different identities, and Em took Slim Shady and he ran with it. He took it way more serious than all of us, that motherfucker."[18] All of which reiterates Eminem's and rap's inherent ironies.

If you listen to *Infinite* one thing you won't hear is the clearly conceived narrating persona of Eminem's later work. The wordplay is complex and the flow intricate, but the speaker lacks characterization and consequently sounds generic if also capable. One recurring claim in this introduction is that rap operates ironically and is always to some degree self-referential. This claim might be construed to imply that persona is the product of the lyrics, but the causal arrow points in either direction: the lyrics emerge from a rapper who exists even as the raps create and recreate that very existence.

By tradition a rapper's persona hews closely (or succeeds best when it does) to his autobiography. "Rap lyrics," Tricia Rose writes, "are closely linked with the author; unlike traditional Western notions of composition in which the composer's text is in a separate sphere from that of the performer, rap lyrics are the voice of the composer and the performer."[19] Jay-Z offers his support in *Decoded*: "The rapper's character is essentially a conceit, a first-person literary creation. The core of that character has to match the core of the rapper himself. But then that core gets amplified by the rapper's creativity and imagination.... And whether it's in a movie or a television show or whatever, the best characters get inside of us. We care about them. We love them or hate them. And we start to see ourselves in them—in a crazy way, become them."[20]

If we think about the writtenness of Eminem we see at least a tripartite construct. So far I've referred to the artist in question as Eminem, whose alter ego is Slim Shady. But of course, the story is more complicated. Marshall Mathers is the author of both personae and is himself a third major persona in the music. Adam Bradley shows how complicated these relationships are even at their least complicated: "Think of Marshall Mathers rapping as Eminem rapping as Slim Shady ... where does the poet's direct expression end and the persona begin? Answering this rests upon how we interpret the 'I' in rap."[21] What minimizes the complication in this reading is that it takes Eminem (et al.) at his implied word that when he raps *as Marshall Mathers* (if we can always be sure when that is) we are to take him at his most "sincere," a term that should be sufficiently problematized by now. Only the most naïve listeners could fail to identify the use of persona even if they cannot identify all its manifestations. For the attentive listener it's always satisfying when Eminem circles back to this subject, whether it's in character, as in "Criminal," which plays off the consequences of taking his lyrics literally, or to comment on the matter, as in "Sing for the Moment."

It's on another song, though, "Till I Collapse," that Eminem gives the real hint of his self-writtenness. After rapping that he'll only rap as long as he maintains his high standard, he says, "because when he can't he will quit writing 'em." The "'em" here refers to raps, but two lines later the word refers to thoughts. And one sees that the earlier "'em" can also refer to "Em," the abbreviated version of "Eminem." The lines offer the alternate interpretation that when Eminem the author loses his ability he'll stop writing Eminem the character (ditto, we can assume, the other personae).

"Till I Collapse" was rapped in 2002 at the height of Eminem's fame and cultural relevance. His drift over the course of the following decade into reclusion supports this reading of a literal statement (for either or both interpretation(s)). The withdrawal might be a necessary consequence of fame—how much easier it is to see ourselves, in the Jay-Z fashion, in the despondency of *The Slim Shady LP* than in the celebrity of *The Eminem Show*. The life becomes a poorer source for the content of the raps, which move first offstage ('04–'09), then in the extreme direction of cartoon and caricature (*Relapse*), then toward a reprisal of new archetypes (recovery, *Recovery*). In their contribution to this volume, Julius Bailey and David J. Leonard consider this latest iteration, which they term Eminem 2.0, in terms of white privilege that as a rapper Eminem is uniquely afforded. What all periods of Eminem's post–*Eminem Show* career demonstrate is a move further away from articulating the cultural moment and closer to *purer* rap-as-rap art-making. Relevance for artistry. Eminem as virtuoso.

Does any of this seem like a surprise from the vantage of 2013? "You know, selling all the records I sold off *The Marshall Mathers LP* out the gate was strange to me. Not that I feel undeserving or anything like that, but I was just like, 'Holy fuck, this is me doin' this.' That's the biggest weirdest thing to live with. I had no choice but to get used to it. But it's still strange."[22]

Writing in 1990 David Foster Wallace could still say about rap that "it's not like good old corporate popular art, whose job was simply to remind us of what we already know."[23] This changed by the laws of capitalism as hip hop became one of the major forces in mainstream culture, but even so rap music retains perhaps the most viable threat to the status quo in its posturing and potential for subversion when it isn't itself promoting conspicuous consumption. Eminem has profited like no other rapper from rap's mainstreaming, but while he does not rap much about material success, he makes career moves aimed at it, and as he does he neutralizes the just-don't-give-a-fuck threat of Slim Shady, whose claim now must come with an asterisk amending "as long as it doesn't hurt sales."

This isn't news. In 2003 William Bowers wrote, "No matter how 'real' he is, now Eminem is a commercial for *8 Mile* is a commercial for Shady Records is a commercial for Eminem's albums is a commercial for MTV is a commercial for a 'life style' is a commercial for Eminem is a commercial for…"[24] The feedback loop is dangerous for an artist who aspires to threaten, because it has been true since Eminem received his endorsement from the *New York Times* and the rest of the mainstream American media that "Eminem makes corporate advertisers comfortable, and for that reason the black hip-hop community has something to worry about. In America, mainstream media is targeted at the most desirable consumer group: whites, ages eighteen to thirty-four, particularly females. Eminem is authentic. Eminem is good-looking, gifted, popular, and Eminem is white. He is a marketing man's dream figure."[25] Unless his music somehow finds a way in the future to take real risks to subvert this relationship (as fans with long memories hope there is), Eminem (unlike Kanye) will maintain as another disposable product sanitized by the forces of consumerism.

This acceptance and "safety" has everything to do with race. As Farai Chideya says, "there was a long wait for the great white hope of rap. When he did appear, the problem for me was that he received all this analysis and psychoanalysis that black rappers never got. If you look at somebody like Tupac who now has been given this kind of psychoanalysis posthumously, when he was alive he was a 'bad boy,' that's all people thought of him. There was no effort in the media to deconstruct who he is or where he comes from. But as soon as Marshall Mathers appeared they all said 'Oh, this troubled white youth. May we lay you down on the couch? What is your problem?'"[26] Even during those few years we feared Eminem we didn't ignore or ghettoize him. Instead, we were fascinated with him. Steve Bramucci recounts such a fascination from the evolving perspective of a young fan turned discerning listener in his essay "The Farther Reaches of Human Proficiency."

I wanted to write this introduction without mentioning Elvis, but when considering the different ways black and white artists are treated in American culture he's unavoidable. In *Black Noise* Tricia Rose writes, "the fact that a significant number of white teenagers have become rap fans is quite consistent with the history of black music in America and should not be equated with a shift in rap's discursive or stylistic focus away from black pleasure and black fans. However, extensive white participation in black culture has also always involved white appropriation and attempts at ideological recuperation of black cultural resistance."[27] She continues later, "There is abundant evidence that white artists imitating black styles have greater economic opportunity and access to larger audiences than black innovators. Historical accounts of the genres often position these subsequently better known artists as the central figures, erasing or marginalizing the artists and contexts within which the genre developed."[28]

Eminem has copped to all this in song after song, most explicitly in "White America," wherein he explains how his minority status inside hip

hop was inverted as he along with hip hop reached the majority-white mainstream. Music-focused Dr. Dre is by all accounts the one who was willing
to "look past" race. In his capacity as Eminem's mentor, Dre encountered
some resistance to working with, and enabling, the first legitimate white
rap star, to which he responded, "I don't give a fuck if you're purple; if you
can kick it, I'm workin' with you."[29] Fast forward to Eminem's near-universal
acceptance into rap's pantheon and the difficult questions of race have less
to do with a white guy's right to rap and more to do with how the audience
listens and who that audience comprises.

　　Henry Louis Gates, Jr., writes in *Signifying Monkey* that language is
how blacks can have something of their own without social reform.[30] This
history is traced back to plantations and slave ships when coded speech
was a necessity. But what does it mean for whites to adopt a language that
has developed in response to, and in defiance of, power they hold? Whether
it's born of sincere cultural and aesthetic admiration, whether it's a genuine
social and political show of solidarity, or whether it's more visceral than that
and rap just seems to be the only music that really "speaks to you,"[31] you can
see how it risks coming across as threatening or exploitive. And regardless,
the authenticity rap represents is always, for the white speaker, borrowed
and therefore *inauthentic*. David Foster Wallace essays this awkward gawk-
ing cum appropriation in *Signifying Rappers*:

> each innovation, new Scene and genius born of a "suffering" we somehow
> long to imagine, even as we co-opt, overpay, homogenize, make the best of
> that suffering song go to stud for our own pale performers.
> 　So an easy analysis, through the fast trains' glass, of rap as the latest
> occasion for the postliberal and highly vicarious guilt we find as exhilarat-
> ing as it is necessary—that we like to play voyeur, play at being kept, for
> once, truly outside.[32]

It's one thing for the white voyeur to read this in a book by, quoting
from *Signifying Rappers*'s back cover, "white, educated, middle-class" authors;
it's another thing, too close for comfort, to have it pointed out *in medias res*,
where the thing in question is the music in question. What can the white
Eminem fan say when listening to "White America" except, "I know, but he's
not talking about me. He's talking about those other…." Eminem's existence
hastens (or at least once hastened) whites' relation to rap from voyeur to vic-
ariously accepted insider, but Eminem's lyrics instruct caution. His participation in hip hop also demonstrates for his audience that one's persona is
(largely) constructed. Miles White analyzes just such construction, particularly of the Slim Shady persona, vis-a-vis race in his contribution here, "The
White Negro Gone Mad." Taking a different angle of approach to race, Sylvie

Laurent considers Eminem's self-identity as white trash. These analyses demonstrate the power of Robert Christgau's claim that "No rapper has ever made clearer, especially to young whites who view black rappers as romantic outlaws, that hip hop is a verbal construct, not to be taken literally."[33]

Now as true as Wallace's assessment was when he was writing in 1990, and even as Eminem was rapping in 2002, it's less true amidst today's rap's ubiquity and relative democracy. Jay-Z meets (produces?) Jay Gatsby; soccer moms sing along to Lil Wayne (and not just to his verse on Eminem's "No Love"); everyone, even Justin Bieber, gets to be in rap songs (and not just as Eminem punch lines).

I don't know that things with Eminem are any easier for black writers. In fact, Farai Chideya suggests they're probably worse: "I think that black people who consistently write about this stuff get tired of nobody listening to them, because mainstream audiences don't read it. There is this tendency to only value the voice of the white critic, no matter what the situation."[34] And she is one of the black critics who was willing to be interviewed for Anthony Bozza's Eminem biography. According to Bozza, this a small group: "Celebrating Eminem, for some, is not simple. Perhaps it is for this reason that only four of the sixteen African-American critics, academics, and artists whom I approached for interviews for this book agreed to talk to me."[35] These rates approximate the responses I got in soliciting the essays in this volume. Such reluctance to give attention to Eminem is one of the perspectives voiced in Kyle "Guante" Tran Myhre's dialogue "He Is Whatever We Say He Is" that appears as an appendix and synthesizes many of the contentious attitudes toward the rapper.

Do you care how white I am or the contributors might be? What about that it's the white rapper who gets to be the subject of this book? While Eminem deserves a book like this as much as any rapper does, there are many who deserve it equally. This book was inspired by Julius Bailey's book *Jay-Z: Essays on Hip-Hop's Philosopher King*, and I hope to soon see similar anthologies devoted to Rakim, Tupac, Biggie, Outkast, Nas, Kanye,[36] Talib Kweli, and other rappers whose voices over beats have provided our era's most dynamic poetry and art.

Chapter Notes

1. Which according to the Eminem of "We're Back" (*Eminem Presents the Re-Up*) was the plan: to go mainstream and make it big. This gloss on Eminem's early career is more a reading of the collective reception of him than of his actual art, which always operates on multiple levels of meaning and accessibility, the pop singles always (in part) misdirections that conceal the "real" content. Then again, everything after *Infinite* was put out on a major label deeply invested in *reception*.

2. With the exception of Rodman, from 2006, all works in this book are new.

3. Norman Mailer, *Advertisements for Myself* (Cambridge, MA: Harvard University Press, 1992), 353.

4. Trusting I'm not alone, I have forgone previews and merely indicated connections as they occur in this introduction.

5. http://www.daveyd.com/whatisrapdav.html.

6. Adam Bradley, *Book of Rhymes: The Poetics of Hip Hop* (New York: BasicCivitas, 2009), 11

7. Chuck Klosterman, *Sex, Drugs, and Cocoa Puffs: A Low Culture Manifesto* (New York: Scribner, 2003), 183.

8. Tricia Rose, *Black Noise: Rap Music and Black Culture in Contemporary America* (Middletown, CT: Wesleyan University Press, 1994), 124.

9. M. L. Elrick, "Eminem's Dirty Secrets" in Hilton Als and Darryl A. Turner, eds., *White Noise: The Eminem Collection* (New York: Thunder's Mouth Press, 2003), 11.

10. Paul Clemens, "Breakdown," *New York Times* (February 24, 2013).

11. Bradley, 101.

12. Bradley, 110.

13. Jay-Z, *Decoded* (New York: Spiegel and Grau, 2010), 26.

14. Bradley, 32.

15. Adam Bradley and Andrew DeBois, eds., *The Anthology of Rap* (New Haven: Yale University Press, 2010), xxv.

16. Whet Moser, "Why Eminem Should Get the Grammy" in Als, 175.

17. Jeff Chang, *Can't Stop Won't Stop: A History of the Hip-Hop Generation* (New York: St. Martin's Press, 2005), 318.

18. Bozza, 19.

19. Rose, 87.

20. Jay-Z, 292.

21. Bradley, 164.

22. Eminem, quoted in Bozza, 99.

23. Mark Costello and David Foster Wallace, *Signifying Rappers* (Hopewell, NJ: Ecco, 1990), 31.

24. William Bowers, "8 Mile" in Als, 19.

25. Bozza, 183.

26. Bozza, 177.

27. Rose, 5.

28. Rose, 6.

29. Bozza, 198.

30. Gates, xix.

31. Tricia Rose sounds prophetic considering it was in 1994 that she wrote: "As more and more of the disenfranchised and alienated find themselves facing conditions of accelerating deterioration, rap's urgent, edgy, and yet life-affirming resonances will become a more important and more contested social force in the world" (105).

32. Wallace and Costello, 69.

33. Robert Christgau, "What Eminem Means—And Doesn't" in Als, 145.

34. Bozza, 264.

35. Bozza, 264.

36. Julius Bailey's edited volume is *The Cultural Impact of Kanye West* (New York: Palgrave Macmillan, 2014).

Race ... and Other Four Letter Words: Eminem and the Cultural Politics of Authenticity

Gilbert B. Rodman

End of the world: Best rapper's white, best golfer's black.
—Chris Rock

Gaps

Describing the work on race and racism done at the Centre for Contemporary Cultural Studies at the University of Birmingham in the 1970s, Stuart Hall writes:

> We had to develop a methodology that taught us to attend, not only to what people said about race but ... to what people could not say about race. It was the silences that told us something; it was what wasn't there. It was what was invisible, what couldn't be put into frame, what was apparently unsayable that we needed to attend to.[1]

As Hall explains it, the Birmingham School took this particular turn because they came to recognize that analyzing media texts in order to identify and critique the ways that people of color were routinely misrepresented, stereotyped, and demonized was simply not an effective way to struggle against racism. The problem here is *not* that media representations didn't matter in the United Kingdom then—or that they don't matter in the United States today. On the contrary, people of color continue to be regularly depicted as dangerous criminals who threaten to destroy the existing social order; as exotic primitives to be feared, despised, and controlled; as helpless children dependent on charity from the technologically superior West; and as

17

fetishized objects readily available for white appropriation—and as long as images like these remain in heavy circulation, it's vital that cultural critics continue to identify and critique them.

But it's also not enough. Implicit in the focus on "bad" representations, after all, is the notion that enough "good" representations will solve the problem. Perhaps the clearest example of the fundamental flaw in this philosophy can be found in *The Cosby Show*. Although *Cosby* presented a far more uplifting public image of black people than had previously been the norm on U.S. television, those "kinder, gentler" fictions didn't translate very well into better living conditions for *real* black people. In fact, the widespread popularity of *Cosby* may actually have made it easier for large segments of white America to believe that the Huxtables' upscale lifestyle was more representative of black America than was really the case, which, in turn, suggested that there was no longer a socio-economic gap of any real significance between white and black America—or, more perniciously, that if such disparities *did* exist, it was because poor blacks had "failed" to live up to the impossibly picturesque example of Cliff and Claire and their designer-sweater-wearing children. What's ultimately at issue here is not the (in)accuracy of *Cosby*'s representations of black America—after all, it's not as if sitcoms about white families provide us with consistently faithful reflections of white America either—but rather what is *not* represented: in the absence of a range of images of black people at least as broad and varied as the standard prime time depictions of whites, *any* single program, no matter how positive or enlightened or uplifting, carries a representational burden that it can't possibly bear in full.[2]

Following Hall, then, I want to suggest that racism, as it currently lives and breathes in the United States, depends at least as much on the gaps in contemporary public discourse on race as it does on flawed media representations of people of color. There are, of course, more of these silences than I can do justice to in this essay, and so I won't say as much here as I might about how the "national conversation" on race (such as it is) frequently uses racially coded language (*crime, welfare, the inner city*, etc.) that studiously avoids explicit references to *race*; or how diligently that discourse steers clear of addressing the actual question of *racism*; or how, when racism *is* actually acknowledged, it's too often reduced to a matter of individual prejudice and bigotry, rather than recognized as a set of systematic and institutional discriminatory practices.[3] As important as these silences are, my concern here is a different sort of gap in mainstream U.S. discourses on race: the one that transforms the common, pervasive, and age-old phenomenon of racial blending (in its multiple and various forms) into something invisible, aberrant, and novel.

For instance, the notion that race is a historical invention (rather than a biological fact)—and the corollary notion that racial categories are fluid and variable—is neither recent news nor an especially controversial idea among scientists and scholars who study race.[4] Nonetheless, even in reputable mainstream media discourse, this well-established fact can be treated as if it were a still untested theory—or, at best, an unresolved question.[5] Similarly, men and women from "different" racial groups have come together (even if such unions have not always been characterized by mutual consent) to produce "mixed race" babies for centuries. Yet it wasn't until the 2000 census that the U.S. government officially recognized that "check one box only" is an awkward instruction for many people to follow when asked to identify their race.

The phenomenon of cultural exchange between "different" racial populations also has a long and tangled history, but such exchanges are still often treated as if they were a dangerous new phenomenon. This is especially true in cases where the borrowing that takes place is recognizably more about love than theft:[6] where whites take up black styles, forms, and/or genres, not to claim them as their own nor to transform them into something "universal" (and thus something dehistoricized, decontextualized, and deracinated), but in ways that suggest genuine respect for—and even deference toward—black culture. Arthur Jafa maps out a historical trajectory of such reverent borrowing that encompasses the influence of African sculpture and photography on Picasso's invention of Cubism, improvisational jazz on Jackson Pollock's abstract painting, and rhythm and blues (R&B) on Elvis Presley's early brand of rockabilly:

> In each of these instances, and despite the seemingly inevitable denial that occurred once influence became an issue, the breakthrough nature of the work achieved was made possible by an initially humble, and thus by definition nonsupremacist, relationship to the catalytic artifact at hand. Just as Beethoven was humble in the face of the body of work that had preceded him, these artists were each students of the work under whose influence they had fallen, students in a fashion which white supremacy would typically make unlikely.[7]

The "seemingly inevitable denial" that Jafa mentions is the discursive move that tries to reclaim the art in question as a fundamentally white phenomenon that can be embraced by the dominant culture without any acknowledgment of the aesthetic and cultural miscegenation that originally gave rise to it.[8]

This essay focuses on a contemporary example of reverential cultural borrowing: hip-hop superstar Eminem and the public controversies that swirl around him. As a white man working in a musical idiom dominated by black aesthetic sensibilities—and who does so without trying to evade or denigrate the black gatekeepers who are the genre's primary critical arbiters—Eminem poses a significant threat to the culture's broader fiction that this *thing* we call "race" is a fixed set of natural, discrete, and non-overlapping categories. And it's *this* facet of Eminem's stardom—his public performances of cultural miscegenation—that is the unacknowledged issue hidden at the core of the various moral panics around him.

Norm

Why is it that the only forms of popular culture that apparently have some sort of direct effect on audiences are the *dangerous* ones? No one seems to believe that more Meg Ryan movies will transform the United States into a land of sweetly perky romantics, yet the sort of virtual violence depicted in *The Matrix* could be cited as an "obvious" inspiration for the very real violence that took place at Columbine in 1999. Few people seem willing to claim that popular computer games like *The Sims* will produce a world of brilliant and creative social planners, but it's almost a given that graphically violent games like *Mortal Kombat* will generate armies of murderous super-predator teens bent on terror and mayhem. *The Cosby Show* (as noted earlier) was unable to usher in an era of racial harmony and tolerance, but edgy cartoons such as *South Park* will supposedly turn otherwise angelic, well-adjusted children into foul-mouthed, misbehaving delinquents. And in spite of several decades of pop songs extolling the virtues of peace, love, and understanding, we're not a visibly kinder, gentler, more tolerant people ... but we can safely blame Eminem's brutal, homophobic, misogynist raps for corrupting our youth, poisoning our culture, and unraveling the moral fabric of the nation.

Or so the story goes. I make these comparisons not to argue that we should be unconcerned with the content of our mass media fare nor to suggest that Eminem's music plays an entirely benign role in contemporary U.S. culture. It would be going too far, after all, to claim that popular music has no recognizable impact on social values, or to suggest that, behind his foul-mouthed, criminally psychotic facade, Eminem is really just a misunderstood, lovable little ragamuffin. Rather, I raise the question of Eminem's allegedly harmful influence precisely because the broader discourse around him is far too saturated with overtones of controversy for me to safely ignore the issue. In this climate, any public statement about Eminem is implicitly obligated to focus on his multiple offenses against good taste, common decency, and fundamental moral values.[9] Commentators who "fail" to emphasize such issues—especially those who dare to suggest that Eminem might actually have talent worthy of praise—are themselves subject to stringent critique for ignoring the "real" (and, apparently, the only) story.[10] I don't want to dismiss the moral concerns of Eminem's detractors out of hand, but I also think that, too often, they manage to ignore what's genuinely novel (and important) about Eminem. In the midst of the moral panic that surrounds Eminem, however, it's rhetorically difficult to get to those other questions without first addressing the agendas set by the dominant discourse.

Most of the public debate about Eminem over the past several years has focused on the offensive, antisocial, irresponsible, dangerous, violent, misogynistic, and/or homophobic nature of his lyrics—and there's plenty of grist to be found for this particular mill. Listen to Eminem's first three major label releases and—among other things—you'll hear him insult his fans, drive with a fifth of vodka in his belly, assault his high school English teacher, encourage children to mutilate themselves, kidnap and kill his producer, shoot cashiers during armed robberies, rape his mother, and (at least twice) murder his wife with sadistic brutality. In the hyper-masculine world of Eminem's music, women are invariably "sluts" and "bitches" and "hos," and men he disapproves of are routinely derided as "pussies" and "faggots." It's not surprising, then, that Eminem has been roundly condemned from the right as a despoiler of common decency and morality, and from the left as an obnoxious promoter of a culture of violence that terrorizes women and gays.[11]

Nonetheless, I want to suggest that what matters about the controversy surrounding Eminem is not what it reveals, but what it conceals. To be sure, there are real and important issues at stake in the public furor over Eminem, especially around the questions of misogyny and homophobia. Cultural criticism, however, is not—or at least it shouldn't be—an all-or-nothing game, where *any* aesthetic or political flaw necessarily renders a particular work wholly irredeemable, in spite of what laudable qualities it might possess (and, of course, the reverse is equally true). Eminem's music contains more than its fair share of misogynistic and homophobic lyrics, but simply to reduce it to these (as many critics do) doesn't help to explain Eminem: it merely invokes a platitude or a soundbite to explain him *away*.

Much of the moral panic here involves a disturbing sort of scapegoating, where Eminem is made into a bogeyman for social ills that are far larger and far older than any damage that he might have been able to do in a mere five years or so of musical stardom. Reading Eminem's critics (from both the left and the right), one gets the impression that he has singlehandedly opened up a previously untapped well of bigotry and violence, and that the very novelty and uniqueness of his brand of poison has somehow overwhelmed the aura of peace-loving tolerance that otherwise characterizes the day-to-day life of U.S. culture.

The major complaints lodged against Eminem are the latest in a long history of complaints about the excesses of the mass media. And it would be easy to respond to this very traditional sort of condemnation of the dangers of popular culture with the very traditional litany of rebuttals: that is, to note that mass media effects are rarely as direct or powerful as the "violent lyrics produce violent crime" equation implies, or that the social ills in question arise from an impossibly tangled knot of multiple causes, or that audiences may be using all this "dangerous" media fare to channel their *pre*-existing antisocial attitudes into relatively harmless fantasies. Whatever merits there might be in such rhetorical strategies (all of which can be found in popular defenses of Eminem's music),[12] they ultimately don't do much to change the basic question at hand ("Does Eminem's music pose a threat to public health and safety?"). They merely answer that question in the negative, while leaving the original "moral panic" frame intact.

And that frame desperately needs to be broken. Part of the nature of a moral panic, after all, is that it presents an exaggerated threat to the social order as a way to draw attention away from genuine cracks and flaws in that order.[13] In the case at hand, it's worth noting that mainstream U.S. culture is already rife with misogyny and homophobia, and was so long before Eminem was born: enough so that his hyper-masculine lyrical excesses may actually be the *least* transgressive, *most* normative thing about him. This doesn't get Eminem off the hook when it comes to his particular renditions of these problematic cultural norms—not at all—but it does suggest that the real stakes in this particular discursive struggle are not those visible on the surface: that Eminem is being taken to task for transgressions that are too disturbing, too unsettling, and too threatening to mainstream U.S. culture to be openly acknowledged. And so what I want to do for the rest of this essay is to tease out some of *those* silences in the public debates about Eminem: silences that, to my ears anyway, scream out for attention quite loudly.

Role

A significant portion of the case against Eminem revolves around the question of his status as a role model for his (supposedly) youthful audience.[14] He doesn't just depict antisocial violence in his music, the argument goes, he personifies it in compelling fashion through the use of first-person narratives. News stories about domestic violence, for instance, are safe (in part) because they're presented with a sufficiently distanced tone so as not to glorify the brutality involved. Eminem, on the other hand, gives us the story from the batterer's point of view—and does so with a wildly manic glee—that sends the message that it's perfectly okay for men to beat, torture, and kill their wives. Such, at least, is the major rap against Eminem: that his music is simply far too real in its violence and hatred to actually work as safe entertainment.

Buried not very far beneath the surface of this critique, however, is a dicey set of assumptions about the relationship between art and reality. When it comes to the aesthetics and politics of popular music, one of the trickiest words that a songwriter/vocalist can utter is "I." In some cases, the use of first-person address is a straightforward form of autobiographical witnessing, whereas in other cases, it's clearly a temporary adoption and performance of a fictional persona. Taken as an abstract question of form and style, it's relatively easy to recognize that the lines between the autobiographical and the fictional "I" are often hopelessly blurred. True stories, after all, must still be dramatized and performed in their telling, and purely fictional tales often involve honest expressions of their interpreters' experiences and personalities.

When one gets down to specific cases, however, many of those nuances wither away. Tellingly, they often do so in ways that afford already-valorized forms of musical expression more artistic license than other, "lesser" musical genres enjoy. In this respect, mainstream rock, folk, and country musicians have much more liberty to use the first person to utter violently aggressive, sexually provocative, and/or politically strident words than do artists working in genres like dance or rap. Which means—not coincidentally—that the artists most frequently denied the right to use the fictional "I" tend to be women and/or people of color.

For example, John Lennon—while still a lovable mop-top, no less—could sing about preferring a woman to her being with another man ("Run for Your Life").[15] Johnny Cash could boast that he'd "shot a man in Reno just to watch him die" ("Folsom Prison Blues"). Bob Shane (of the Kingston Trio) could stab a woman to death for unspecified reasons and regret nothing other than that he was caught before he could escape to Tennessee ("Tom Dooley"). Eric Clapton could gun down a sheriff in the street without audible remorse or regret ("I Shot the Sheriff"). And Bruce Springsteen could undertake a murderous rampage across Nebraska in which he killed "ten innocent people" with a sawed-off shotgun ("Nebraska").

All of these musical crimes were generally understood to be acceptable forms of dramatic musical fiction—or, at least, none of them sparked any significant wave of moral outrage from the public at large—and all demonstrate quite clearly what Michel Foucault calls "the author function":

> Everyone knows that, in a novel offered as a narrator's account, neither the first-person pronoun nor the present indicative refers exactly to the writer

or to the moment in which he [sic] writes but, rather, to an alter ego whose distance from the author varies, often changing in the course of the work. It would be just as wrong to equate the author with the real writer as to equate him [sic] with the fictitious speaker; the author function is carried out and operates in the scission itself, in this division and this distance.[16]

The musicians cited above are all understood to be "authors" in Foucault's sense of the term (even when, as in Clapton's case, they're singing other people's songs), and so their most violent musical narratives are readily interpreted as artistic fictions.

Musicians who "fail" to be white, straight, economically privileged, and/ or male, however, are frequently and forcefully denied comparable artistic license, even when (or perhaps *especially* when) they're working within artistically valorized musical genres such as rock. For instance, when Madonna or Prince sing about sexual escapades in the first person, they're made into poster children for why CDs need parental warning labels—with "critics" such as Tipper Gore leading the charge to police the musical soundscape.[17] When Alanis Morissette hurls bitter musical invective at a duplicitous ex-lover ("You Oughta Know"), rock critics are quick to accuse her of being an "angry woman" and a "man hater"—whereas male rock stars who offer venomous musical kiss-offs to former girlfriends (e.g., Bob Dylan, Elvis Costello) are lauded as visionary poets. When Ice-T or N.W.A. use music to narrate revenge fantasies about firing back at criminally violent police officers, they're met with public outrage forceful enough to cancel national concert tours and expunge the offending songs from already released albums—and in Ice-T's case, the backlash's racism is underscored by the public framing of his offending song ("Cop Killer") as an example of (everything that's wrong with) gangsta rap, even though it came from an album released by his speed metal band, Body Count. In cases like these, the possibility that these musicians are invoking the fictional "I" is one that the dominant public discourse largely refuses to recognize or accept. "Common sense," it seems, tells us that John Lennon didn't *really* want to kill his first wife when he wrote "Run for Your Life," but that "Cop Killer" *must* be taken as a literal expression of the truth about Ice-T's felonious desires.

Part of Eminem's musical brilliance, then, is his ability to recognize this double standard and to use the tension between the fictional and the autobiographical "I" to fuel his art. His first three nationally released albums— 1999's *The Slim Shady LP*, 2000's *The Marshall Mathers LP*, and 2002's *The Eminem Show*—find him self-consciously sliding back and forth between (a) his "real life" identity as Marshall Mathers (who describes himself as "just a regular guy"); (b) his professional alter ego, Eminem (the self-assured, swaggering rap star); and (c) the fictional character, Slim Shady (the evil trickster persona that *Eminem* (rather than Marshall) sometimes adopts). For example, in "Role Model" (from *Slim*), Eminem complains that his critics can't see through the fictions he's constructed and that the villainous demon they're railing against (Shady) doesn't really exist. In "Stan" (from *Marshall*), Shady explains—with great sensitivity, no less—to an over-zealous fan that the violence and venom found in Eminem's music is "just clowning." And in "Without Me" (from *Eminem*), Marshall notes that his fans (and perhaps even his critics) clearly prefer Shady to him. As Tom Carson describes it:

> So obsessed with identity that he's got three of them, he uses his alter egos' turf fights to create an arresting conundrum: perspective without distance. Juggling scenarios to flash on not only his reactions but his perceptions about his reaction, even as he baits you about *your* reactions, he analyzes himself by dramatizing himself, and the effect is prismatic because nothing is ever resolved. At one level, a line like "How the fuck can I be white? I don't even exist" ["Role Model"] ... is just another deft reminder that "Eminem" is a persona. But when it comes sideswiping out of the racket, it can sound downright, um, existential—an inversion of the central conceit of Ralph Ellison's *Invisible Man*.[18]

Given the frequency with which Eminem's music involves first-person narratives, cynical observers have wondered whether Eminem is simply too egotistical to rap about anything other than himself. But this fairly common reading of Eminem's art—and of rap in general—points to a fundamental failure to recognize the historical connection between the deliberately over-the-top lyrical posturing of hip hop and the longstanding oral traditions of boasting, toasting, and playing the dozens found in African American culture: oral traditions that themselves weave together authentic self-expression and performative hyperbole in ways sophisticated enough to make the "I" being invoked by the speaker impossible to parse neatly.

When push comes to shove, then, whether Eminem really means what he says in his songs is, quite literally, an example of the canonical loaded question: "Have you stopped beating your wife yet?" Without wanting to dismiss Eminem's real-life outbursts of physical violence (which are a separate issue altogether), I think that a better question to ask is this: Why do so many people find it so extraordinarily difficult to envision Eminem (and other rappers) as someone who might have enough creativity, intelligence, and artistry to fashion and perform a convincing fictional persona? To be sure, such a rethinking of Eminem's art doesn't have to result in either respect or approval: one can, after all, still be disturbed and offended by fiction. For that matter, many critics are simply unable to recognize what Eminem does as *art* in the first place, apparently assuming that *art* and *abrasiveness* are mutually exclusive categories.[19]

Nonetheless, at the root of the widespread, collective inability to see Eminem as an *author*, as an *artist*, as a *performer*, we find a cultural bias at least as disturbing as the goriest of his musical fantasies: a bias that rests on the prejudicial notion that "some people" are wholly incapable of higher thinking and artistic creativity—and that their ability to create "fiction" is limited to making minor modifications to their otherwise unvarnished personal experiences. In this case, those "some people" are rappers—which is, in turn, a thinly disguised code for "African Americans" in general. Here, then, is another one of those problematic discursive silences, where criticizing "rap" or "hip hop" becomes a way to utter sweeping condemnations of black people and black culture without ever having to explicitly frame such commentary in racial terms.

To be sure, this particular slippage is partially enabled by the discourses of authenticity that play a crucial role in rap aesthetics and hip-hop culture. Critically successful rappers, after all, typically have to establish that they have an "authentic" connection to "street life" and/or "the hood," and they will often justify the violent themes, drug references, and profane language in their music as honest reflections of the real life environments from whence they came. At the same time, however, the dominant aesthetics of rock, folk, and country *also* depend heavily on questions of "authenticity," but they manage to do so without any serious expectations that the "authenticity" of the musicians in question must be read as "autobiography."

Quite the contrary, as a rock star like Bruce Springsteen can use his small-town, working-class upbringing as a license to compose authentic *fictions* about that culture. The "authenticity" of a song like "The River" (to take but one example) clearly doesn't depend on the lyrics' faithfulness to Springsteen's personal experience. We know full well that the rock star who we hear on the radio and see on MTV didn't get his high school girlfriend pregnant and wind up trapped in a life of chronic unemployment, melancholic depression, and shattered dreams. In cases like Springsteen's—that is, those typically found in rock, folk, and country contexts—even when one's "authenticity" is unmistakably connected to biographical facts, that connection actually authorizes musicians to adopt dramatic personae and invent *fictional* scenarios, and the "truth" of those fictions is rarely measured by their proximity to real events.

Perhaps more crucially, we need to remember that authenticity must always be *performed* in order to be recognized and accepted as such. It's not enough for Springsteen's fans and critics simply to know that he comes from a working class background: in order to maintain his status as an "authentic" working class icon, he must continue to dress and talk and perform in ways consistent with mythical standards of "working-class-ness" long after his own daily life has ceased to resemble the lives he sings about.

There's a pernicious double standard at work here that affords white musicians the freedom to separate their "authenticity" from their real lives, a freedom that black artists rarely enjoy. Of course, as a white man, Eminem seems an odd person to fall victim to such a bias ... but that actually leads directly into the next part of my argument.

Race

Is Eminem the Elvis of rap: a white man who makes black music credibly, creatively, and compellingly? Or—alternately—is Eminem ... the Elvis of rap: a white man who's unfairly achieved fame and fortune by making black music, while black artists with equal (if not greater) talent languish in poverty and obscurity?[20]

Obviously, I've rigged the question so that the answer is inescapable— Eminem *is* the Elvis of rap—but then the question of racial identity as it relates to Eminem's music (which has dogged his career from the start) has been a rigged one all along. After all, no matter what answer one decides upon, to take the question's basic premise at face value is to start from an essentialist (and highly problematic) assumption: namely, that the musical terrain can be neatly divided up into non-overlapping territories that match up perfectly with the "natural" racial and ethnic categories used to identify people. black people make black music, white people make white music— and one dare not cross these lines lightly.

Lest there be any confusion, let me make it clear that my critique of these assumptions is not simply an argument for music as some sort of "color-blind" sphere of cultural activity. On the contrary, questions of race and racial politics are absolutely crucial to understanding *any and every* major form of U.S. popular music since the rise of minstrelsy. Where essentialist models of musical culture run aground is in failing to recognize that the history of U.S. popular music involves an extended series of intermingled and creolized styles that have nonetheless been mythologized as if they were racially pure forms. Jazz, for instance, commonly gets pegged as "black music," despite the fact that early jazz drew heavily on the instrumental structures of European military marching bands. Similarly, rock has come to be widely understood as "white music" despite the central roles that the blues, R&B, and black gospel all played in its birth.

Insofar as they help to shape the musical terrain in significant fashion, these racialized ways of categorizing music are very real—and very powerful—but they are not simply natural facts. Rather, they are culturally constructed *articulations*: processes by which otherwise unrelated cultural phenomena—practices, beliefs, texts, social groups, and so on—come to be linked together in a meaningful and *seemingly* natural way.[21] Although it may still make sense to talk about rap as "black music," it only does so if we acknowledge that such a label bespeaks, not some sort of essential blackness at the music's core, but broad and tangled patterns of musical performance, distribution, and consumption that *historically* have been *associated with* African Americans.

Given this, there's no inherent reason why a white man like Eminem can't still be a critically acclaimed rapper, but we can still ask meaningful questions about the relationship of Eminem's music to the broader terrain of U.S. racial politics. In the end, however, the actual questions that critics have asked about Eminem's racial authenticity tell us more about the racism of the culture in which Eminem operates than they do about Eminem himself. As was the case with Elvis before him, questions about Eminem's racial authenticity perpetuate the larger culture's tendency to reduce all racial politics to the level of the (stable, coherent, essentialized) individual. Framing the issue as one of "what's a white man doing making black music?" helps to deflect attention away from the racism of the culture industry, and allows us to duck difficult—yet significant—questions about institutionalized racism and popular music that deserve to be addressed more openly and directly. For instance:

- Why *does Billboard* still segregate its charts along racial and ethnic lines, carving out separate categories for "R&B/Hip-Hop" and "Latin" music in ways that implicitly proclaim the "Hot 100/200" charts to be the province of white America?
- Why *do* rap acts have to pay higher insurance premiums for their concert tours—often high enough to prevent many rappers from touring at all—even when actual incidents of violence and property damage at hip-hop shows are no more common or severe than those at rock or country concerts?[22]
- Why *can't* a genre with as large a fan base as rap—according to the RIAA, it's been the second best-selling music in the United States (behind rock) every year since 1999[23]—manage to get radio airplay in proportion to its popularity, even in major urban markets?

If we're going to treat racism in the music industry with the seriousness that we should, *these* structural and institutional issues are the sorts of questions we should focus on first. After all, if the musical terrain is racially segregated to such an extent that a white rapper (or a black rocker) constitutes a noteworthy transgression—and it is—it's only because the larger institutional forces in play actively work to maintain the tight articulations between specific racial communities and musical genres.

Questions about Eminem's racial authenticity also make it easier for critics to simply ignore *what* he says entirely—from his most violent and disturbing narratives to his most trenchant and insightful socio-political commentaries—by simply denying him the moral right to speak at all (at least in his chosen genre/idiom). Focusing on whether Eminem should make "black music" does little to address questions of racial politics and racism meaningfully. Instead, depending on how one answers the "should he or shouldn't he?" question, such a focus underscores one of two problematic ideas: (a) the essentialist/segregationist notion that black and white music, black and white culture, black and white people should each keep to their own kind, or (b) the naive, "color-blind" myth that race is simply irrelevant to popular music and is thus something that we can ignore completely. Either way, such arguments amount to a form of magical thinking: that is, they attempt to deal with very real—and very complicated—questions of the relationship between race and culture by reducing them to pithy soundbites that transform race into a nonissue.[24]

Perhaps most crucially, though, questions about Eminem's racial authenticity mask a more subtle, but no less disturbing, agenda—one that's about maintaining rigid lines between the races when it comes to behaviors, attitudes, and politics: lines that Eminem violates deliberately, forcefully, repeatedly, and threateningly. And *these* are forceful threats that Eminem *should* follow through on more fully.

Bête

Race *is* at the heart of the Eminem uproar—but not in the way that it's typically framed. The problem with Eminem isn't that he's just another white man ripping off black culture—he's not the new Vanilla Ice—it's that he manages to perform "blackness" and "whiteness" *simultaneously*, blending the two in ways that erase precisely the same racial boundaries that white America has worked the hardest to maintain over the past several centuries.

Perhaps the easiest road into this piece of my argument goes through Miami and draws on another controversial rap act: 2 Live Crew. When their 1989 album, *As Nasty As They Wanna Be* first went gold (i.e., sold 500,000 copies), there was no public outcry, no lawsuits, no obscenity trials, no moralistic hand-wringing over what havoc this "dangerous" music was wreaking upon its audiences, because the bulk of those sales were in predominantly black and Latin "inner city" markets. Where 2 Live Crew ran into a buzzsaw of controversy was when they started to "cross over" to white audiences in significant ways. It's no coincidence that their infamous obscenity trial took place not in Dade County (i.e., Miami, the urban market that the band called home and the site of their strongest fan base) but in Broward County (i.e., the much whiter, much richer, much more suburban county just north of Miami). As has long been the case, white America has only really cared about the allegedly dangerous effects of popular culture when its own children were the ones purportedly in harm's way. "Hip hop," as Eminem sagely reminds us, wasn't a problem when it was found in black neighborhoods such as Harlem, but only after it crossed over to white America.

The moral panic over Eminem and his music is much the same phenomenon, only on a larger and more threatening scale. Eminem, after all, has reached a loftier level of stardom than 2 Live Crew ever dreamed of, and so his cultural and political impact (real or imagined) is of a much higher magnitude. 2 Live Crew faded back into the woodwork pretty quickly after the flap over *Nasty* died down. Eminem, on the other hand, is already one of the top 100 selling artists of all time, with more than 25 million units sold as of June 2005.[25] More important than sheer sales figures, however, is the perceived source of Eminem's threat. His music hasn't "crossed over" from black to white: it's come *from within* white America, publicly giving the lie to the conceit that there's a neat and immutable line that separates white from black—with all the dark, dirty, dangerous stuff allegedly living on the "other" side of that line.

Put another way, the vision of itself that mainstream white America works overtime to perpetuate is a vision largely devoid of hate, violence, and prejudice.[26] White America generally ignores or dismisses such attitudes, behaviors, and practices when they manifest themselves in its own ranks, while actively projecting them onto a broad range of marginalized Others: black bodies, brown bodies, lower class bodies, foreign bodies, and so on. At best (if you can call it that), when white America has to face its own warts and blemishes, it tries to find ways to explain them away as exceptions, as aberrations, as deviations ... *anything* but as a common and pervasive aspect of white America's normal condition.

And Eminem clearly knows all this. For instance, he begins "The Real Slim Shady" with a sneering line that calls his race-baiting critics to task for their inability to understand that someone could walk and talk and rap and act the way that he does and still be white. Even more bluntly, on "The Way I Am," he rails against white folks intent on trying to fix his racial identity in ways that allow *them* to maintain *their* illusions about the stability of race, rapping that he's lost patience with cocky whites who would dismiss him as a "wigger."

To be sure, Eminem is not the first artist to blur these lines—not by a long shot—but the manner in which he does so is rare for someone at his level of public visibility. Unlike Vanilla Ice, for instance, Eminem's investment in hip hop comes across as the sort of genuine passion of a lifelong fan, rather than as a temporary mask that can be (and, in Ice's case, was) removed at the end of the show. Unlike the Beastie Boys, Eminem comes across as someone who cares as much (if not more) about maintaining the overall integrity of hip-hop culture as he does about his commercial success. As Carl Rux puts it, "Eminem may have been born *white* but he was socialized as *black*, in the proverbial hood—and the music of the proverbial hood in America for the last twenty-five years has been hip-hop music."[27]

Historically speaking, this sort of deviance from the heart of whiteness has been met in three different ways. The race traitor in question has been reassimilated, rendered invisible, and/or excommunicated. And so Eminem's *real* crime may simply be that he's too popular to be ignored, too brash to be pulled back into the bosom of unthreatening whiteness, and so he must be branded as a demon, a deviant, a monster, a *bête noire*—who's all the more *bête* for "failing" to be *noire*—and then the demon must be cast out, lest his racially blurred performance come to be accepted as a viable option for other members of the white club.

A crucial aspect of this threat to hegemonic whiteness is the way that Eminem's unwavering self-presentation as "white trash" works to unsettle the dominant cultural mythology that equates "whiteness" with middle-class prosperity. If Rux is right to claim that Eminem was "socialized as black," to a large extent, it's because of the strong correlation between "race" and "class" in U.S. culture. The blackness in Eminem's background that Rux points to is rooted in the fact that Eminem's childhood poverty placed him in the disproportionately black "hood" of inner city Detroit. And so it's significant that a number of Eminem's detractors play "the race card" in order to steer the broader conversation away from the sort of cross-racial, *class-based* alliances that Eminem's popularity suggests might be possible.

This practice was especially pronounced with respect to *8 Mile*, Eminem's first foray into Hollywood acting, where a number of critics complained that the film took unfair swipes at the black bourgeoisie. For example, writing about the film in the *New Republic*, Justin Driver complained that,

> far from untethering hip-hop from race, Eminem's class bait-and-switch simply replaces the fact of blackness—i.e., skin color—with an idea of blackness that equates being black with being poor, angry, and uneducated. Eminem is perpetuating precisely the idea that animated Norman Mailer's 1957 essay "The White Negro." ... Eminem would likely object to Mailer's

racist posturing, particularly in light of his steadfast refusal to utter the word "nigger" in any context. "That word," he says, "is not even in my vocabulary." Unfortunately, judging from the evidence, neither is the term "black middle class."[28]

Somewhat more gracefully—at least insofar as he doesn't repeat Driver's curious error of implicitly treating Eminem as the film's author—but still problematically, Roy Grundmann wrote that

> despite its honorable intentions, the film ends up exploiting the social reality of the inner-city black people it portrays. It turns them into profitable spectacle, while remaining silent on the causes of their oppression. At the same time, the film is openly hostile towards the *Ebony* magazine set, which it juxtaposes with Rabbit's white working-class identity.[29]

Insofar as (a) the film's principal villains *are* black and middle class, (b) their class position *is* the pivotal distinction that marks them as threats to the community, and (c) the *real* black middle class is hardly the principal force working to keep the *real* working class down, there's some merit to these critiques … and yet it's a perversely narrow-minded and—to be blunt about it—suburban way to read a film that (a) defies Hollywood convention by centering its story on working class people, (b) refuses to cater to the still far too common stereotypes that portray poor people as thugs and criminals, (c) avoids the trap of representing the middle class as primarily white and/or idyllically benign, and (d) depicts strong examples of working class solidarity across racial lines. In the eyes of critics worried about the film's open hostility "towards the *Ebony* magazine set," cross-racial alliances are apparently a laudable and welcome goal when it comes to the middle class—but undesirable, disturbing, and threatening when it happens amongst the lumpen proletariat. The sort of critiques that Driver and Grundmann offer might be more compelling if the film's narrative presented an unambiguous vision of class mobility for whites at the expense of cross-racial friendships. Tellingly, however, *8 Mile* ends on a much more subtle note. Rabbit/Eminem may win the big rap battle against the middle-class black poser, but he *doesn't* ride off into the sunset with a new recording contract in his pocket and guaranteed stardom before him, while his black posse remains stuck in the ghetto: instead, he leaves the club where he's just scored his big triumph so that he can go back to *finish his shift* at the factory where he makes his living. This isn't the triumph of white exceptionalism over the black bourgeoisie: it's a surprisingly honest (for Hollywood, anyway) acknowledgment that having aesthetic talent doesn't guarantee that one will have financial success. More importantly, it's an ending that leaves Eminem's character firmly embedded in the same community where he grew up.

Rage

Part of what makes *8 Mile* such an interesting film is the way it nego-tiates a relatively nuanced understanding of the intersections of race and class in U.S. culture. In moving toward my conclusion, though, I want to focus on a slightly different class-related question—one that turns the harsh glare of the spotlight (or is that a *search*light?) back on *us* as cultural critics: namely, the perceived impropriety of what are popularly (if not entirely properly) understood to be lower class forms of expression, and the con-current inability of much of the professional managerial class (including us academics) to accept that smart, insightful, and valuable thoughts can come out of "coarse," "inarticulate," and "obscenity-laced" mouths.

And Eminem's is an unabashedly coarse mouth. *Fuck, shit, piss, cum, tits, cock, dick, balls, asshole, cunt, pussy, ho, bitch, slut, faggot, jack-off, cock-sucker, motherfucker.* All these—and much, much more—are mainstays in Eminem's lyrical lexicon. Significantly, the one time-honored example of linguistic crudity that Eminem emphatically and self-consciously *won't* use is "nigger," but that isolated gesture of political sensitivity, no matter how sincere it is, doesn't manage to save Eminem from being roundly castigated—and dismissed out of hand—for the unrepentant crudeness with which he expresses himself otherwise.

I'm not the first critic (by any means) to point to the role that class prejudices play with respect to whose speech we value and whose we don't. bell hooks has written on multiple occasions about her undergraduate years at Stanford, and how her "failure" to conform to bourgeois standards of class-room decorum—standards that she'd never encountered growing up in rural Kentucky—marked her as a "bad" student, in spite of her articulateness and intelligence.[30] Laura Kipnis's work on *Hustler* points to the ways in which politically progressive critics who would otherwise applaud the magazine's stinging jabs at big business and big government nonetheless manage to dismiss *Hustler*'s political commentary because of the "low class" nature of the magazine's satire.[31] And Lauren Berlant argues that dominant U.S. media representations of political protest promote a nefarious double standard: one where "political emotions like anxiety, rage, and aggression turn out to be feelings only privileged people are justified in having."[32] Poor folks and women and people of color, she argues, must play the role of "the well-behaved oppressed" if they have any hopes of having their political voices heard (much less taken seriously).

Eminem, of course, may never have read hooks or Kipnis or Berlant (or the like)—but that's actually part of my point. His intelligence and wit and keen sense of the political terrain may not derive from the sort of "book learning" that we tend to value in academic settings, but his intellect is no less real for that. Nor is it less insightful simply because it comes in a package that includes four-letters words and unchecked rage. I don't think it's a coincidence, though, that so many critiques of Eminem's music focus on the foulness of his language—and I suspect that at least some of the controversy around him would go away if only he could make his points in more polite and genteel fashion.

But why should he? Especially since many of his sociopolitical critiques *are* angry ones—and often justifiably so. I don't want to simply romanticize Eminem as some sort of organic intellectual or working class hero—that would be precisely the sort of patronizing elitism that I'm trying to guard against here—but I *do* want to suggest that, as cultural critics, *we* could stand to be more self-reflective about our own class position and biases, and about how readily we dismiss potentially valuable cultural criticism simply because it comes from someone who says "motherfucker" in public without flinching.

And there *is* thoughtful—and even progressive—cultural commentary to be found in Eminem's music: from pointed quips about a litigation-happy culture[33] to extended rants against Bush's war on terror,[34] from biting critiques of racism in the music industry[35] to scathing indictments of the classism that made Columbine a "national tragedy" when daily violence in inner city schools can't make the news at all.[36] And while no one's likely to confuse Eminem with Public Enemy anytime soon—political statements remain a sidebar for him, rather than his primary agenda—he's also a more multifaceted and politically engaged artist than his detractors seem able or willing to recognize.

None of this is meant to draw some sort of magical shield around Eminem and his music, nor do I want to suggest that he's not fair game for criticism himself. He clearly understands that language is a powerful tool— and a powerful weapon. In "Sing for the Moment," he raps that words can "be great," "degrade," or worst of all "teach hate." And so the sensitivity that he shows when it comes to avoiding "the N-word" is something he could conceivably apply to his unabashed use of the word "faggot" as a general term of insult. And one might hope that someone who displays the sort of intelligence that Eminem does in his rhymes could also recognize that if he *really* wants to provide a better life for his daughter, as he frequently claims, he might want to reconsider his tendency to portray women as bitches and sluts who (at best) are nothing more than "good fucks."[37]

That being said, I don't want to argue for some sort of simple trade-off here, where we'll agree to forgive Eminem for the violent misogyny of, say, "Kill You" or "'97 Bonnie and Clyde" because the penetrating and insightful sociopolitical critique found in, say, "The Way I Am" or "Square Dance" makes up for his more disturbing narratives. But I'm even more leery of the reverse trade-off that it seems we may be too eager to make: the one where we let our distaste for Eminem's most disturbing messages simply trump the valuable contributions he *does* have to make to a broader set of conversations about race, class, media, and politics.

Arguably, a large part of what scares many people about Eminem is that they look at him and see bits of themselves that they'd prefer not to acknowledge. After all, it's not as if he single-handedly invented misogyny or homophobia or violent fantasies out of thin air: those were all present in U.S. culture in significant ways long before Eminem was born, and it's the rare person raised in such a culture who can legitimately claim to be completely free of all such failings. But part of what I think that we—as cultural critics—should value about Eminem is precisely that we can look at him and see bits of ourselves that we *should* acknowledge. And if we happen *not* to be particularly proud of some of those facets of ourselves, that's fine. But, in such a scenario, we should go about the difficult task of working to change those unsavory aspects of our personalities and lifestyles, rather than simply pretending they're not there and/or projecting them onto Other, more marginalized people.

Put another way, when it comes to current public discourses around both race (in general) and Eminem (more specifically), too many scholars and critics (i.e., people like us) fail to adequately acknowledge their own roles—however passive or implicit those might be—in shaping and maintaining some of the more disturbing forms of racial hierarchy and disenfranchisement. I think it's perfectly fine for cultural critics to hold Eminem's feet to the fire for his more egregious lyrical excesses, but only if they—*we*—are also self-reflexive enough to do so in ways that aren't ultimately about trying to protect *our* positions of privilege at the expense of others.

A good example of what this sort of nuanced criticism looks like comes from *Ms.*, in which Joan Morgan carefully registers her concerns with the misogynist aspects of Eminem's music, but then, in terms that resonate strongly with Stuart Hall's admonition to attend to "the silences" in the discourse, she deliberately refuses to join the chorus of voices demanding Eminem's censure. "At best," she writes, "hip-hop is a mirror that unflinchingly reflects truths we would all much rather ignore.... A knee-jerk reaction to violent hip-hop is often a case of kill the messenger. In the end, it's silence—not lyrics—that poses the most danger."[38] When it comes to Eminem, there are many such silences that deserve to be filled with productive noise, but let me point to three of the biggest.

With respect to gender and sexuality, the silence we most need to shatter is the one that pretends that Eminem's degradation of gays and women is abnormal. After all, the "clean" versions of Eminem's albums that Kmart and Wal-mart (those stalwart retail institutions of middle America) were willing to sell didn't delete the misogyny and homophobia: just the drug references and profanities. Mainstream U.S. culture has a *long* way to go before it can hold Eminem's feet to the fire on this front without hypocrisy.

With respect to class, the silence that Eminem's highly visible "white trash" pride should help dispel is the one around white poverty. While people of color still remain far more likely to be poor than whites are, the vast majority (68 percent) of the people living below the poverty line are white. That's certainly not the face of poverty one is typically shown by the mainstream media, however, which prefers to pretend that whiteness and affluence go hand in hand.

With respect to race, the silence that Eminem is best positioned to help us break is the powerful taboo against miscegenation: cultural, metaphorical, or otherwise. Given the ongoing apoplexy and fear that have dominated the mainstream discourse on "the browning of America," there's a lot of value to be learned from a figure who manages to blue the lines between black and white music, black and white culture, black and white performance with ease, with talent, and—perhaps most importantly—with a large dose of humility about his whiteness.

And if, as a culture, we can't break those silences, then we're in very deep trouble indeed.

Coda

In an earlier draft of this essay, that last sentence served as my closing thought. But then, suddenly, the ground on which I was working shifted beneath me: not quite so dramatically that I needed to start over from scratch, but enough so that I couldn't just pretend that the changes in the terrain hadn't happened. This is one of the occupational hazards of studying contemporary culture (popular or otherwise). It's a constantly moving target, which makes it difficult (if not impossible) to pin one's objects of study down with any descriptive or critical finality. In the case at hand, the shift in the terrain resulted from the fall 2004 release of Eminem's fourth major-label album, *Encore,* and the unprecedented *lack* of controversy that it inspired.[39] In the face of apparent public indifference to Eminem's latest efforts to push middle America's moral panic buttons, I had to wonder what had happened to hip hop's most controversial superstar. Was the moral panic over? Had Eminem finally won over his former detractors? Or had he simply lost his edge?

Encore was clearly a commercial success—it sold more than four million copies and, even though it wasn't officially released until November, it was still one of the 100 best-selling albums of 2004—but as both an aesthetic endeavor and a public provocation, it failed. Badly. The most generous critics routinely described the album using adjectives like "spotty," "uneven," and "inconsistent," and the only public controversy involving Eminem since its release—the presence of his phone number in Paris Hilton's hacked cellphone address book—found him playing an incidental and supporting role in someone else's drama, rather than his more accustomed role as an instigator and gadfly.

In many ways, though, *Encore*'s failure is potentially more interesting than any of Eminem's previous successes, as it helps to demonstrate the extent to which his career actually *is* fueled by a considerable artistic talent. While his detractors often prefer to understand Eminem as completely talentless—or, perhaps more generously, as someone who wastes his talent on unworthy, amoral endeavors—the double-edged failure of *Encore* underscores how tightly his skills as an *auteur* and a *provocateur* are intertwined with one another. Horror stories such as "'97 Bonnie and Clyde" and "Kim" bothered people as viscerally as they did not simply because of the violent misogyny visible on their surfaces, but because they were compelling and powerful works of art.[40] *Encore*, on the other hand, fails as art largely because it doesn't try very hard to get under its listeners' skin—and where it does make an effort to provoke, it largely fails because Eminem sounds like he's just going through the motions.

More crucially for my purposes, though, *Encore*'s shortcomings demonstrate how much his artistry depends on the race-blurring aspects of his musical performance. Explaining what distinguishes Eminem from most other white rappers, Tom Carson writes that those other artists "deracinate" the music by

> keeping the beats but redefining the attitude as frat-boy acting out. What makes Eminem more challenging is that he's audibly assimilated hip-hop as culture. His nasal pugnacity is unmistakably the sound of a white kid for whom this music was so formative that he never heard it as someone else's property.[41]

Encore ultimately falls apart because Eminem seems to have drifted away from his culturally miscegenated roots and toward a sort of frat-boy prankster aesthetic that was largely absent in his earlier work. Where once he had used music to feud with worthy public targets like censorious politicians and corporate bigwigs (or even compellingly dramatic private targets like his mother and his ([ex-]wife), now he's picking on the likes of Michael

Jackson and Triumph the Insult Comic Dog. And where once he wielded his profanity-filled pen like a keenly honed sword, now he's building entire tracks around the slap-happy adolescent joys of farts, belches, and retching.

The major exception to this downslide—and the song that critics commonly cited as one of the few tracks that helped to elevate the album from "muddled" to "uneven"—is "Mosh." Released as the album's second single, just prior to Election Day in the United States, the song is interesting enough musically, even if it doesn't quite live up to the best of his previous efforts. It lacks the playfulness and catchy beats of "The Real Slim Shady"; it doesn't flow as smoothly or effortlessly as "The Way I Am"; it doesn't have the same thrilling, in-your-face edginess that characterizes "White America," but it's also something Eminem has never given us before: a full-fledged protest song. "Fuck Bush," Eminem proclaims, "until they bring our troops home," with the rest of the song—and the video that accompanies it—explicitly beckoning the nation to come together and vote "this monster, this coward that we have empowered" out of office. As noted above, Eminem's music has never been completely apolitical, but it has also never made politics its central theme as directly or insistently as "Mosh" does.

"Mosh" doesn't manage to save *Encore* (any more than it managed to help defeat Bush), but as a rhetorical gambit, it's pointed enough to suggest that Eminem might, in his own way, be the Madonna of his generation: a controversial—and seemingly dismissible—pop star who turns out to be a much more outspoken figure when it comes to political issues than most observers (fans included) would have imagined possible. One early believer in Eminem's potential for politically progressive musical agitation was Tom Carson:

> Right now, dissing his would-be censors aside, our hero's political acumen is roughly on a par with Daffy Duck's. But with his flair for topicality, a few more skids in the Dow could turn him as belligerent as Public Enemy's Chuck D, and wouldn't *that* be interesting?[42]

And though most of *Encore* sounds more like "Daffy Duck" than anything Eminem had ever released before, the forceful pugnacity of "Mosh" provides reason to believe—or at least hope—that Eminem might someday really turn out to be "our hero" after all.

Chapter Notes

1. Stuart Hall, "Race, Culture, and Communications: Looking Backward and Forward at Cultural Studies," *Rethinking Marxism* 5(1): 15.

2. For more on the racial politics of *The Cosby Show*, see Michael Eric Dyson, *Reflecting Black: African American Cultural Criticism* (Minneapolis: University of Minnesota Press, 1993), 78–87; Herman Gray, *Watching Race: Television and the Struggle for Blackness* (Minneapolis: University of Minnesota Press, 1995), 79–84; and Sut Jhally and Justin M. Lewis, *Enlightened Racism: The Cosby Show, Audiences, and the Myth of the American Dream* (Boulder, CO: Westview, 1992).

3. There are many sources for more detailed arguments about these particular discursive silences and evasions, but some of the best are bell hooks, *Where We Stand: Class Matters* (New York: Routledge, 2000); Peggy McIntosh, "White Privilege: Unpacking the Invisible Knapsack," reprinted in Paula S. Rothenberg, ed., *Race, Class, and Gender in the United States: An Integrated Study*, 4th ed. (New York: St. Martin's, 1998), 165–9; Beverly Daniel Tatum, *"Why Are All the Black Kids Sitting Together in the Cafeteria?" and Other Conversations About Race* (New York, Basic, 1999); and Patricia J. Williams, *Seeing a Color-Blind Future: The Paradox of Race* (New York, Noonday, 1997).

4. A small portion of this literature includes Maurice Berger, *White Lies: Race and the Myths of Whiteness* (New York: Farrar Strauss and Giroux, 1999); Richard Dyer, *White: Essays on Race and Culture* (New York: Routledge, 1997); Ruth Frankenberg, *White Women, Race Matters: The Social Construction of Whiteness* (Minneapolis: University of Minnesota Press, 1993); Paul Gilroy, *Against Race: Imagining Political Culture Beyond the Color Line* (Cambridge, MA: Harvard University Press, 2000); Noel Ignatiev, *How the Irish Became White* (New York: Routledge, 1995); Noel Ignatiev and John Garvey, *Race Traitor* (New York: Routledge, 1996); George Lipsitz, *The Possessive Investment in Whiteness: How White People Profit from Identity Politics* (Philadelphia: Temple University Press, 1993); Michael Omi and Howard Winant, *Racial Formation in the United States: From the 1960s to the 1980s* (New York: Routledge, 1986); David R. Roediger, *Towards the Abolition of Whiteness* (New York: Verso, 1994); Beverly Daniel Tatum, *"Why Are All the Black Kids Sitting Together in the Cafeteria?" and Other Conversations About Race* (New York, Basic, 1999); and Patricia J. Williams, *Seeing a Color-Blind Future: The Paradox of Race* (New York, Noonday, 1997).

5. For example, see Sharon Begley, "Three Is Not Enough: Surprising New Lessons from the Controversial Science of Race," *Newsweek* (February 13, 1995): 67–69; Robin Marantz Henig, "The Genome Is Black and White (and Gray)," the *New York Times Magazine* (October 10, 2004): 46–51; and Nicholas Wade, "Race-Based Medicine Continued," the *New York Times* (November 14, 2004): section 4, 12.

6. And, of course, here I'm borrowing (with love) the phrase *Love and Theft* that Eric Lott used as the title of his groundbreaking book on blackface minstrelsy.

7. Arthur Jafa, "My Black Death," in Greg Tate, ed., *Everything but the Burden: What White People Are Taking from Black Culture* (New York: Harlem Moon, 2003): 250.

8. Also see Todd Boyd, *The New H.N.I.C. (Head Niggas in Charge): The Death of Civil Rights and the Reign of Hip Hop* (New York: New York University Press, 2003): 122–127 for a nuanced discussion of the differences between "imitation" and "influence" with respect to white artists working in black idioms.

9. As Zadie Smith sardonically notes, "Every article ever published on Eminem can be paraphrased thus: Mother, Libel, Guns, Homosexuals, Drugs, Own Daughter, Wife, Rape, Trunk of Car, Youth of America, Tattoos, Prison, Gangsta, White Trash." Zadie Smith, "The Zen of Eminem," *Vibe* (November 2002): 96.

10. For instance, both Eric Boehlert ("Invisible Man: Eminem," reprinted in Nick Hornby and Benjamin Schafer, eds., *Da Capo Best Music Writing 2001: The Year's Finest*

Writing on Rock, Pop, Jazz, Country, & More (Cambridge, MA: Da Capo, 2000): 119–127) and Michael Hoyt ("An Eminem Expose: Where Are the Critics?," *Columbia Journalism Review* 67 (2000)) complain that critics simply have routinely dismissed and/or glossed over Eminem's most offensive lyrics, even while the public controversy raging around Eminem remains the perennial focus of much of what's been written about him in the mainstream press over the past several years.

11. For example, see Eric Boehlert, "Invisible Man: Eminem," reprinted in Nick Hornby and Benjamin Schafer, eds., *Da Capo Best Music Writing 2001: The Year's Finest Writing on Rock, Pop, Jazz, Country, & More* (Cambridge, MA: Da Capo, 2000); Ethan Brown, "Classless Clown," *New York* 153 (June 26/July 3, 2000); Anthony DeCurtis, "Eminem's Hate Rhymes," *Rolling Stone* (August 3, 2000): 17–18; Christopher John Farley, "A Whiter Shade of Pale," *Time* (May 29, 2000): 73; Sasha Frere-Jones, "Haiku for Eminem," reprinted in Jonathan Lethem and Paul Bresnick, eds., *Da Capo Best Music Writing 2002: The Year's Finest Writing on Rock, Pop, Jazz, Country, & More* (Cambridge, MA: Da Capo, 2001): 138–140; and Michael Hoyt, "An Eminem Expose: Where Are the Critics?," *Columbia Journalism Review* 67 (2000).

12. For example, see Tom Carson, "This Land Is His Land," *Esquire* (December 2002); N'Gai Croal, "Slim Shady Sounds Off," *Newsweek* (May 29, 2000); Brian Doherty, "Bum Rap: Lynne Cheney vs. Slim Shady," *Reason* (March 5, 2001); Richard Kim, "Eminem—Bad Rap?," *The Nation* (March 5, 2001); Joan Morgan, "White Noise," *Ms.* (August/September 1999); Carl Hancock Rux, "Eminem: The New White Negro," in Greg Tate, ed., *Everything but the Burden: What White People Are Taking from Black Culture* (New York: Harlem Moon, 2003); Zadie Smith, "The Zen of Eminem," *Vibe* (November 2002); and Josh Tyrangiel, "The Three Faces of Eminem," *Time* (June 3, 2002).

13. Sociologist Stan Cohen describes a moral panic

> as a condition, episode, person or group of persons emerges to become defined as a threat to societal values and interests; its nature is presented in a stylized and stereo-typical fashion by the mass media; the moral barricades are manned [sic] by editors, bishops, politicians and other right-thinking people; socially accredited experts pronounce their diagnoses and solutions; ways of coping are evolved or (more often) resorted to; the condition then disappears, submerges or deteriorates and becomes more visible. Sometimes the object of the panic is quite novel and at other times it is something which has been in existence long enough, but suddenly appears in the limelight. Sometimes the panic is passed over and is forgotten, except in folklore and collective memory; at other times it has more serious and long-lasting repercussions and might produce such changes as those in legal and social policy or even in the way society conceives itself [quoted in Stuart Hall, Chas Crichter, Tony Jefferson, John Clarke, and Brian Roberts, eds., *Policing the Crisis: Mugging, the State, and Law and Order* (New York: Holmes & Meier, 1978): 16–17].

In extending and updating the notion of the "moral panic" as a category of social analysis, Angela McRobbie notes

> that at root the moral panic is about instilling fear in people and, in so doing, encouraging them to try and turn away from the complexity and the visible social problems of everyday life and either to retreat into a "fortress mentality"—a feeling of hopelessness, political powerlessness and paralysis—or to adopt a gung-ho "something must be done about it" attitude. The moral panic is also frequently a means of attempting to discipline the young through terrifying their parents. This remains a powerful emotional strategy [Angela McRobbie, *Postmodernism and Popular Culture* (New York: Routledge, 1994): 199].

14. As far as I can tell, Eminem's detractors have simply assumed that his primary audience consists of minors, but I've yet to see any hard data offered in support of this

claim. This is a time-honored, if not exactly honest, rhetorical device when it comes to moralistic condemnations of popular culture. Framing the issue as one of "protecting children" not only carries more affective weight than "protecting young adults," but it also implicitly absolves the critics invoking such rhetoric from the need to actually pay attention to what real audiences have to say about their media choices. I don't doubt that Eminem's fanbase includes a significant number of minors, but the claim that Eminem's audience is mostly children needs to be backed up with something more than the knee-jerk assumption that popular culture (or, more narrowly, hip hop) is "just for kids."

15. Lennon quite possibly borrowed this line from Elvis Presley's version of "Baby, Let's Play House."

16. Michel Foucault, "What Is an Author?" Translated by J.V. Harari, reprinted in James D. Faubion, ed., *Aesthetics, Method, and Epistemology: Essential Works of Foucault, 1954–1984, Vol. 2* (New York: New Press, 1999), 215.

17. Gore's self-proclaimed fandom for artists such as the Rolling Stones—who didn't exactly make sexually prim music in their heyday—only serves to underscore the fact that there was something more than just sexually provocative lyrics at stake in her attacks on what she called "porn rock."

18. Tom Carson, "This Land Is His Land," *Esquire* (December 2002): 88.

19. Novelist Zadie Smith rebuts this attitude by noting that

> Salvador Dali was an asshole. So was John Milton. Eminem's life and opinions are not his art. His art is his art. Sometimes people with bad problems make good art. The interesting question is this: When the problems go, does the art go, too? Oh, and if that word 'art' is still bothering you in the context of white-trash rapper from Detroit, here's a quick useful definition of an artist: someone with an expressive talent most of us do not have ["The Zen of Eminem," *Vibe* (November 2002): 88].

20. For a more extended discussion of the racial politics of Elvis' stardom, see Gilbert B. Rodman, "A Hero to Most? Elvis, Myth, and the Politics of Race," *Cultural Studies* 8(3): 457–483.

21. For an extended definition of "articulation" as the term is most commonly used in cultural studies, see "On Postmodernism and Articulation: An Interview with Stuart Hall," *Journal of Communication Inquiry* 10(2): 45–60.

22. For a more extended discussion of this practice, see Tricia Rose, "Fear of a Black Planet: Rap Music and Black Cultural Politics in the 1990s," *Journal of Negro Education* 60(3): 276–290.

23. See http://www.riaa.com/news/marketingdata/pdf/2003consumerprofile.pdf.

24. For an especially cogent version of this argument with respect to the blues, see Paul Garon, "White Blues," in Noel Ignatiev and John Garvey, *Race Traitor* (New York: Routledge, 1996).

25. See http://www.riaa.com/gp/bestsellers/topartists.asp.

26. For more extended versions of this argument, see Jim Goad, The Redneck Manifesto: How Hillbillies, Hicks, and White Trash Became America's Scapegoats (New York: Touchstone, 1997); bell hooks, Teaching to Transgress: Education as the Practice of Freedom (New York: Routledge, 1994); bell hooks, Where We Stand: Class Matters (New York: Routledge, 2000); Eric Lott, Love and Theft: Blackface Minstrelsy and the American Working Class (New York: Oxford University Press, 1995); and Patricia J. Williams, Seeing a Color-Blind Future: The Paradox of Race (New York, Noonday, 1997).

27. Carl Hancock Rux, "Eminem: The New White Negro," in Greg Tate, ed., Everything but the Burden: What White People Are Taking from Black Culture (New York:

Harlem Moon, 2003): 21. Also see Todd Boyd, The New H.N.I.C. (Head Niggas in Charge): The Death of Civil Rights and the Reign of Hip Hop (New York: New York University Press, 2003: 127–129.

28. Justin Driver, "Class Act," the *New Republic* (November 25, 2002): 42.

29. Roy Grundmann, "White Man's Burden: Eminem's Movie Debut in *8 Mile*," *Cineaste* (Spring 2003): 30–35.

30. bell hooks, Teaching to Transgress: Education as the Practice of Freedom (New York: Routledge, 1994); bell hooks, Where We Stand: Class Matters (New York: Routledge, 2000).

31. Laura Kipnis, *Bound and Gagged: Pornography and the Politics of Fantasy in America* (Durham, NC: Duke University Press, 1999); Laura Kipnis "(Male) Desire and (Female) Disgust: Reading *Hustler*, in Lawrence Grossberg, Cary Nelson, Paula Treichler, eds., *Cultural Studies* (New York: Routledge, 1992).

32. Lauren Berlant, "The Face of America and the State of Emergency," in Cary Nelson and Dilap P. Gaonkar, eds., *Disciplinarity and Dissent in Cultural Studies* (New York: Routledge, 1996): 408.

33. See the third verse of "Sing for the Moment."

34. See the second verse of "Square Dance."

35. See the second verse of "White America."

36. See the second verse of "The Way I Am."

37. For example, one of the anonymous reviewers of this essay seemed willing to accept my general argument concerning the racial politics underlying the moral panic around Eminem, but still expressed discomfort at the lack of an unequivocal condemnation of Eminem's sexism and homophobia. Given that the version of this essay read by reviewers already refused to whitewash (pun fully intended) Eminem's more unsavory lyrics, it's hard not to read such a critique as an example of what Patricia J. Williams has called "battling biases": a form of analytical paralysis in which progressive outrage at one form of political injustice is blindly used to reinforce the less-than-progressive status quo along a different axis. "Upon occasion," Williams notes, "the ploughshare of feminism can be beaten into a sword of class prejudice" (*Seeing a Color-Blind Future,* 32). The recognition that Eminem's music is more complicated than a straightforward expression of patriarchal privilege doesn't require us to erase Eminem's sexism and homophobia from critical discussions of his public personae. At most, it might require us to inject a bit of productive nuance to our understanding of Eminem's sexual politics. Laura Kipnis's commentary on the tangled class/gender politics of *Hustler*, for instance, could just as easily be used to describe the misogynistic aspects of Eminem's music: "Doesn't this reek of disenfranchisement rather than any certainty of male power over women? The fantasy life here is animated by a cultural disempowerment in relation to a sexual caste system and a social class system" (*Bound and Gagged,* 151). Such an analysis doesn't let Eminem's violent sexism off the hook—any more than Kipnis simply ignores *Hustler's* objectification of women—but it also refuses to pretend that our analysis of Eminem's music and stardom can safely be reduced to a single strand of identity politics.

38. Joan Morgan, "White Noise," *Ms.* (August/September 1999): 96.

39. Michael Jackson complained that the video for the album's first single, "Just Lose It," was defamatory insofar as it included a satirical swipe at Jackson with respect to the still-pending child molestation charges against him. This "controversy," however, died down almost as quickly as it surfaced.

40. Tori Amos' cover of "'97 Bonnie and Clyde" may be the clearest illustration of the artistry inherent in Eminem's song. In the context of an album (*Strange Little*

Girls) where she covers a dozen songs written by men that explicitly construct powerful visions of masculinity, Amos's performance of Eminem's musical fantasy is simultaneously a critical (feminist?) appropriation of the narrative and an absolutely eerie embodiment of it.

    41. Tom Carson, "This Land Is His Land," *Esquire* (December 2002): 88.
    42. Tom Carson, "This Land Is His Land," *Esquire* (December 2002): 90.

Beats by Em

Ben Hoerster

It would be difficult to argue with anyone positing Eminem as one of the greatest rappers of all time. Even music fans who are turned off by certain controversial aspects of his lyrical content, his distinct vocal tone, or perhaps even the color of skin, are at the very least going to be able to recognize his athletic, almost gymnastic, abilities as a rapper. His vocal delivery conveys a sense of lyrical dexterity matched only by the greats. He creates intricate, mathematical rhyme patterns and makes it look easy. Given the tremendous scale of his talents as a vocalist and lyricist, not to mention his oversized persona, it's easy to see why his skills as producer and beatmaker are overshadowed. However, an examination of his work in this realm reveals Eminem as a talented producer with a plethora of skills, that he has honed to create monster hit records in three decades and multiple eras of hip hop.

Eminem's skills as a producer are different than those that make him a great MC. On the mic, Eminem is a singular entity, presenting his personal stories and sketching ideas that are integral to his own narrative. In contrast, his musical productions throughout the years are almost always the result of collaborations. As an MC, his dexterous vocal delivery is matched by few (Naughty by Nature's Treach and Jay-Z, both stated influences, come to mind). As a musician, he doesn't possess those abilities. He can create a complex, racing lyrical passage and perform it, making it look easy, but he doesn't have the "chops" to pluck out a guitar phrase or bass line in the same way. He nonetheless has found success working with other musicians and producers to construe his musical ideas. He possesses other tools as a producer that have contributed to his successes, including an ear for catchy melodies and a fair amount of perfectionism that binds him to the studio, where he patiently and meticulously tweaks sounds to create unique tones.

Eminem's strength in, and compulsion for, collaboration has been the key element of his success as a producer, demonstrating the powerful effectiveness of working together. The coherent musical statement presented in his music is created by him shaping and being shaped by his collaborators. From his earliest days working with fellow Detroit citizens Proof and Mr. Porter in the early 1990s through the following decades creating music with Luis Resto, Eminem has used his collaborative skills to push new boundaries musically and sonically while maintaining certain musical elements that define his unique sound.

At this point, identifying Eminem-involved productions is an easy task. There are several elements consistently present in his works that help define his sound. His revelatory, political, and confessional tracks use brooding, minor chord phrasing to amplify his intense emotional tenor. When he's not exploring these darker themes, Eminem relies on pizzicato instrumentation and bubbling, bouncing melodies to back his humorous anecdotes and pop culture takedowns. The meticulously crafted, deliberately artificial tones he creates add the important sonic dimension to the surreal environment he inhabits. His warm, thick synthesized bass lines roll and pulsate during up-tempo numbers and trudge when he slows things down. These musical elements didn't manifest in a vacuum. His development as a producer took shape as a result of the work and influence of two key collaborators.

Dr. Dre would eventually play an enormous role in shaping Em's aesthetic, but before connecting with him, the Bass Brothers were key influences in the development of Eminem's signature sound. The Bass Brothers, Jeff and Mark Bass, recognized Em's talents early on, first signing him to their label in 1992 after hearing him freestyle on a Detroit radio station and inviting him to their studio for free recording time. At this time, the Bass Brothers were working with local Detroit artists on demo recordings, including early Em appearances on Basement Production (later Soul Intent) albums *Steppin onto the Scene, Still in the Bassmint,* and *Soul Intent.* In addition to their work capturing the burgeoning hip-hop scene in Detroit, the brothers also worked with funk music legend George Clinton and electronic group Tycie and Woody. The Bass Brothers as well as Eminem's friends Mr. Porter and Proof helped Eminem record his earnest first attempt at an LP, *Infinite.* The Bass Brothers were the executive producers of *Infinite,* which was released in 1996. Eminem had two co-production credits on the album, for "Maxine" and "Jealousy Woes II." In addition to their work early on, the Bass Brothers have remained consistent collaborators throughout Eminem's long career. These early recordings give a glimpse into the influences they were absorbing and exploring at that time.

Stylistically, the music Eminem is credited with shows tacit influences of beats made by early '90s production teams like Da Beatminerz and Tribe

Called Quest and producers such as Pete Rock and Detroit's own J Dilla. In this era, these producers and others were mining old jazz records looking for rich, warm tones to sample like the sounds made by the Fender Rhodes electronic keyboard, and mid-tempo musical phrases to loop. Laid back melodies were often matched with sharp, snapping snare drums, crisp high hats, and booming kick drums. This was a change from the de rigueur in production aesthetics present in the early '90s when producers such as The Dust Brothers and the Bomb Squad were cramming as many samples as they could into their compositions and creating hectic, claustrophobic sound-scapes. These warm, airy samples were perfect templates for the new breed of virtuosic MCs led by Nas, Biggie, and members of the Wu-Tang Clan.

Earlier productions from Eminem's collaborators at this time explored those warm jazzy sounds, occasionally filtering them through their own lenses but usually just composing near facsimiles of works by other artists.[1] For example, the song "Maxine" from *Infinite* is very similar to AZ's song "Rather Unique" produced by Pete Rock, recorded in 1995. Both songs have at their core a sophisticated musical phrase employing the signature Rhodes keyboard, propelled by a sharp crack of the snare and warm thump of the kick drum. Eminem and his collaborators weren't only exploring this con-temporary sound. They were also looking back and experimenting with sounds and techniques from different parts of the country and from pre-vious eras. On Soul Intent's self-titled third album, one can hear homage to Public Enemy producers the Bomb Squad as well as influential West Coast producers the Boogiemen and DJ Muggs. These efforts demonstrated the ability of Eminem's crew to effectively use the same hectic, dense drum loops and multilayered sounds and songs with high BPMs. But at this point, Em's music had not yet developed a coherent sound. His team was show-casing their ability to produce music with diverse influences. And rap music as a whole was beginning to change stylistically. Eminem and his collabo-rators were able to adapt to these changes effectively.

Hip-hop artists near the close of the century began to abandon the use of samples more and more. This change was partly driven by artists and record labels fearing litigation from copyright holders and partly driven by the abuse and overuse of certain sampling techniques by producers such as Diddy (Puff Daddy at the time) sampling entire phrases of musical com-positions that were top ten hits barely more than a decade prior. One egre-gious example is Puff Daddy's 1997 single "Been Around the World." On that track, he conspicuously cribs the Nile Rodgers guitar hook from David Bowie's smash hit "Let's Dance" from the mid-'80s and then interpolates the chorus from Lisa Stansfield's hit single "All Around the World" in the same song.

The move away from sample-based music was also instigated by other factors, including the rise in popularity of southern music. Southern rap music is a diverse segment of the culture, but one characteristic largely consistent across its constituents is that it doesn't rely on samples the way rap from the West Coast and East Coast has. It is unclear why southern music developed this way, but several influential production crews from the South helped shape the style. One of these groups was Organized Noize; they used live instruments and programmed drum patterns to create hits for Outkast and Goodie Mob. Other key artists who contributed to shaping this southern sound of hip hop were 2 Live Crew, DJ Spanish Fly, a legendary Memphis DJ who is credited as a forefather to crunk and trap music, and Mannie Fresh, a workhorse producer and DJ from New Orleans who was strongly influenced by early 1980s electro-hop coming out of L.A.

Producers such as Pharrell Williams and Chad Hugo of the Neptunes, Timbaland, and Dr. Dre began to experience success using original compositions as well. Likewise, the Bass Brothers increasingly began to move away from using samples. Because they were already adept at playing instruments and were plugged into the larger music scene in Detroit outside of rap music, they easily made this transition. Another factor that contributed to their success was the opportunity they had to work with engineers who collaborated with Motown artists and producers during the height of the music label's success. Working with these musicians gave the Bass Brothers the tools that allowed them to recreate some of the desired sounds and tones they and other producers had previously captured via sampling.[2] The beats credited to them on *The Marshall Mathers LP* demonstrate their ability to recreate bass and keyboard tones with the same warmth and smoothness as those made during Motown's heyday.

The Bass Brothers (consistent with hip hop as a whole) didn't completely abandon sampling and although their use was far less frequent, they went on to have great success using samples. For example, their well-placed usage of Aerosmith's popular "Dream On" for Eminem's song "Sing for the Moment" helped ground his message in a familiar context. Sampling this classic arena rock song also helped bolster Em's crossover appeal and the song's anthemic feel added some firepower to his live show setlist. Not satisfied with merely sampling the tune though, Eminem hired Aerosmith's guitarist Joe Perry to play the guitar solo that closes the track out.

Early on, during the production of *The Slim Shady EP* in 1997 and *LP* in '99, Eminem began expressing a clearer message to his collaborators about what he wanted his music to sound like. Luckily for him, the Bass Brothers were more than capable of helping him achieve that. Eminem told *Mix* magazine in 2000, "They came up with fatter, thicker-sounding beats than anything I'd had before." At the same time, Dr. Dre was moving toward production techniques that eschewed the use of samples, although for Dre this was more of a return to form. Before his work on *The Chronic* and subsequent work with Death Row artists, Dre was a member of World Class Wrecking Crew, where his productions were largely sample-free and were firmly planted in the West Coast electronic scene populated by other artists such as Egyptian Lover.[3] But by the start of the '90s, his use of samples was significantly increasing. Dre began demonstrating an ear for discovering compelling funk samples and matching them to the right artists, as evidenced by his production work for the D.O.C. on his song "Funky Enough," which samples the opening bars of the Sylver's song "Misdemeanor." By the time of Dre's solo debut, *The Chronic,* he had plunged full on into sample-based music and completely changed the aesthetic aims of the style by adding sophisticated engineering touches that added sparkle to the source music, a contrast to other contemporary producers like the Bomb Squad and Cypress Hill, who were still emphasizing the gritty, dusty elements of their sourced materials.

The early '90s saw Dre continuing to develop and grow this style, but in just a few years he was already moving away from sample use. His earth-rattling song "Natural Born Killaz," featuring former N.W.A. groupmate Ice Cube, showed the success he was capable of while avoiding samples. Again Dre developed and honed this style during the late '90s on albums by Nas and Nas's ill-fated group, The Firm, as well as on compilation albums produced by Dre and his newly formed record label, Aftermath.

Aftermath is where Eminem would ultimately land after Dre heard Eminem's demo tape. When Eminem debuted on Aftermath with *The Slim Shady LP,* Dre fluently demonstrated his masterful production, which he subsequently further showcased on his own much-delayed sophomore album, *Chronic 2001.* It's worth mentioning here that Dre, too, was a producer whose effectiveness as a collaborator was key to his enormous success. Eminem had opportunities to watch this and learn from Dre's collaborative process with other artists.

Now that Eminem had hooked up with Dre and brought his collaborators the Bass Brothers with him, the three entities blended and melded their styles together to create a coherent vision in *The Slim Shady LP.* Eminem was involved in the production in multiple ways. Jeff Bass, in an interview with *Mix* magazine, described Eminem's influence over the direction of the compositions by humming phrases for bass lines or guitar licks. It's true that Em was collaborating with two accomplished producers, not to mention Dre, but it's clear that they were open to taking cues from Eminem. Em used these experiences to learn more about production techniques and song composition.

Music created for *The Slim Shady LP* was designed to match Eminem's energy at the time. And because that energy could change in an instant, the album featured a dynamic blend of sounds reflecting the polarities of Eminem's psyche. The Bass Brothers, already used to crafting songs with Em in mind, were now somewhat freed from the financial constraints involved in making music and were able to devote more time to crafting songs and working with engineers to tweak tones that more successfully complemented Eminem's moods and themes. Dre too worked to match Em's sound.

Given the task of creating what would be Eminem's momentous debut, Dre found an obscure sample tailor-made to soundtrack the arrival of a transcendently skilled rapper seeming to come out of nowhere. Labi Siffre's buoyant phrasing on his song "I Got The" crept along at a snail's pace and provided plenty of open space for Em to insert his personality and charisma throughout his debut single, "My Name Is."

Subsequent releases increasingly featured production work from Eminem. He maintained his collaborative relationship with The Bass Brothers and Dr. Dre but also sought out new musicians and songwriters as he developed as a producer. On this journey he would ultimately plant himself at the dead center of popular music, producing some of the biggest hits of the decade.

Eminem's skills and prowess as a producer seem to have developed in service to two simultaneously occurring needs. First, Eminem—who was already expanding his empire into other ventures (artist development, cinema)—knew that producing music for both himself and artists in his stable would lead to more revenue. Second, and perhaps more importantly, Eminem needed to create beats and rhythms that would help match the intensifying intricacies of his flow. Songs like "Without Me" and "Cleanin' Out my Closet" are examples of his efforts to create beats to synch with his rhyme patterns.

By all accounts, Em is a studio rat. Numerous reports speak of the time and care he puts into crafting his verses. In an interview with Zadie Smith, Eminem dismisses the notion that some rappers are able to write verses in twenty minutes.[4] Em says that although he may get a rough draft down quickly, he will continually revisit and revise the rhymes and couplets over days and weeks. It seems likely that he would take as much care with his musical compositions.

Creating his own soundscapes allowed his verses to merge with them more completely and discretely. For someone who pioneered a rhyme style and thematic oeuvre, it is a testament to his abilities as a producer and musician that he was able to craft music that would complement it. By 2002, a year that featured the release of both *The Eminem Show* and the soundtrack to the movie *8 Mile*, Eminem was taking more control over the production work and hitting his stride as a producer. Still maintaining his habit for collaboration, the Grammy-nominated *The Eminem Show* had him collaborating with his usual cast of characters: Dre, The Bass Brothers, Luis Resto, and others.

Eminem wasn't satisfied working the boards only on his own solo efforts, though, and started to create beats for other artists. His production work on two pivotal albums in the early 2000s is demonstrative of his status as a heavyweight producer at the time. Everyone knows about Em's verses on "Renegade," the song he constructed for Jay-Z's return-to-the-foundation-themed album, *Blueprint*. According ex–Jay-Z-rival Nas on his song "Ether," Eminem "murdered" Jay on his own track. No easy feat for any rapper, especially considering Jay-Z was hitting his own peak right about that time. Nas wasn't the only one who felt Em outshined Jay on the track. But it was not just his stellar verses that piqued the listener's attention; the music Em laid down for Jay was well suited for both artists. The dark, brooding, menacing melody builds and crescendos repeatedly throughout the song. The instrumentation used here was smoother than on other tracks he produced at the time. This may have been the result of mixing and mastering, which would have required the composition to fit more with the soul-sampled aesthetics of the other beats on the album.

Blueprint is often noted as a return to form for rap as a genre. Moving away from the style of synth-heavy electronic music popular in rap at the time, Jay-Z's fourth album was seen as reminiscent of the Golden Era ('92 – '96) sound molded by Dr. Dre, RZA, DJ Premier, and many others. It showcased beats from Kanye West and Just Blaze featuring glimmering soul samples, sped up and bolstered by additional drums. *Blueprint* was a statement. Jay-Z wisely tapped Em to contribute to this album as well, despite Eminem's disparate musical style. The beat Em delivered ran counter to the album's core narrative. However, its appearance on the record isn't forced. It fits in the album, and credit should be given to Em for his ability to give Jay a song that would work in the context of such a soulful, return-to-form album.

Perhaps flattered by Nas's declaration of him as victor in the imagined competition between Nas and Jay on "Renegade," Eminem agreed to produce a song for Nas's album *God's Son* the following year. "The Cross" doesn't have a place in hip-hop lore the way "Renegade" does but its dynamic, epic musical qualities helped it go toe-to-toe with the other tracks on *God's Son*. Producing tracks for Nas and Jay-Z during their feuding years served several purposes. Em demonstrated that he could deliver productions that were clearly in his own style but that were also myopically designed for the artists he was giving them to. He effectively revisited this feat again, and even upped the ante, when he created the music for Tupac's emotionally heavy track "Runnin'" featuring the Pac-foe Notorious B.I.G. Both rappers had been deceased for several years and hearing them together on a song over Em's melancholic composition had a healing effect on listeners and fans still grieving over the loss of these two iconic rappers. These two high-profile placements set Eminem up to be one of the most highly sought-after producers of the mid-'00s.

Throughout the decade, Eminem produced a plethora of songs for himself, for artists affiliated with his label, including Obie Trice, 50 Cent, and D12, and for other major stars in hip hop such as T.I., Jadakiss, and Akon. One assignment in particular that indicated his ascension into the company of hip-hop's elite producers was when he was tapped in 2004 to produce Tupac's posthumous release *Loyal to the Game*. He worked with Luis Resto to produce every song on the album outside of the bonus tracks. Eminem successfully met the daunting task of creating compelling music for lyrics recorded over a decade prior by hip-hop's most iconic figure. Noah Callahan-Bever, in his review of the album for *Vibe* magazine, described beats that "oscillate from dark and brooding to spine-tingling and epic" and lauds his efforts by calling his production choices "an ideal fit for 2Pac's impassioned, if at times grandiose, lyrics."[5]

What Em brought to the table during this period was an ear for unique, unconventional sounds that he would manipulate and compose to create music that resonated with both rap fans and pop fans. *The Eminem Show* released in 2002 was the most concentrated demonstration of these elements. This album was stuffed with compelling musical compositions tailor-made to support and add context to the subject matter of his raps. There is no nuance here. His song "Square Dance," with lyrics of frustration and adversity is placed on top of a beat full of unrelenting tension. His confessional lyrics on "Cleanin' Out My Closet" are presented on a busy, loose drum pattern and wandering piano loop, which combine to add dramatic weight to his words. "Hailie's Song" uses a similar formula to great effect. The fact that some beats on the album are repetitive is not necessarily a weakness. On the darker, edgier songs, repetition gives the listener an effect similar to that of a march—it's easy to imagine an army of Stans or the group of wannabe Slim Shadys from his MTV Video Music Awards appearance marching along to songs like "Square Dance," "Sing for the Moment," and "Till I Collapse." And the use of repetition on the more confessional songs urges the listener to lean in and become captivated by Em as storyteller. Of course Em is a man of contrasting moods and he balances the darkness with the fun "Without Me," which features synthesized tones grounded by a pulsating bass line.

The Eminem Show and his production work on the *8 Mile* soundtrack demonstrated that he could make music fit certain moods, and he did so for many artists throughout the first decade of the millennium. He showed he could create a beat tailor-made for a certain artist that remained permeated by his DNA as a producer. This is most evident on Jay-Z's "Moment of Clarity"—even when completely redone by Danger Mouse for his *Grey Album,* it is clear that its genesis is thanks to none other than Marshall Mathers. At this time, Eminem was also cultivating a collaborative relationship with his touring keyboard player Luis Resto. Outside of Em's monumental work with Dr. Dre, his collaborative relationship with Resto has given life to some of the most compelling and successful music of Eminem's career. The monster smash "On Fire," created for Lloyd Banks, showed his ability to match contemporary tastes while still maintaining a strong musical identity. This song also showcased his ability to craft party songs. Later in the decade he would do himself one better with the pop radio staple "Smack That" with Akon.

During this period, Eminem also focused on creating more dynamic songs. His collaborations with Resto allowed him to craft songs with more complex phrasing and song structure. These two would ultimately work together to create Em's most popular songs, too, including "Lose Yourself" and "Not Afraid." Producing smash hits in 2010 required more than just an ear for beats and a decent reputation. To have a song played consistently on the radio requires focus groups and rigorous testing from radio program directors. Surviving in this era means Em has developed all of the tools necessary to be a producer: the ability to find samples, program drum beats and create sounds; knowing which artists to work with; finding talented musicians to help you realize the sounds in your head, and developing and maintaining relationships with other producers and studio engineers to stay on the cutting edge of production techniques. For Eminem, it also requires staying true to his roots. His loyalty to early collaborators such as Dre and the Bass Brothers is clear, as he has collaborated musically with both throughout his long career.

It's difficult to anticipate how Eminem's career will develop moving forward. He has left himself with little to prove. He has demonstrated an ability to produce commercially successful hits, reaching the top quarter of Billboard's Hot 100 chart more than twenty times. Perhaps more impressive than his commercial feats has been his ability to produce several iconic songs that have connected strongly with music fans and have made room for themselves in a hip-hop canon staunchly defended by hip-hop classicists with little interest in productions made after the Golden Era. However, rap music continues to progress. In the past Eminem adapted cleverly by finding new songrwriters and producers to collaborate with. Rap music continues to transform and is shifting into a new era. The genre's current aesthetic characteristics reveal an accelerated move from its organic roots toward a sound increasingly defined by synthesized instrumentation and mechanical beats. This is a sound Eminem has helped to shape and define, so it is likely that he will continue to find success in the current soundscape. Little is known about his next album, projected to come out in late 2013. One intriguing development is that he has been collaborating with No I.D., a veteran Chicago producer who got his start producing soulful, sample-based music for the rapper Common. Throughout his long career No I.D. has developed into a versatile artist; he has a great ear and is a master with a sampling machine. He also is adept at working with musicians, utilizing them to add texture and bolster his sample based music as well as creating original compositions. The pairing of these two seems promising, and working with a new producer who has stylistic differences but a similar pedigree to past collaborators should serve to reinvigorate Eminem. Once again it appears Eminem will lean on his skills as a collaborator to find his way back to the top of the charts.

Chapter Notes

1. This isn't to say there is anything wrong with this. Artists in all forms hone their craft by working through the influences of their predecessors. Eminem has acknowledged that he developed his skills as a rapper by rapping along to his favorite artists.

2. Gary Eskow, "The Bass Brothers and Eminem," *Mix* (August 2000).

3. Dre Productions at this time include seminal electro-hop song "Supersonic" by JJ Fad.

4. Zadie Smith, "The Zen of Eminem," *Vibe* (November 2002).

5. Noah Callahan-Bever, "2Pac *Loyal to the Game* Review," *Vibe* (March 2005).

The Fanatic Lyric:
Eminem as Poet

Aaron Apps

This essay begins with a difficult task: to describe Eminem's lyricism without referring to the lyrics themselves as they contort, spasm over beats, and form in between bars. The lyrics can't appear on the page at any length because they are too expensive to publish, thanks to copyright law. It's a problem that leaves me as a reader and writer in an eddying, troublesome conundrum that is hard to swim out of. How does one describe the mechanics of poetry without tearing into the engine case to see how the pistons move? How does one show the magnificent engineering of the gasoline driven line within the machine without showing the schematics? How does one say anything about a verse without quoting the verse itself? Such a constraint throws a wrench into all efforts aimed at close reading.

As I pondered how to approach the lyricism in Eminem's songs with no access to the verse itself, I realized that not having access to the lyric opens up a much wider space of discourse about Eminem. I'm approaching his work as poetry with an emphasis on the verse, from the perspective of a poet, but there is always much more to poetry than rhymes, cadences, and metaphors. Shutting the valve off to one area in the engine floods another area and creates a new set of possibilities, a new approach. And, just maybe, the lyric unto itself becomes more of a crutch than a guide. There is so much to Eminem's lyricism that isn't in the tight construction of the bars that is equally, if not more, important to his body of work as a poet.

Besides, I'm critical of contemporary New Formalism (an approach to reading and writing poetry that focuses entirely on close readings of the rhetoric within poems) for its strict focus on the verse itself as an immunologically abstracted thing, as something separated off from the world entirely. I'm skeptical of New Formalism because its interest in rhyme, meter, and diction is set always over and above the content and politics of the poem, and this move that focuses on the workings of the poem has a politics of its own that attempts to keep writing in the domain of the self-referential, self-contained aesthetic object. But surely hip hop can't be contained in such simplistic aesthetic borders. Hip hop samples, steals, defaces, quotes, and is always already political. Hip hop is hostile and contentious territory. When I look at my predicament through this lens, when I accept the mess of influences and outside refuse, not having access to the lyrics themselves seems like a gift rather than a curse. Close reading the metaphors and rhyme patterns in a few verses would be almost too easy; in their place I'm left with Eminem as a complicated, porous figure who creates verses that are shockingly dexterous, I'm left with Eminem "the Poet."

So, in Eminem's case, what does it mean to be a Poet? Eminem is a popular figure as much as he is a lyricist, and all of the controversy that surrounds him makes the task of talking about him as just a lyricist troubled work. One can't draw up an easy immunological border between the perceived pubic *auteur* and the lyric crafted between the bars of blood-beating beats. Eminem is a "Poet" in the capitalized sense of the word. He expands beyond the borders of the song outward into his image and the public's multifaceted ideas of his image. The figure, the image, the specter of "Eminem" has all of the allure, style, and excess of poets of historical and biographical note such as Rimbaud, Keats, Plath, and Byron. Marshall Mathers isn't just another rapper who constructs shockingly tight rhymes into musical bars, Eminem is as much myth as he is man, and he becomes a myth to his listeners much like the above poets. Eminem crafts or comports into images as much as he creates music. The lyrical skill that can be teased out via close reading is there in Eminem's work, it's there in excess, but it feels equally honest to step back from its intricacies in in order to circle around the "Poet" or "Rapper" as a proper noun. That circling feels like a truer gesture toward getting at the rhymes. That tangential meandering toward a center through the spectacle of Eminem's persona gets closer to the truth of the lyric.

As I sidestep the intricacies of the lyric in order to talk about public persona, I want to mention and hold up scholarly efforts that delve into the lyric because they are accomplishing important work in terms of pushing rap into the realm of poetry, where it deserves to be. Lyrically intricate rap verses deserve to be elevated both for their complexity and for their social and economic content. Eminem creates poetry of worth and substance in this sense, but Eminem is his own monster, his own amorphous body of pop- and socio-cultural problems. I want to acknowledge that rap is poetry, and that Eminem is among the most skilled living writers of verse (literary poets, slam poets, and rappers combined) from the outset of this argument in order to elide the work of proving his artistic merit as it happens in the gears of the words in the engine of the verse. I want to do this both because I can't quote from the songs, and because to merely quote and close read rhymes would be problematic. Instead, I'll focus in on Eminem, a figure with his own set of influences, and his mythos. What happens when we crack open the myth and turn the rapper back into a man? What happens when we take the public persona and fold it back into the rhymes? How do they relate? How do they clash? Where do we as listeners and viewers end up in relation to the performance as we sit back engulfed in the flood of images and lyrics? How do Eminem's underground roots connect to the glistening leaves of his pop persona?

To do this work, to make these connections, to step into the pastiche of his image in order to get at the reality of his lyrics, I want to cut Eminem down a few notches in order to build him back up. I want to see into and through the gleam of his cultural cache in order to see both what's great about his lyrical skill and what about it makes it bridge over to a wider audience. I'll say this: I think it's too easy to posit that Eminem's mass appeal is *strictly* a product of race. I think the problem is more complicated, and is rooted to a degree in the style and content of his lyrics. Again, the lyrics are important, but I want to take a different angle in as to why they are.

Eminem isn't made of the same matter as Macklemore, Riff Raff, Paul Wall, Asher Roth, Yelawolf, Mac Miller, El-P, nor are any of those rappers cast from the same matter as one another. Sure, race is a factor; Eminem appeals to a struggling white audience, and connects to that audience in a strangely personal way that effervesces with a kind of sincere effect, but that's not all that makes him tick, that's not all that makes him successful. The threads Eminem connects to his audience make his success understandable quantitatively. Simply put: in terms of sheer numbers (not demographic percentages), there are more white than non-white people irking out a living in poor and lower-middle-class conditions. And suburban kids outside of those conditions often imagine themselves in such conditions, or are only a generation removed from them. It's a perspective that strikes a major chord with a large consuming audience. Eminem is the perfect coat of paint for the consumer—it's not just that he's white, it's that he presents aspects of that audience's struggle back to it in ways that are deeply appealing. Eminem is seductive to the helplessness, anger, and alienation that this audience feels.

But it's not just race or class connecting Eminem to a particular audience; it's also the style of his lyric—the way the rhymes are constructed, and the hype that surrounds them. The approach and stylistic choices he deploys in his verses are tied to a certain energy that reflects class distinctions and social struggle, but I think the approach and craft is itself essential to Eminem's appeal. There's something specific to Eminem. Any of the aforementioned artists are invested in portraying the challenges of a hard-lived existence, even Asher Roth, who openly claims his suburban roots, has a political edge if you look past his radio tracks, yet none of them even come close to Eminem's initial or continued success. There's something strange and particular about Eminem, and there's something seductive about him. I'm tempted to say that it is the fantasized violence and anger that the songs contain, but even that feels too easy, too concrete. Sure, that violence is tempting, but it alone isn't enough to draw in the massive success and respect that Eminem has gleaned both within the industry, and especially within the larger music-consuming audience. Even if Eminem's actual experiences don't overlap with the audiences in any concrete way, the sense of overlap is more palpable, and seemingly more real. This is the audience who buys Eminem records in excess and supports his legacy, and they're passionate about him. There's something very particular about Eminem that gives him an extra boost in his audience's eyes, and it isn't a singular thing. It's not just race. It's not just marketing. It's his whole body of authorial work that creates the mystique. It's Eminem the Poet, proper.

Nor is Eminem's success a simple matter of lyrical skill (even though I'm putting an emphasis on that point within this essay). Yes, he *is* a great lyricist—he blows me away sometimes with the razor edge of his craft, that's undeniable—but there are *multitudes* of great lyricists like Ice Cube, Andre 3000, Big L, Kendrick Lamar, Rakim, Lauryn Hill, Lil Wayne, Big Daddy Kane, Ludacris, Talib Kweli, Scarface, etc. Not to mention other thoroughly canonical figures like Jay-Z, Tupac, Nas, and Biggie. So, why is Eminem viewed as unequivocally "the best" by such a large body of the listening public? Why does such a large portion of the purchasing audience flock to Eminem and not to any other number of rap greats?

I admit that I'm often critically drawn to the reactions people have to songs and videos as they are released, and as they begin to pick up momentum as cultural objects. In short, I like to read internet comments because they provide a strange lens into the fan community. As I scroll through people's cursory reactions on YouTube and on forums, there is often someone ranting unprovoked about Eminem's greatness in relation to whatever video or article is at hand; it's a strange dynamic within the fan community, and one that I as a listener don't understand. Or, I potentially understand it in terms of the racial and socioeconomic dimensions of the popular listening community; I just don't understand it in terms of lyricism itself. In fact, the attitudes of such fans make me exude a curmudgeonly affect toward Eminem as a public figure. Sure, he's lyrically impressive even at his worst—

even *The Relapse* (widely acknowledged as Eminem's worst album, even by himself in several interviews) includes tight rhyming constructions and multiple voices that echo the best of high Modernist poetry in terms of sheer lyrical skill—but these are features that you can find in most rap that is invested in the lyric. What makes Eminem stand out? Is it because he is the most skilled "white" MC we've ever seen? I don't think that in and of itself is enough. Then, what gives?

Before I got caught up in the strange problem of writing about the lyric without quoting it, I was caught up in the problem of writing about Eminem himself. When I mentioned to a colleague that I was writing about Eminem's lyrical ability, and that I was a bit hesitant about doing it because I felt he already had too much credit as a figure, the colleague in question cornered me and was adamant about how Eminem's greatness was "a given, acknowledged by everyone," and said that I was "just being contrary." The same thing happened when I mentioned my hesitancy about the article to my Intro to Fiction students at the University of Minnesota. One of them responded with utter sincerity, "yeah, but Eminem is *so* great." Maybe I am giving into a contrary tendency, but while I don't deny that Eminem is both lyrically skilled and culturally important, I just don't think he deserves to be held above any of the aforementioned artists. Creating an essay that fetishized Eminem's lyricism and *only* fetishized his lyricism felt like bad territory to tread into even before I came to terms with any formal limitations.

It's not just disrespectful to these other artists to call Eminem the greatest lyricist. What's worse is that it's disrespectful in a way that's not interesting or generative. As a poet, I like it when writers, critics, and academics slander and tear apart the figures in canonical anthologies in order to include women, people of color, and people of different class backgrounds—it makes the whole effort of anthologizing more honest and permeable, it runs against New Formalism. Calling rap poetry on par with the rest of contemporary, oft-academic poetry functions in a similar way: the action that includes it in the academy changes our perception of the poetry being produced and propagated by the academy. Tossing rap up into the poetic stratosphere is a win-win situation—such acts make things more inclusive and create a space where we can look at literature for reasons other than its high-thrown status as literature, as cannon. Texts like Adam Bradley's *Book of Rhymes: The Poetics of Hip Hop* and Jay-Z's *Decoded* are important because they expand the borders and expectations of what we consider poetry by considering rap to be on equal footing with literary attempts at genre.

The motivations for calling Eminem "the greatest living lyricist" (rhetoric that is always filled with hyperbole), on the other hand, feels conservative and stifling. It's a gesture that is disrespectful to many other voices within hip hop that we should be listening to—whether those are the prophetic lyricists who have come from harsh backgrounds into places of fame, or the highly politicized voices of the underground. It seems wrong to merely write about Eminem using the same approach as Adam Bradley or Jay-Z. It seems wrong to articulate Eminem's lyrical skill in a way that fetishizes both the lyric and the artist given strange space he occupies within our popular imagination. If I take the poetic significance of rap as a given, as an *a priori* state, where then does Eminem stand in the pantheon of lyricists? Is he, as most of the anonymous internet claims, the greatest living MC? Of course not, and who cares? But then how do I answer the previous question? Where does he stand amid rap's many great lyricists? Where do I position him within that vast spectrum? And, why does he remain so much more seductive than other MCs of his lyrical ability?

I don't have an easy answer to either question, but I do have an anecdote that might help tease out some of the rhetoric that tangentially surrounds the question of Eminem as a lyricist. I like to think that I might ironically (in terms of distance, rather than comedy) circle around Eminem's position as a lyricist for the duration of this essay in order to trace the contours of his lyricism both in terms of cultural origins and public perceptions. When I taught a hip hop course at the University of Minnesota titled *Prophets of the Hood*, a course that used rap lyrics to focus in on the existential nihilism that is produced in the face of political and social oppression, at some point the students devolved into playground antics of deciding who were the top ten rappers of all time. While such list making is ultimately silly and hopelessly subjective, it does hold some cultural weight within the hip-hop community given that MTV's "Hottest MC" list or *The Source*'s coveted "5 Mics" rating can make or break a rapper's career, and within the auspices of the classroom it brought out some noteworthy dynamics between my students in terms of the relationship between audience and race. To be a bit reductive for the sake of brevity, there was a sharp racial divide between the students in the class in terms of how they perceived Eminem's significance: the white students thought Eminem was one of the best rappers of all time, and the students of color didn't even put him in their top ten. Everyone acknowledged Eminem's skills as a lyricist. Sure, it was a self-selecting audience of students who decided to take a summer course focused especially on creative writing and hip hop (in the state of Minnesota), but it also seems quite apropos in retrospect. The students who didn't hold Eminem on a pedestal posited a multitude of rappers for the top spot, which seemed much more honest and aesthetically diverse. When we finished off our top MC tangent, everyone (Eminem fans and skeptics alike) started ragging on Lil Wayne. He wasn't making anyone's top ten, lyrical skills or not. I'm not exactly sure why, but I think it has to do with the way they related to Lil Wayne—as easily consumable and complicated as his verses may be, they lack any emotional or political root. Being all spectacle and lyrical skill with no point through which the audience can relate to him, Lil Wayne doesn't make the cut. While Eminem, on the other hand, uses emotional sincerity and a connection to a certain economic background in excess, and he definitely finds a connection to his audience through that sincerity.

Audience connection aside: Eminem is still the lyricist Nas cited on "Ether" as having enough lyrical skill to tear down Jay-Z on his own album (on *Blueprint*'s "Renegade") during their historic rap battle. And now, more than ten years later, Jay-Z and Eminem have a co-sponsored DJ Hero game called the "Renegade Edition" that recalls that historic track. Eminem's reputation as a lyricist runs deep and is widely accepted, but the move that puts him in a position to stand between two of the great MCs as the bar on which their own lyrics are judged against each other's is what backs up fans' claims to Eminem's greatness. But it's not just the lyricism as a singular thing that is driving audiences in mass to Eminem's side to become devoted fans, there's something more to it as I've already intimated. I want to posit that connection is rooted in Eminem's origins in battle and live-performance rap. That approach to hip hop as central force in the development of his lyrical voice, combined with an ability to cross over to the mainstream because of his race, skill, and connections to Dr. Dre's popular audio productions pushed him the him the extra mile to not only cross over but to enter the popular ether as a dominate force. Signing to Interscope Records pushed him to the next level, but being rooted in a certain cultural lineage allowed him to prosper. Eminem's approach to rap is rooted in a certain style, and that style gives him a platform to launch from.

Of course, the above list of things (race, class, image, etc.) that allowed for Eminem's success within the mainstream sounds like a hodgepodge rather than a singular root cast deep into the soil. Eminem's lyrical adroitness is undeniable and much of his legacy is contingent upon that skill, so looking to the origins of that while acknowledging the perfect storm of other factors that allowed him to cross over seems like a reasonable move. It ultimately comes down to how those lyrical origins transfer over to the public persona. Eminem, Slim Shady, and Marshall Mathers do not rely only on swag or persona to connect to the audience, there is always the lyrics to back that persona up. There are always those verses that touch, prod, and shock the listener, both with their content and with their skill. There is always something at stake in the background. There is always verse between the bars that prevents the audience from classifying Eminem as another joke in the league of Vanilla Ice. Eminem has "cred" as a rapper; no one denies that he is the real deal.

But there is also a certain style and accessibility to Eminem's verse that makes it cross over easier on a mass scale, and I think that accessibility is equally rooted in his experiences as a battle rapper in small Detroit clubs. His skillfulness is always already rooted in the sense of performance and raw skill that such environments demand, and unlike many other MCs with similar roots, Eminem was able to transfer that skill built around live, intimate, high-pressure performances into an active and successful writing practice. This positions him in a strange place—he's not *just* a battle rapper or freestyle rapper, although he has those skills in his toolkit at any moment, he is also an adept writer who can craft complicated metaphors and narratives into verse.

The combination of both sides of the lyrical coin in one artist is rare, or, at least, the fluidity with which Eminem is able to flip between the two sides of the coin is rare. To get an idea of how this difference between the two approaches to the lyric plays out in other artists we might contrast Black Thought of The Roots and Pusha T of Clipse in order to see how these two approaches to the lyric stand apart. Black Thought rhymes in a more straightforward manner that's invested in the sound of the flow over the beat, while Pusha T's style leans more toward metaphor and complexity. In short: Black Thought provides a smooth delivery while Pusha T provides a dense one—they're both experts operating on different poles of the lyrical spectrum, and they both have radically different approaches and styles. Pusha T's lyrics are harder to access and more veiled in their metaphorical intricacy such that they demand multiple listens just to tease out their densely wrought meanings, while Black Thought's lyrical constructions tend to be more straightforward and dexterous in terms of delivery. When I return to a Black Thought verse it is because I'm surprised by the smoothness of the delivery, not because I didn't understand it (at least usually). What is so impressive about Eminem is the way he is able to shift between these two juxtaposed lyrical poles.

Eminem's recent EP collaboration with Royce da 5'9" *Hell: The Sequel* under the group name Bad Meets Evil shows Eminem at his most lyrically playful and metaphorically complex, but even in the atmosphere of a semi-competitive collaborative work Eminem writes in a mode that is accessible to the listener. Tracks like the violent narrative "Stan" from the *Marshall Mathers LP* or the essayistic protest song "Mosh" also hover between the two poles of complexity and straightforwardness in wonderful ways; the listener slides along with the message, floating with it as it rides the beat, sputtering as the lyrics release clever jabs. Eminem jumps into slick and straightforward flows at one moment, and then gets caught up in the complexity of an extended metaphor in the next. At his best, he mixes the two seamlessly.

This might be a strange place to go in order to further illustrate my point, but I want to take a look at Eminem's Nike Air Jordan "The Way I Am" sneakers.

In the song that the sneakers take their lyrics from, "The Way I Am," Eminem reacts to the media's influence on his life from various angles. He laments the reaction of activists to his homophobic and sexist lyrics, as well as to the public's pop-like perception of him as an artist. *The Way I Am* is also the title of Eminem's memoir that features the same multi-colored and overlaid lyrical scrawls on several of its graphic, well-designed pages. These spastic, random collections of words written in Eminem's handwriting feel resonant with his lyrical origins, and having those lyrics printed on sneakers feels all the more fitting. I can imagine the sneakers squeaking on the floor of a freestyle club, worn on the feet of a body pressed closely against other bodies with thick smoke snaking in the air and shifting DJ beats pounding in the ears. The music fades to silence and then an MC introduces the two rappers who are going to battle. Their lyrics flood over the body and the crowd reacts booing, yelping out expletives, oohing and awing at every clever bar thrown back and forth between two rappers engaged in competitive lyrical combat.

The form of the lyrics on the shoes, spastically scrawled, overwritten (palimpsestic), worn on the body, and still ringing with clarity, feels as though it somehow gets at the roots of Eminem's approach. They represent (if you'll allow the pun) the way he is. Eminem's lyrics make sense to the listener on the first go, but they are also crafted and spastically overlaid in their rhyme and metaphor. Eminem has both a smoothness of delivery to hook the listener, and the complexity of lyric to hold them there for multiple listens. The fact that the shoes are part of a massive marketing campaign through the Nike Corporation feels somehow true to Eminem's body of work as well. As much as he rails against his image, as much as he connects to a more working-class audience, he still is a media object that has been traded on *TRL* in excess right alongside N'Sync—his ability to cross over to a wider audience is also part of his body of work. And as much as I want to avoid dwelling on the media-oriented aspects of Eminem for too long, both because I've already mentioned it and because it does have its troublesome elements, when I see the massive stadiums full of people that Eminem is able to fill in Detroit when he does a homecoming tour, I think the honesty of that poor and working-class battle rap stage is still there, at least the heart of it is, even as it has exploded in size to include such a massive and wide-ranging audience. Even if he does reach a substantial following, it is a following that gleans its members from a vast number of backgrounds, and it includes the working class folks Eminem claims roots in.

And it all comes back to battle rap: the battle rap performance stage is the platform that allowed Eminem to cross over in the first place, and it's what keeps his lyrical approach exciting. There is a need to be sharply clever, and to have a razor-edged wit, but there is also a need to do it in a way that is understandable to the audience in the immediacy of the moment. When that clear delivery gets combined with the mad and obsessive desire to create lyrics that stand up against some of the most complicated verses ever made, the result is an artist who has both credibility on the lyrical end of the spectrum and a level of unprecedented accessibility.

There's a wonderful MTV video of Eminem freestyling with his now deceased friend Proof from early in his career that speaks well to the intimacy that's at the core of Eminem's practice.[1] The two rappers slide back and forth, rhyming, calling on each other to take over at certain points as they slide into and out of lyrical energy together. As they rap, Eminem references his own life growing up in Detroit, and points out the windshield of the car at his old house (they're parked in front of one of his childhood homes for the interview). The combination of this intimacy of place and performance with an artist who stands on top of the *TRL* charts for record periods is what makes Eminem stand out. And it's the intimacy that makes him so successful, at least in any sustained sense. It's what allows listeners to enter a world that relates to their own.

It's not *just* that he's white, *TRL* friendly (in an ironic way, but *TRL* friendly nonetheless), or of a certain economic class—it's that he's all of those things, while simultaneously being the sort of lyricist who is able to blend together complicated lyrical skill with a wonderful and accessible delivery. It also remains true that the Eminem is also always larger than the lyric itself; he is always the public Poet with a seductive backstory and comic delivery. He dresses up like Britney Spears, hosts shows on MTV, and fetishizes violence, but he also simultaneously is rooted in a working-class authenticity that comes through in the rhymes. And as much as I can drift away from the lyric itself in order to talk about public reception, I feel always drawn back to it in an inescapable feedback loop.

Without his lyrical skill and roots in battle rap, Eminem would both lack the credibility to exist as a rapper within the rap community, and he would lack the ability to create such simultaneously seductive and complex songs. Eminem is a Poet with a huge public persona, but what is a Poet without their poetry?

Chapter Note

1. http://www.youtube.com/watch?v=k-2kk6s1axk.

The Black Vernacular Versus a Cracker's Knack for Verses

Darin Flynn

Who would have ever thought that one of the
greatest rappers of all would be a white cat?
—Ice-T, Something from Nothing:
The Art of Rap[1]

Slim Shady's psychopathy is worthy of a good slasher movie. The sociolinguistics and psycholinguistics behind Marshall Mathers and his music, though, are deserving of a PBS documentary. Eminem capitalizes on his linguistic genie with as much savvy as he does on his alter egos. He "flips the linguistics," as he boasts in "Fast Lane" from Bad Meets Evil's 2011 album *Hell: The Sequel.*

As its title suggests, this essay focuses initially on the fact that rap is deeply rooted in black English, relating this to Eminem in the context of much information on the language of (Detroit) blacks. This linguistic excursion may not endear me to readers who hate grammar (or to impatient fans), but it ultimately helps to understand how Eminem and hip hop managed to adopt each other. The second part of the essay focuses on Eminem's craft. My take is novel, I think, though some fans may find themselves reading what they already know. That's actually my aim: to make explicit some of what fans know (and love) implicitly. The idea is to contribute to an understanding of how and why Eminem's music is appreciated.

Eminem Sociolinguistics: An Intro

The intro to "Above The Law" on *Hell: The Sequel* brings up the gap between the rich and the poor: the former "get richer," Claret Jai sings proverbially, while the latter "stays poor." Of special interest is that the Detroiter sings "stays" in the intro, but "stay" when she repeats the same line in the chorus. I can think of no better introduction than this to sociolinguistics. As one expert of this field, Sali Tagliamonte, remarks, "the use of verbal -s in contemporary standard English dialects ... only occurs in third person singular. Why? Nobody knows for sure. That's just the way it is."[2] By contrast, in some of the colonial dialects that the early black slaves were exposed to, verbal s could optionally extend to other persons in the present-habitual ("I/you/we/they smokes").[3] As a consequence, verbal -s was possible in all persons in the vernacular of slaves and ex-slaves, and this usage persists to this day among many blacks in the South.

Let's now come back to Detroit, which black southerners flocked to during the Great Migration of the early twentieth century. Northern whites— even working-class ones—restrict -s to third-person singular verbs in "habitual" contexts ("I/you/we/they smoke," not "I/you/we/they smokes"). According to renowned sociolinguist Walt Wolfram, this restriction has spread to black English dialects in northern cities like Detroit:

> [T]here is a kind of dialect levelling in which traditional, localized Southern features may be reduced or lost. For example, in urban Northern AAVE [African American Vernacular English] there is no evidence of 3rd plural -s in *The dogs barks* even though this trait was a characteristic of some earlier regional varieties in the South.[4]

However, Jai's intro in "Above The Law" demonstrates that verbal -s still persists beyond the third-person singular in her Detroit dialect. As Wolfram's remark suggests, this timeworn pattern is rare—it is absent in black children, for instance[5]—so it is noteworthy that Eminem uses it on occasion. For example:

- "...that Nas and Jay does" ("Monkey See Monkey Do," *Straight from the Lab* bootleg)
- "I sprays the facts" ("The Re-Up," *Eminem Presents the Re-Up*)

Jai's intro-line also subtly points out that non-standard grammar is favored by the lower classes, who mostly "stays poor," whereas it is avoided by the upper classes who "get rich" (not "gets rich"). This point can be emphasized by focusing on the use of verbal -s in third-person singular. Northern white American dialects not only restrict -s to third-person singular verbs in habitual contexts, as just mentioned, but also require it ("she smokes," not "she smoke"). In contrast, -s is frequently absent from third-person singular verbs in black English dialects ("she smoke a lot"). Importantly, in his landmark study of four dozen black Detroiters,[6] Walt Wolfram found that verbal -*s* is absent at very different rates depending on social class. Working-class speakers omitted verbal -*s* at much higher rates (56.9–71.4 percent) than middle-class speakers (1.4–9.7 percent). The charts in Figure 1, adapted from Wolfram, illustrate this sharp social stratification. The first chart shows that the rate of -*s* absence varies according to age, too: younger speakers omit -*s* more often. The second chart additionally shows that the rate of -*s* absence varies according to gender: male speakers tend to omit -*s* more frequently.

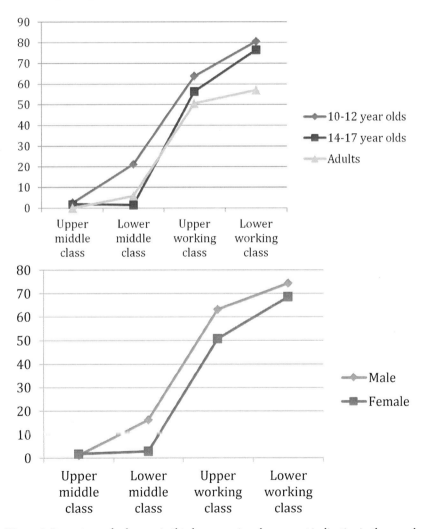

Figure 1. Percentage of *s* absence in third-person singular present indicative in the speech of Detroit blacks according to class.

Wolfram studied nine other distinguishing features of black English in Detroit and found them to pattern according to broad social categories in much the same way as verbal -*s* did. For instance, black English uniquely allows *is/are* (*'s/'re*) to be variably absent (e.g., "my dad funny," "we a family," "they singin'"). Wolfram again found that *is/are* absence occurred at very different rates depending on social class. Working-class speakers omitted *is/are* at considerably higher rates (37.3–56.9 percent) than middle-class

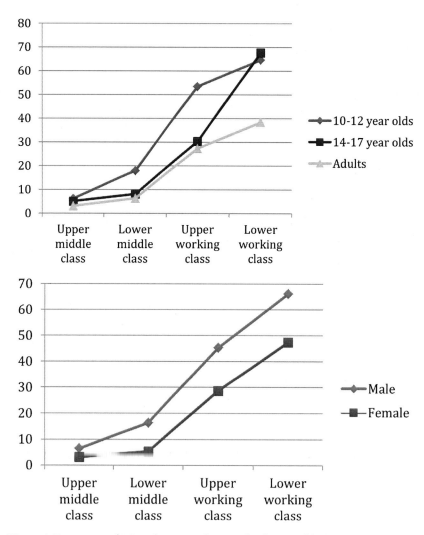

Figure 2. Percentage of *is/are* absence in the speech of Detroit blacks according to class as well as age (first chart) and gender (second chart).

speakers (4.7–10.9 percent). This sharp social stratification can be seen in the charts of Figure 2, adapted from Wolfram. The two charts also illustrate that younger speakers on the one hand, and males on the other, each omit *is/are* more frequently.

In short, Wolfram's study demonstrated that Detroiters usage of non-standard grammar reflects their social structure. However, most language behavior is not fixed within broad social categories like class, age, or gender. Rather, speakers tend to shift their speech style in different contexts. For instance, Wolfram found that working-class Detroiters omitted verbal *-s* and *is/are* at rather high rates during interviews. The latter were conducted in an informal atmosphere to record naturalistic conversation. The speech elicited is described as "not quite casual but not quite formal … the speech used by children to adults and adults to respected strangers … the style in which Americans make their moves up (or down) the social scale."[7] Crucially, the same working-class speakers omitted verbal *-s* and *is/are* at much lower rates when asked to read a couple of pages. The reading passage was a coherent narrative, focused on a conversation about a basketball game, but as a reading task, it elicited a more careful or formal style of speech. The dramatic rate changes are shown in Figure 3, adapted from Wolfram. Such large stylistic shifts suggest that verbal *-s* absence and *is/are* absence are both highly developed linguistic features of the black community in Detroit, and that speakers are consciously aware of them.

So what about the language of hip hop? What style is most appropriate for hip-hop artists to slip into, and do they do it? Rap music is aimed primarily at young urban working-class blacks, as John and Russell Rickford emphasize:

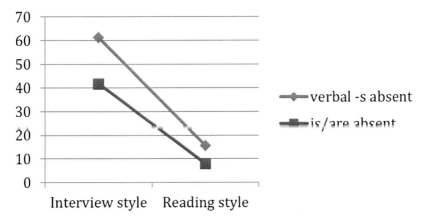

Figure 3. Percentage of verbal *-s* absence and *is/are* absence in the speech of working-class black Detroiters, by style.

There is no question that black talk provides hip-hop's linguistic underpin-
nings.... What many hip-hop heads probably don't realize is that [an act
like] Goodie Mob owes plenty to Spoken Soul [the Rickfords' loving term
for black English]. Not just for sledgehammer lyrics and the style in which
they're delivered, but for its coveted, noncommercial status within the
industry. After all, the Mob is regarded as "real" and truthful because of its
image of fierce nonconformity, and nothing thumbs its nose at conformity
like the unrestrained African American vernacular. Although white suburban youngsters eat up hip-hop's edgy tales of money, sexual adventure,
ghetto life, and racial injustice (and keep ghetto rhymes atop the pop
charts), black urban youngsters are the genre's target audience. And black
urban youngsters follow artists who roam the world implied by the neighborhood language of black urban youngsters.[8]

Moreover, some genres and subgenres (gangsta, hardcore, horrorcore)
target males in particular. This is largely true of rap in general. As Adam
Bradley states: "Rap music is a musical form made by young men and largely
consumed by young men."[9] Altogether, then, it stands to reason that black
MCs will not only omit verbal *-s* and *is/are* in their lyrics, but do so at very
high rates, as per the charts above (Figs. 1–3).

Ideally, one would want to compare an MC's usage of black grammar
in rap versus interviews, to monitor stylistic shifts. This is precisely what
H. Samy Alim did with two black rappers: New Orleans's Juvenile, and
Philadelphia's Eve. Alim first determined the overall rates of *is/are* absence
in two albums: Juvenile's 1999 *That G-Code*, and Eve's 1999 *Let There Be
Eve ... Ruff Ryders' First Lady*. He then recorded interviews with each artist

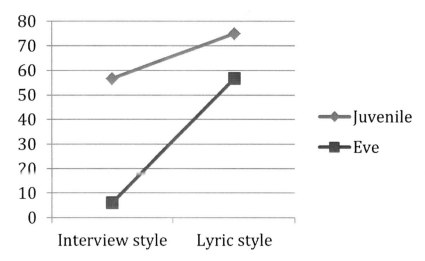

Figure 4. Percentage of *is/are* absence in the speech of Juvenile and Eve, by style.

in 2000 and determined the rates of *is/are* absence in those interviews. I've plotted the results of his study in Figure 4. As Alim states: "We see an increase in the frequency of absence … when moving from the interview data to the lyrical data…. So it is clear that both of these artists display the absent form more frequently in their lyrical data than in their interview speech data."[10]

Alim goes on to argue that rappers are conscious of *is/are* variation and use it to "stay street":

> Hip Hop artists assert their linguistic acts of identity in order to "represent" the streets. This may be viewed as a conscious, linguistic maneuver to connect with the streets as a space of culture, creativity, cognition, and consciousness. If we view Hip Hop artists as social interactants communicating with members of the Black American Street Culture, [*is/are*] variation appears to be conscious—street-conscious (both cognitive and cultural). Hip Hop artists, by the very nature of their circumstances, are ultraconscious of their speech. As members of the [Hip Hop Nation], they exist in a cultural space where extraordinary attention is paid to speech. Speech is consciously varied toward the informal end of the continuum in order to maintain street credibility.[11]

But what about white hip-hoppers? Of the dozen white rappers in Cecelia Cutler's study *Crossing Over: White Teenagers, Hip Hop and African American English* only one displayed any kind of *is/are* absence in his everyday speech style. However, most displayed *is/are* absence while rapping, if only sporadically. For instance, Cutler reports that the late underground rapper Eyedea did not omit *is/are* in his everyday speech style, but did so a little in his performances.[12] In one rap battle, for example, he omitted *is/are* four times out of twenty-five (15 percent), as in "So why Ø you walkin'…?," where Ø indicates an absence. Emimem, too, omits *is/are* in his raps, but not especially frequently. Examples include:

- "some of us Ø cannibals" ("The Real Slim Shady," *The Marshall Mathers LP*)
- "while we Ø comin' out" ("Just Don't Give a Fuck," *The Slim Shady EP*)

In a study of fifteen songs, Julie Dougherty found that Eminem displays *is/are* absence at a rate of 16 percent (N=268).[13] This rate corresponds to the speech of lower middle-class black males in Wolfram's Detroit study (see Fig. 2), but MCs from this social class are expected to display much higher rates of *is/are* absence in their raps (see Fig. 4).

As for verbal *-s*, Eminem very rarely omits it in third-person singular. Here are some examples:

- "everybody wantØ to [wanna] run…" ("Marshall Mathers," *The Marshall Mathers LP*)
- "What difference it makeØ?" (Bad Meets Evil, "Lighters," *Hell: The Sequel*)

Eminem's systematic use of verbal –*s* in third-person singular is similar to what upper middle-class blacks did in Wolfram's study (see Fig. 1), but, again, it sharply distinguishes Eminem from his fellow MCs, who show high rates of –*s* absence in raps. Following are some easy-to-find examples from black MCs in songs with Eminem:

- "She keepØ a sugar daddy"—Royce da 5'9," from Detroit ("Rock City," *Rock City*)
- "…who wantØ to [wanna] die" —Xzibit, from Detroit ("Say My Name," *Man vs. Machine*)
- "she hearØ me" —Bobby Creekwater, from Atlanta ("Shake That," *Curtain Call*)

In sum, Eminem does not "overuse" black English grammar, in spite of being integrated into the black speech community. There may be several reasons for this. First, Cutler points out that white hip-hoppers must be cautious to avoid being labeled inauthentic "wannabe" blacks. For example, in the presentation of black English in the documentary *Voices of North Carolina*, Phonte introduces fellow rapper Joe Scudda:

Phonte: "Yes in hip hop we do have friends, and yes he is a white man. His name is Joe Scudda, and he freestyleØ too…"

Joe Scudda: "What Ø up? / I'm back on the grind again / still remindin' 'em / We Ø in the front where the line beginØ / You Ø in the back where the line goØ in."[14]

Observe how, in just a few bars, Scudda omits *is/are* three times, and verbal –*s* twice (Phonte also does once). I remember thinking, when I first saw the documentary, that Scudda was "overdoing authenticity." White rappers use black grammar because their adopted music genre is black, but most do so in moderation, because they are not trying to be black themselves. Eminem is outspoken about this, notably in "White America," but it is especially obvious from what he always leaves unspoken—the N word, which his black peers use habitually.

Cutler suggests that white hip-hoppers may also avoid overusing black English because normally they do not have native-like control of its grammar. But this is not true of Eminem. Virtually all grammatical features that are unique to black English in Detroit[15] are found in Eminem's lyrics—in correct usage. Some examples have already been given—verbal –*s* absence in third-person singular; verbal –*s* used in other persons; *is/are* absence. Another is so-called "remote" "been." When Eminem says "I been crazy" in "Forgot About Dre," his pronunciation and intended meaning are decidedly black: "been" is markedly stressed, and the sentence means that Eminem was crazy long ago, and still is. Crucially, if the same sentence were used in (non-standard) white English, "been" would not be stressed, and the meaning would also be quite different: Eminem was crazy, perhaps even recently, but he is no longer crazy.[16] Some other examples of Eminem's command of black English follow:

- "Completive" "done"; for example: "she done fed it" ("My Mom," *Relapse*); "they done had enough" ("Elevator," *Relapse: Refill*).
- Invariant "be": "they be actin' maniac" ("Infinite," *Infinite*); "they kids be listenin'" ("Sing for the Moment," *The Eminem Show*).
- "they" for "their"; for example: "they kids" ("Sing for the Moment," *The Eminem Show*); "they veins" ("I'm Shady, *The Slim Shady LP*).
- "ain't" used for "didn't"; for example: "I ain't have to graduate…" ("White America," *The Eminem Show*); "we ain't know" ("Yellow Brick Road," *Encore*).
- Double-negatives with verbs; for example: "Nobody couldn't see" ("Say Goodbye Hollywood, *The Eminem Show*); "Nobody don't care" (2Pac, Black Cotton," *Loyal to the Game*).
- Negative inversion (words inverted in negation); for example: "don't anyone know me" ("Sing for the Moment," *The Eminem Show*); "can't nothing compare" ("Fly Away," *Fly Away* single).
- "finna," an abbreviation for "fixin' to" that means "getting ready to"; for example: "We finna make this" ("Ballin' Uncontrollably," *Straight from the Vault EP*); "finna have a party" ("Shake That," *Curtain Call*).
- "I'mma" for "I'm gonna"; for example: "I'mma hit the cinema" ("Ballin' Uncontrollably," *Straight from the Vault EP*).
- Irregular verb forms; for example: "tooken" for "taken" ("Marshall Mathers," *The Marshall Mathers LP*); "drug" for "dragged" ("Kill You," *The Marshall Mathers LP*); "spitted" for "spat" (Bad Meets Evil, "Fast Lane," *Hell: The Sequel*).
- Discourse words/phrases: not just the usual suspects ("Yo," "Dawg," "You know what I'm sayin?," etc.), but lesser known ones like "son," a term used (paradoxically) for peers ("Infinite," *Infinite*; "Same Song & Dance," *Relapse*).

Another reason that Eminem doesn't overuse black grammar is that he doesn't need to. Alim claims that many MCs use black grammar to an exaggerated degree in order to maintain "street credibility." Instead, Eminem has widely documented—in interviews, music, and film—that he grew up poor, developed authentic relationships in the black ghettos of Detroit, and battled his way to the top from rap's deep underground, with genuine talent. In Ice-T's documentary *Something from Nothing: The Art of Rap*, Redman singles out Eminem as an MC who "been gained" his respect, and remarks: "He was in my hood before he blew up. He was in Newark, he was with the Outsidaz. So he been in the hood before he got on. So I think it always been in him." Eminem embodies the rags-to-riches American dream, of course, but many in the ghettos can still relate to him because (aside from passing references to his Benz) he doesn't overly flaunt his riches, unlike many rappers. Moreover, his tragedy-plagued life and his music remind fans that riches don't ensure bliss.

Though Eminem's ghetto-fandom is important, it is widely believed that most of his fans are middle-class whites. Jonathan Scott offers a warning in this connection:

> Mathers is a poor kid from industrial Detroit, not a middle-class belletrist.... [I]n the context of Eminem criticism—which is becoming intense ... white middle-class critics are attempting to claim Mathers as their own progeny, as yet another great white poet of the great tradition of great white literature. We can forget about them for now, for Mathers himself would doubtless show them the middle finger if faced with their puerile ideas about his art.... To frame it differently ... Marshall Mathers III [is] the first poet laureate of the white working class. And he is first precisely because he is the first white writer to speak on behalf of poor whites not through a white ethnic middle-class immigrant art form but rather through the popular-democratic tradition of Black folks.[17]

It is useful to relate Scott's point to Eminem's language. Below I offer a list of grammatical features that many would assume to be black English, and Eminem may well deploy them as such in his black-rooted music. But these are also linguistic features of Eminem's working-class white background, which he has talked, acted, and rapped about. So in these instances at least, Eminem is not just "talking black" ("Sing for the Moment," *The Eminem Show*); he is also speaking his native white tongue.

- "don't" used for "doesn't"; for example: "she don't understand" ("8 Mile," *8 Mile*); "shit don't phase me" ("Hailie's Song," *The Eminem Show*); "it don't matter" ("Lose Yourself," *8 Mile*).
- "Ain't" used for negative of "have" and "be"; for example: "you ain't seen it" ("The Kids," *The Marshall Mathers LP* [clean version]); "I ain't sniffed since..." (Bad Meets Evil, "Nuttin' to Do," *Nuttin' to Do / Scary Movie*); "My views ain't changed" ("Square Dance," *The Eminem Show*).

- Double/multiple negation; for example: "ain't got no tits!" ("My Name Is," *The Slim Shady LP*); "I ain't goin' nowhere" (" Hailie's Song," *The Eminem Show*); "ain't never met nobody" ("So Bad," *Recovery*).
- "is"/"was" used for "are"/"were"; for example: "how fucked up is you?" ("Stan," *The Marshall Mathers LP*); "they was like,…" ("Cum On Everybody," *The Slim Shady LP*); "you was a mom" ("Cleanin' Out My Closet," *The Eminem Show*).
- Past participle form used for preterit; for example: "I seen the porno" ("Guilty Conscience," *The Slim Shady LP*); "We been ridin' around" (Bad Meets Evil, "The Reunion," *Hell: The Sequel*); "They been waitin' patiently" ("Forever," *Relapse: Refill*).
- Preterit form used for past participle; for example: "I've went to jail" (" Hailie's Song, *The Eminem Show*); "you must have mistook me" ("Cold Wind Blows," *Recovery*); "I would've did anything" ("Space Bound," *Recovery*).
- Preterit form used for adjective; for example: "his ass was rotted" ("Can-I-Bitch," *Straight from the Lab*); "my head is swole" (Lil Wayne, "Drop The World," *Rebirth*); "some are wrote on a napkin" ("Almost Famous," *Recovery*).
- "Them" used for "those" (as determiner); for example: "them baffling acts" ("Tonite," *Infinite*); "them same friends" ("If I Had," *The Slim Shady LP*); "And them shits reach…" ("Remember Me?," *The Marshall Mathers LP*).
- Object pronouns used as subjects; for example: "Them's the people" ("Never 2 Far," *Infinite*); "Him don't give…" (Bad Meets Evil, "A Kiss," *Hell: The Sequel*). Object pronouns are especially common in conjoined subjects; for example: "Me and Hailie danced" ("Bump Heads," *The Singles*); "him and Jeff were still…" (DJ Jazzy Jeff, "When to Stand Up," *When to Stand Up*).
- Verb suffix *-ing* usually pronounced *-in'*; for example: "workin'," "playin'," etc.
- "all's" used for "all as," a working-class (and rural) variant of "all that"; for example: "all's we know" ("2.0 Boys," *2.0 Boys*).

Notwithstanding the above, it must be recognized that Eminem has a distinctly black accent (as he openly acknowledges in "The Way I Am," *Marshall Mathers LP*), in several ways. First, he often changes the "l" consonant to [o] (the GOAT vowel) at the ends of words or syllables. So for instance, "fatal" rhymes perfectly with "Play-Doh" in "Fly Away" (*Recovery*). This is a well-known pronunciation feature of black English. In white varieties of American English, the consonant "l" also acquires an [o]-like quality at the ends of words and syllables, but it rarely changes completely into a vowel.

Second, Eminem frequently drops the "r" sound at the ends of words and syllables, in words like "car," "mother," "Morgan," or "barbecue." Wolfram's study of black Detroiters revealed that middle-class speakers dropped "r" in this way somewhat frequently (20.8–38.8 percent), and that working-class speakers did so even more frequently (61.3–71.7 percent). In her study of fifteen songs, Dougherty found that Eminem drops the "r" sound at the very high rate of 82.1 percent (N=285). This pronunciation pattern puts him in the same range as working-class black males in Wolfram's study. That is, as far as his (non-)pronunciation of "r" is concerned, Eminem has (or takes on) the accent of a working-class black man. This fact really stands out because all whites always pronounce their r sounds in Detroit (unlike in Boston or New York City).[18]

Third, Eminem's pronunciation of "hushing" sounds "sh," "zh," "ch," and "j" (as in "na*tion*," "A*si*an," "lun*ch*," "bu*dge*," respectively) is sometimes closer to "hissing" sounds "s," "z," "ts," and "dz" (as in "na*s*cent," "dai*s*y," "Ri*tz*," "a*dze*," respectively). For instance, listen to the first verse of "Never 2 Far" (*Infinite*) and pay attention to how he pronounces "ri*ch* ... i*tch*ed ... fi*sh* ... uncondi*ti*onally ... ca*sh* ... vi*si*on ... mi*ssi*onless." Similarly, listen to "lun*ch* money ... tea*ch*er, tea*ch*er ... deten*ti*on" in the first verse of "Brain Damage" (*The Slim Shady LP*), or how he says "freedom of spee*ch*" in the intro to "White America" (*The Eminem Show*). This pronunciation pattern is not documented for black English (aside from a few words, like "shrimp" being pronounced "srimp"), but it seems somewhat common among black hip-hoppers, so I assume that Eminem adopted it from the latter. (Outside the hypermasculine hip-hop nation, this pronunciation pattern is sometimes described as sounding effeminate or gay.)

Finally, Eminem regularly pronounces the [aɪ] vowel in such words as "vibe," "high," and "time" as [aa] ("vahb," "hah," "tahm"). This pronunciation is widely associated with southern Americans as well as northern blacks. Like most blacks, Eminem tends to say [aɪ] (not [aa]) before voiceless consonants ("p," "f," "t," "s," "sh," "ch," and "k"). As a consequence, words like "tide" and "tight" do not have the same vowel for Eminem. So for instance, when he is composing a song during the bus-riding scene of *8 Mile*, he instinctively chooses words that end in voiceless consonants, to ensure that the last vowel remains constant as [aɪ] (not [aa]): "real life ... kill mics ... still white ... hate life ... brake lights ... stage fright ... blank like."

Interestingly, Eminem's retention of [aɪ] before voiceless consonants is conservative by Detroit standards. Bridget Anderson reports that most black Detroiters now pronounce [aɪ] as [aa] before voiceless consonant,

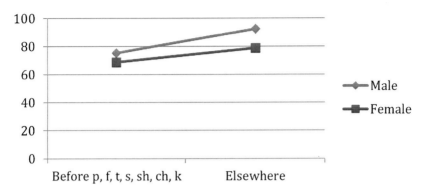

Figure 5. Percentage of [aɪ] pronounced as [aa] in the speech of black Detroiters, by gender and context.

almost as often as they do elsewhere, such that "tight" usually has the same vowel as "tide" (both with [aa]).[19] This is shown in Figure 5, adapted from Anderson.

According to Anderson, blacks adopted the [aa] pronunciation before voiceless consonants from white Appalachians who migrated to Detroit. Evidently, blacks felt an affinity with these working-class whites who, like them, were discriminated against, marginalized, and ultimately "left behind" in Detroit's inner city by other whites. This is the same kind of affinity, it seems, that brought black hip hop and Eminem together—so closely, in fact, that "the Caucasian of rap"[20] is able to tell his rivals, "kiss my black ass!"[21] while his mentor Dr. Dre tells resentful black MCs in particular, "you can kiss … the cracker's ass."[22]

Eminem Psycholinguistics: A Primer

Eminem proclaimed his mission statement in the very first line of the first verse of the first (and title) track of his debut album, *Infinite*, in 1996: to set off "chain reactions" in listeners' brains with his "pen and paper." A hundred million fans later, he can rightfully declare "mission accomplished." But just how did/does he accomplish it, really? The short answer is that Eminem *is* accomplished, period. About three hundred songs are powered by his unrelenting voice. But the question lingers and invites longer answers from different perspectives (hence this book). In this second part of this essay, I offer a one-word answer from psycholinguistics for Eminem's accomplishments: priming. *Priming* refers to a subconscious memory effect whereby one's response to a stimulus is influenced by prior exposure to another stimulus. Homophony is a good first example.

As most people know, a homophone (literally *homo-* "same" + *phone* "sound") is a word or phrase that sounds the same as another. Eminem is famously a homophone because Marshall Mathers realized early in life that M&M's chocolate candy could refer to him. The proper nouns in Slim Shady are also homophonous with adjectives. Homophones are common—representing over forty percent of English words, according to some dictionaries—and we ably use context to get around their ambiguity. However, psycholinguists have discovered that "appropriate and inappropriate meanings are both activated when we hear an ambiguous word.... [C]ontext does affect meaning selection eventually, even though it does not appear to prevent incorrect meanings from being activated in the first place."[23]

For instance, suppose we measure your brain's response to seeing a word on a computer screen after hearing a sentence. Your response to seeing "Hershey's" (as opposed to, say, "Levi's") may be faster after hearing the sentence "Only a few songs on this album are Eminem's." The sentence's influence on your response time is called a "priming effect." It suggests that the sentence-final word causes the meaning "M&M's"—and other chocolate candy by extension—to be activated in your subconscious brain in spite of the disambiguating context. (Similarly, you may respond faster to seeing the word "music" (as opposed to, say, "fashion") after hearing the sentence "Only a few candies in this bowl are M&M's.")

Eminem makes extensive and increasing use of priming and homophony. Specifically, his verses tend to sustain the ambiguity caused by a given homophone. The goal, as stated above, is for his pen and paper to cause chain reactions in our brains. It is not, as some misunderstand, only to make puns. For instance, Eminem's verse in Rihanna's "Numb" (*Unapologetic*) starts with "I'm plastered." The intended slang meaning that he's "high" is clear from Rihanna's preceding singing and it is verbalized in the next line. But the literal meaning related to plaster is also drawn out by a muffled voice that shouts "Drywall!" immediately after. Eminem then recycles the bar that he used to end-rhyme with "drywall" in his previous collaboration with Rihanna ("Love the Way You Lie," *Recovery*). He also uses a line from that song's hook in the next line of "Numb." Our memory carries over the original intents of these recycled bars into "Numb," but Eminem gives them additional meanings here, related to being high—namely, administering a drug test and lying about its result. None of this is meant to be funny, it seems. Eminem aims more directly to sustain simultaneous meanings that are activated in our brains by homophony and associated memories.

This is not to deny that Eminem often uses priming and homophony to convey humor, whether light (for example, "my wheels spoke to her" in Skylar Grey's "C'mon Let Me Ride," *Don't Look Down*) or dark (for example, in "Mockingbird," *Encore*, he raps that he will make a jeweler eat every karat). He notoriously wields them to go Slim Shady on various people: his exes and other women, his rivals and others in the hip-hop industry, political figures and other talking heads, etc. Examples abound, but a current favorite comes from his electrifying verse in 50 Cent's "My Life": Shady silences his critics and gets them to see his way by tearing out their vocal cords, which he then uses to connect their eye sockets to electrical outlets. It's absurd, of course, but it makes sense in the listening moment because "cords" and "sockets" both prime "electricity," and vice versa.

Eminem is especially prone to priming literal meanings in fixed phrases or idioms (again, particularly in more recent songs). One notable example is the Christmas "fuck you" from *Recovery's* "Not Afraid" that makes a gift a curse. The first phrase primes a less idiomatic reading of the two homophones in the second phrase. He achieves a similar (priming) effect when he name-drops Michael Vick and David Carradine before using the idioms "sick puppy" ("Cold Wind Blows," *Recovery*) and "die hard" (Bad Meets Evil, "Welcome 2 Hell," *Hell: The Sequel*), respectively. In "Richard" (Obie Trice, *Bottoms Up*), he repeats a memorable hook line from "Lose Yourself" (*8 Mile*) but the preceding line of "Richard" newly injects sexual innuendo into its expressions ("only get one shot," "chance to blow"). In "Won't Back Down" (*Recovery*) the expression "turn me down" has its usual idiomatic meaning of rejection, but its literal meaning is also primed by a decrease in the song's volume at the end of the preceding line.

Eminem has also become legendary in his use of homophones to play off more than two meanings in his lyrics. To give just a few recent examples:

- "Dick" in the hook of "Richard" (Obie Trice, *Bottoms Up*) refers to the nickname, to Eminem being a jerk, and to his penis—all at once.
- In the second verse of "Won't Back Down" (*Recovery*), "little pricks" refers to small punctures from needles, to Eminem's competitors being diminutive jerks, and to their tiny penises, again simultaneously.
- In his verse in "Above The Law" (Bad Meets Evil, *Hell: The Sequel*), Eminem intends the phrase "I am–Bush" to mean (in that one line only) that he is (George W.) Bush, that he is timid ("bush" is slang for "pussy"), and that he ambushes.
- In the second verse of "Not Afraid" (*Recovery*), "getting capped" refers to Eminem's mysterious rival getting killed, but his choice of words in the preceding bars primes two other concurrent meanings: his rival getting a royal cap atop his head,[24] and his rival getting his teeth sealed or covered.

- In his third verse in "A Kiss" (Bad Meets Evil, *Hell: The Sequel*), Eminem uses "beaver" as the slang term for vagina, but again, his choice of words in the preceding bars primes two other meanings. He draws out the literal meaning of "beaver" by saying "a damn" (obviously homophonous with "a dam") just two words earlier. And he appeals to the memory of Beaver from "Leave It to Beaver" by mentioning "cleavers" in the previous line—the Cleavers being Beaver's family on the show.

The last example deserves special attention. "Leave It to Beaver" and its key characters—including each of the Cleavers—are rapped about in the hard-fought exchange between B-Rabbit (Eminem) and Lotto (Nashawn "Ox" Breedlove) in the *8 Mile* movie. After the battle, B-Rabbit confides to Cheddar Bob (Evan Jones): "Yo, that Leave It to Beaver line almost killed me." So, many fans are well primed to get the Theodore "Beaver" Cleaver reference in "A Kiss."[25] Now, Eminem is such an unrestrained artist, and so cognizant of homophony and priming, that he reads into the name Beaver Cleaver what few others have dared to in over a half-century, and he primes that warped reading in a song by Bad Meets Evil. Eminem leaves no doubt that he is the second of this duo. In particular, he amplifies the evil of female genital mutilation (if that were possible) by evoking the cute innocence that is "Leave It to Beaver" in the subliminal background. That evil-highlighting background is further strengthened by Eminem's overlapping reference to beavers, which are conspicuously cute furry animals. Incidentally, "damn" (like "beaver") does triple-work here: its homophony with "dam" primes "beaver" in the same line; its hell-associated meaning ("damnation") also primes several words in the next line ("demon," "behemoth," and "evil"); and it is used in a fixed phrase as a swear word.

Like it or not, this is horrorcore rap at its finest. It is a Detroit-born genre that Eminem honors with his Slim Shady persona and his extraordinary lyrical skills. Eminem is rightfully proud of his own lyrics, and he is famously hostile toward fatuous lyricists (see "Syllables," *Syllables* single). The mutilation-by-cleavers threat in "A Kiss" is aimed at female pop artists, for instance. Specifically, he taunts Katy Perry (think "Boom! Boom! ... Moon! Moon!" repeated fourteen times) and Lady Gaga (think "You're Lebanese, you're Orient!") by name, before using the word "divas" at the end of a line. The next few lines end in a different compound rhyme, but each contains an internal rhyme that closely matches "divas": "cleavers," "beaver," and "Evil." These four words are dispersed across four lines and also diverge in meaning, but they are mind-linked because they rhyme (especially in Eminem's black accent). The goal—apart from rhythm and flow—is for the listener to combine the obvious meanings of these words (including the slang meaning of "beaver") into a single, horrifying concept. The same lines also contain other internal near-rhymes ("demon," "behemoth," "seethin'," etc.), which further strengthen the rhythm, flow, and concept.

The foregoing all takes place in under five seconds, and serves to illustrate that priming also works between words that are not identical but similar in sound. In particular, psycholinguistic experiments show that rhyming words prime each other. For example, try completing the following sentence:

The man walked into the bank and slipped on some ice. He'd gone to deposit his payment and nearly broke his _____.

Possible completions include "ankle," "foot," "arm," etc. If "payment" is replaced by "check" in the sentence, you are more likely to end it with "neck"—a rhyme-priming effect. This effect is documented for everyday speech,[26] but is much stronger in rap, of course. For example, Eminem famously conjured the N-word (without saying it) in "Criminal" (*The Marshall Mathers LP*) by ending one line in the word "quicker," and ending the following line in the non-rhyming word "word," priming his listeners to "fill in the blank" (as in the sentence above). Relatedly, in "Till I Collapse" (*The Eminem Show*) he even avoids a euphemism for the N-word by substituting "wizzle" for "nizzle" in Snoop Dogg/Lion's well-known expression "for shizzle, my nizzle."[27] Parenthetically, this expression is immediately preceded by another interesting application of rhyme-priming. Eminem hesitantly compares his resounding success to "pop fizzing up," playing off the homophony of "pop." Crucially, "fizzle" is a synonym of "fizz," with an alternative meaning: while soda pop fizzes (up), pop music fizzles (out). And so our hip-hop-primed minds and ears virtually anticipate Eminem's next move: he fills the next two lines with *-izzle* suffixes/rhymes.

What about words (or phrases) that do not rhyme perfectly? These are important in any discussion of Eminem because he attaches special importance to them himself (see, for example, "Yellow Brick Road," *Encore*). Such words can prime each other, too. Joe Stemberger reports that people are better at using irregular verbs like "fall" or "freeze" in the past tense when the subject happens to prime the right vowel—"the check fell," "the chrome froze"—and they tend to make mistakes when the subject happens to prime the wrong vowel—"the chalk falled," "the cream freezed."[28] Eminem jokingly illustrates this kind of priming mistake in "Kill You" (*The Marshall Mathers LP*): he says "tweece" before correcting himself ("twice"), following a string of words with [i] (the FLEECE vowel), including "80 G's a week" in the same line.[29]

More subtly, Eminem is known for "bending" words in ways that would sound odd out of context, but not in his raps, again thanks to priming. In Dr. Dre's 2011 single "I Need A Doctor," for example, he fiddles with the pronunciation of [ʌ] (the STRUT vowel) in "son" so that it better assonates/ rhymes with [ɔ] (the THOUGHT vowel) in three preceding words in the same bar. If these words did not precede it, Eminem's pronunciation of "son" would be odd. Similarly, in 50 Cent's "My Life" he alters [ɪ] (the KIT vowel) in "electricity" to align it with the verse's assonance in [ʌ]. In Funkmaster Flex's "If I Get Locked Up" (*The Tunnel*), he rhymes "baked" with "degrees" by changing the latter's last vowel to [e] (the FACE vowel). Again, priming is crucial to pulling this off. In the same song he changes "sedation" to "sedadation" to sound-align it with "medication," which appears in the previous line. In "The Way I Am" (*Marshall Mathers LP*), some words are stressed on the wrong vowel (for example, "the inDEX/ or pinKY") due to the strong anapestic rhythm of the song (recall that even the piano goes "plink-plink-PLINK" throughout). In all these cases, a preceding sound structure is carried over partially to a following word, a form of priming.[30]

Of course a string of words with the same vowel (assonance) usually primes actual words with their conventional pronunciations in the rapper's mind. For instance, in "Sing For The Moment" (*The Eminem Show*) Eminem says "he don't" in the middle of a line that has [o] (the GOAT vowel) in four preceding words, whereas in "Love You More" (*Encore*) he uses "doesn't" as this word is preceded by "cuz" and "puzzle." The word "again" in particular takes on a variety of pronunciations depending on the vowels in words before or after it in the verse. Another example is "root," which he tends to pronounce with [u] (the GOOSE vowel; for example, "It's Okay," *Infinite*; "If I Had," *The Slim Shady EP*; "The Lunch Truck Battle," *8 Mile*) but he pronounces it with [ʊ] (the FOOT vowel) in some songs, for the sake of rhyming. For instance, he adopts this pronunciation at the end of one bar in the 2000 single "Quitter" because the preceding bars end in words with [ʊ] ("hood," "woods"). This is a legitimate pronunciation in many parts of the U.S., but even listeners who are unfamiliar with it are primed by preceding words, so they either don't mind or don't notice.

Not surprisingly, black English provides much of the variation in Eminem's words. For example, in verses that assonate in [ɪ] (the KIT vowel), he tends to substitute [ɪ] for [ɛ] (the DRESS vowel) before nasal sounds ("pen," "Eminem") and likewise he tends to substitute [ɪ] for [i] (the FLEECE vowel) before the "l" sound ("real," "dealer").[31] Both are pronunciation features of black English. In the same way, he usually pronounces "thing" with [ɪ] but he adopts the black "thang" pronunciation in "When I'm Gone" (*Curtain Call: The Hits*), to force a rhyme with "pain." Like most whites, he also says "aunt" as "ant"—for example, he rhymes "Aunt Peg" with "pant leg" in "Scary Movies" (*Bad Meets Evil, Nuttin' to Do / Scary Movies*)—but he takes on the black pronunciation of "aunt" in "Guilty Conscience" (*The Slim Shady LP*), where he rhymes "aunt's cribs" with "blonde wigs." Relatedly, he adopts the black pronunciation of "ask" as "aks" in a verse of "The Reunion" (Bad Meets Evil, *Hell: The Sequel*), where this word is surrounded by other "aks" sequences: "backseat/ ... taxi/ ... Maxi ... actually ask me/ ... smacks me." In "Jimmy Crack Corn" (*The Re-Up*) he even appropriates rapper Chingy's notorious "urr" accent to rhyme "care" with "absurd"/"sir"/etc.[32] He also pronounces "scared of you" as "scurred of you" in the 2009 single "The Warning," to adjust to rhymes in preceding lines: "occur to you" and "prefer to do."

Consonants are also an important source of priming. For instance, your brain responds more strongly to a word if you were just exposed to another word that begins with the same consonant or consonant group (alliteration). The brain response in question is somewhat negative, however. Whereas speakers tend to produce rhyming sequences like "pick tick" or "cattle battle" somewhat faster than normal, they tend to produce alliterating sequences like "pick pin" or "cattle cutter" somewhat slower.[33] Moreover, some recent studies show that, when all else is equal, speakers tend to avoid pairing alliterative words in sentences. For instance, speakers prefer "Patty handed an animal to the child" or "Hannah passed a hamster to the child" over "Patty passed an animal" or "Hannah handed an animal" or "Patty handed a hamster."[34]

Perhaps for the reason above, Eminem seldom uses alliteration, except when the repeated consonants are useful to convey particular meanings or effects. In "No Love" (*Recovery*), for example, the alliterative phrase "drool or dribble a drop" appears after a line that ends in the homophone "spit," slang for "rap." Eminem uses alliteration here to emphasize the alternate literal meaning of "spit," by exploiting the fact that our English-speaking minds associate *dr* with liquid. Compare "drool," "dribble," "drop," "drip," "drivel," "drizzle," "drench," "drain," "draft/draught," "drink," "drunk," "dram," "dreg," "driblet," etc. (Sound-meaning pairings like *dr* "liquid" cause words with these consonants to prime each other.)[35]

Eminem also makes dramatic if scarce use of consonance (the repetition of consonants regardless of position). Notably, in "Kill You" (*The Marshall Mathers LP*) he delivers a sequence of ten "v"s ("I invented violence...") that culminate in his rendition of a chainsaw "vrinnn vrinnn VRINNN!" He especially favors the repetition of so-called "vulgar" consonants. These are sounds that are articulated with the lips ("p," "b," "f," "v," "m") or with the back of the tongue ("c/k," "g," "ng") or with both ("qu/kw," "gu/gw," "w/wh"), which are hugely overrepresented in vulgar words, at least in English.[36] Good examples include not only swear words ("piss off, goddamn mu'fuckin' cocksuckers!") but also slurs of all types ("spic," "spook," "wop," "mick," "gook," "polack," "guido," "kike," "canuck," "paki," "cracker," "wigga," "pig," "cop," "fag," "fop," "punk," "wacko," etc.) as well as taboo body parts and functions ("boob," "bum," "cock," "prick," "pecker," "muff," "poontang," "cum," "frig," "bang," "wank," "screw," "bugger," "crap," "poop," "puke," etc.). Eminem knows this instinctively and he purposely primes profanity into some appropriate songs by overusing "rude" consonant sounds. As a striking example/exercise, get the lyrics of "Square Dance" (*The Eminem Show*), among other things a dis song against Canibus, and underline or circle all "vulgar" consonant sounds.

Finally, we briefly consider the subtlest type of priming—one that relies neither on sound or meaning, but only on grammar. Here's an easy example: if you call a store that closes at 5 o'clock and ask, "What time do you close?," the storekeeper is likely to say, "5 o'clock." But if you ask, "At what time do you close?," the more likely response is, "At 5 o'clock." That is, the grammar of your question primes the storekeeper's grammar. It is clear that Eminem is aware of grammatical priming. For instance, one line in a "A Kiss" (Bad Meets Evil, *Hell: The Sequel*) has the purposely convoluted construction: "Him don't … do him?" In more usual black English, the beginning of this line would be "He don't…" and the ending would be "do he?" (as Kuniva asks in "Hallie's Revenge," *Straight from the Lab*). Eminem asks "do him?" rather than "do he?" (or "does he?") in order to force a rhyme with two other lines ("…to 'em" and "…through him"). Crucially, at the beginning of the line, he also says, "Him don't…" rather than "He don't…" (or "He doesn't…"), apparently in order to prime us for "do him?" at the end of the line.

I also have the impression that Eminem recycles grammatical constructions through much of his lyrics, something that is predicted by grammatical priming. For example, in the outro of "Mockingbird" (*Encore*) he uses two double-object constructions in a row ("buy you a mockingbird … give you the world") and then switches to a series of sentences with prepositional phrases ("buy a … ring for you … sold it to ya"). In his second verse of "Renegade" (Jay-Z, *The Blueprint*), he uses the grammatical frame "__ as __" in both bars of the "cake/Dixie" line, and he uses the frame "__ with __" in both bars of the "Mormons/Catholics" line. Repeating grammatical structures like this improves a song's flow at an abstract level.[37] A study is needed to see if his use of the various grammatical features listed in the first part of this essay also primes him to reuse them in a verse.

To summarize, psycholinguistic experiments reveal that hearing or saying an utterance causes a huge variety of words and phrases that are related in sound, meaning or structure to be activated in the subconscious brain. The strongest evidence for such "priming effects" may well come from rappers like Eminem who can quickly assemble clever and intricate verses while freestyling or battling. As psycholinguists have observed:

> [T]he primary purpose of language is to convey information from a speaker to a listener. The results of our experiments indicate that the choice of words used to convey this information depends on a lexical access process that is influenced by a combination of form and meaning. Perhaps the "special" examples of language..., such as poetry, are in fact a natural consequence of this property of lexical access. If so, then poetry, puns, and other forms of wordplay should not be viewed as exceptions to normal language use. Indeed, they may provide useful insights into the organization and operation of human language.[38]

What sets Eminem apart is his ability to set off chain reactions in our brains with his music. The lyrical choices made by his pen and paper are of such quality and quantity that his listeners are caught in a crossfire of sounds, meanings, and structures that prime themselves and each other.

Conclusion

Much like Eminem consciously primes our subconscious brains with his lyrics, my essay aimed to make explicit a selection of what his fans already know implicitly. Specifically, by documenting some of the sociolinguistics and psycholinguistics in his music, I hope to have contributed to an appreciation of Eminem, "the first poet laureate of the white working class."[39] That individualized appreciations like this are sorely needed in today's hip hop is apparent not only from its endless detractors ("How can you listen to this crap?") but also from some of its listeners. For example, Eminem was included twice in a recent list of worst rap lyrics from the last year or so.[40] The first entry is his "butt police" line in Rihanna's "Numb" (*Unapologetic*). Eminem repeats "rear" twice to evoke police sirens as well as a female's rear end. That is, "butt police" primes two word meanings and he manages to build both into the next line with a single non-ambiguous word. This is ingenious and entirely characteristic of both his wordcraft and his Shady persona, yet his creativity is not only unappreciated, but assessed as "the worst."[41]

Eminem's second inclusion in the "worst rap lyrics" list is his "spaghetteven" line in 50 Cent's "My Life." Eminem's wordplay is again the focus of derision, but there is much going on here worth appreciating. One point of interest is his pronunciation of the first syllable of "spaghetti"/"spaghetteven." He causes its unaccented vowel to assonate with other vowels—both accented and unaccented—throughout much of the verse. This may be the first time that a rapper (or any poet) has successfully anchored a verse in largely unaccented internal rhymes. This lyric is also significant in that Eminem transforms spaghetti from the comfort food that he might've thrown up in his insecurity before a battle ("Lose Yourself," *8 Mile*) to the power food that currently fuels his revenge on critics. Fans can only appreciate this change in connotation, whether it should have come from two decades of rapping experience, or from a split-second schizzo-switch to Slim Shady. Certainly Eminem listeners are now primed to hear "spaghetti" in a new way. I would even venture that spaghetti is only a few mentions away from becoming to Eminem what Campbell's soup was to Andy Warhol. (Google Eminem + spaghetti to convince yourself.) The general point I am getting at is one made long ago by Tim Brennan, whose rhetorical questions serve well as an envoi:

> What if one claimed that the pleasures of rap—like the colors of Da Vinci and the polyphonies of Bach—had to be learned, deliberately, as in the art appreciation courses? Or that those who could not, at least by projection, understand such pleasures were in some basic sense uneducated? … How can one get to the tactical point of insisting on rap's formal expertise when the very sense of it as art is so weak?[42]

Chapter Notes

1. Paul Toogood, producer, *Something from Nothing: The Art of Rap* (Beverly Hills, CA: Indomina, 2012).

2. Sali Tagliamonte, *Analysing Sociolinguistic Variation* (Cambridge, UK: Cambridge University Press, 2006), 181.

3. Shana Poplack and Sali Tagliamonte, "Back to the Present: Verbal -s in the (African American) English Diaspora," in Raymond Hickey, ed., *Legacies of Colonial English: Studies of Transported Dialects* (Cambridge: Cambridge University Press, 2004).

4. Walt Wolfram, "The Grammar of Urban African American Vernacular English," in Bernd Kortmann and Edgar W. Schneider, eds., *Handbook of Varieties of English* (Berlin: Mouton de Gruyter, 2004), 322.

5. Lisa J. Green, *Language and the African American Child* (New York: Cambridge University Press, 2011), 214.

6. Walt Wolfram, *A Linguistic Description of Detroit Negro Speech* (Washington, D.C.: Center for Applied Linguistics, 1969).

7. Ibid., 17

8. John R. Rickford and Russell J. Rickford, *Spoken Soul: The Story of Black English* (New York: Wiley, 2000), 87.

9. Adam Bradley, *Book of Rhymes: The Poetics of Hip Hop* (New York: Basic Civitas, 2009), 189.

10. H. Samy Alim, *Roc the Mic Right: The Language of Hip Hop Culture* (New York: Routledge, 2006), 121.

11. Ibid., 124.

12. Cecelia Cutler, Crossing Over: White Teenagers, Hip Hop and African American English (PhD diss., New York University, 2002).

13. Julie Dougherty, "My Name Is: The Linguistic Construction of Slim Shady, Eminem, and Marshall Mathers" (Masters essay, Georgetown University, 2007).

14. Neal Hutcheson, producer, *Voices of North Carolina* (Raleigh, NC: North Carolina Language and Life Project, 2005).

15. Wolfram, "The Grammar," 322.

16. Green, *Language*, 100.

17. Jonathan Scott, "Sublimating Hiphop: Rap Music in White America," *Socialism and Democracy* 18 (2004): 144.

18. Eminem also drops some *r*'s between vowels; when he first pronounces "story" in "Yellow Brick Road" (*Encore*), or when he says "lyrics" in the single "Syllables," to give just two examples. In northern cities this pattern is unique to black English.

19. Bridget Anderson, "Dialect Leveling and /ai/ Monophthongization Among African American Detroiters," *Journal of Sociolinguistics* 6 (2002): 86–98.

20. "Session One," *Recovery* [deluxe version].

21. "The Re-Up," Eminem Presents the Re-Up.

22. Dr. Dre, "I Need A Doctor," single.

23. Matthew J. Traxler, *Introduction to Psycholinguistics* (West Sussex, UK: Wiley, 2012), 117.

24. As in: "to be provided with a (royal) cap." Princeton's WordNet also defines "capped" as an adjective with the meaning "covered as if with a cap or crown especially of a specified kind." Compare "cloud-capped mountains"; "brown-capped mushrooms"; "snow-capped peaks."

25. Also not lost on at least some fans is the otherwise obscure fact that Beaver, who is identified with Eminem in the B-Rabbit vs. Lotto battle, was played by an actor with the same last name (Jerry Mathers).

26. David Rapp and Arty Samuel, who conducted the study, took numerous precautions to ensure that participants' rhyme-priming was not "built-in" in any part of their experiment. David N. Rapp and Arthur G. Samuel, "A Reason to Rhyme: Phonological and Semantic Influences on Lexical Access," *Journal of Experimental Psychology* 28 (2002): 564–571.

27. The foregoing relates to the phenomenon of rhyming slurs—when people use a short phrase to conjure a slur that the phrase rhymes with. For example, racists use the phrase "pitch and pine" to conjure the rhyming slur "shine" for blacks. Similarly, "Jew" is conveyed by "fifteen and two," "box of glue" or "pot of glue." Rhyming slurs are common in British and Australian English. A well-known Cockney example is "trouble and strife" for "wife." See Antonio Lillo, "From Alsatian Dog to Wooden Shoe: Linguistic Xenophobia in Rhyming Slang," *English Studies* 82 (2001): 336–348.

28. Joseph P. Stemberger, "Phonological Priming and Irregular Past," *Journal of Memory and Language* 50 (2001): 02–95.

29. Elsewhere, he actually embraces such priming mistakes precisely because they improve the rhyme or rhythm of the song. In "Shake That" (*Curtain Call*), for instance, he changes "shit-faced" to "shit-face-ted" immediately after the similar-meaning word "wasted." This is a priming mistake, but he retains it because it improves rhyming. In "Fast Lane" (Bad Meets Evil, *Hell: The Sequel*) he uses the marked past tense form "spit-ted," which fits better than "spat" with the surrounding vowels and rapid rhythm of the verse. (He uses "spat" elsewhere, for example in the single "Fly Away.")

30. Eminem also gets away with such bending because our brains restore words

to their original "stored" pronunciations when we listen anyhow. For instance, psycholinguistic research has long shown that if you edit a recording by substituting a cough noise for a vowel or consonant in the middle of a word, listeners will hear the edited word as if it had been pronounced perfectly and as if the cough had happened just before or after it (Traxler, *Psycholinguistics*, 69). Our brains proffer "top-down" information like this so that speech can remain intelligible even in very noisy acoustic conditions. "Sound restoration effects" are especially important in rap music, where speech must compete for our ears with loud beats, samplings, etc.

31. Eminem's verse in "The Re-Up" (*Eminem Presents the Re-Up*) is a good example. In "Not Afraid" (*Recovery*) his black English rendering of "feelings" as "fillings" is primed not by [ɪ] but by the word "teeth" in the previous bar, and it sets up two other dentistry double entendres in the next line.

32. Chingy hails from St. Louis, Missouri, where some blacks naturally pronounce [ːɜ] (the SQUARE vowel) as [ɜː] (the NURSE vowel) such that, for instance, "there" becomes "thurr," "e'erbody" becomes "urrbody," etc. Chingy also occasionally pronounces [r] (the NEAR vowel) as [ɜː], so that "here" becomes "hurr."

33. Christine A. Sevald and Gary S. Dell, "The Sequential Cuing Effect in Speech Production," *Cognition* 53 (1994): 91–127.

34. T. Florian Jaeger, Katrina Furth and Caitlin Hilliard, "Incremental Phonological Encoding During Unscripted Sentence Production," *Frontiers in Psychology* 3, no. 481 (2012): 1–22.

35. The priming effect is especially strong with certain sound-meaning pairings, like *gl* "light/vision" ("glimmer," "glisten," "glitter," "gleam," "glow," "glint," etc.) and *sn* "nose/mouth" ("snore," "snack," "snout," "snarl," "snort," "sniff," "sneeze," etc.). See Benjamin K. Bergen, "The Psychological Reality of Phonaesthemes," *Language* 80 (2004): 290–311.

36. "Vulgar" is an example in itself. See Roger W. Wescott, "Labio-Velarity and Derogation in English: A Study in Phonosemic Correlation," *American Speech* 46 (1971): 123–137.

37. Grammatical priming is difficult to apply because rhyme takes precedence over grammar in rap. Eminem illustrates this while poking fun at pretentious grammar in one of his Wake Up Show freestyles: "I'm back out looking for someone of to beat the crap out" (Sway & King Tech, *Wake Up Show Freestyles Vol. 5*).

38. Rapp and Samuel, "A reason to rhyme," 570. Seth Lindstromberg and Frank Boers also demonstrate that rhyming, assonance and alliteration are especially common in fixed phrases and idioms. For example, "When the cat's away, the mice will play" could be worded differently, as in "When the cat's gone, the mice will play," but it's not. Seth Lindstromberg and Frank Boers, "Phonemic Repetition and the Learning of Lexical Chunks: The Power of Assonance," *System* 36 (2008): 423–436.

39. Scott, "Sublimating Hiphop," 144.

40. "The 20 Worst Rap Lyrics of 2012," last modified December 17, 2012. http://www.aux.tv/2012/12/the-20-worst-rap-lyrics-of-2012/. Note also generally negative comments below article.

41. Eminem's "butt police" line is also derided in "Numb: Rihanna & Eminem Team Up For Hazy Track Off *Unapologetic*," last modified November 18, 2012. http://www.huffingtonpost.com/2012/11/18/numb-rihanna-eminem-unapologetic_n_2155381.html. Comments there are generally negative, too.

42. Tim Brennan, "Off the Gangsta Tip: A Rap Appreciation, or Forgetting About Los Angeles," *Critical Inquiry* 20 (1994): 665.

The Melodic Nature of Rap and the Importance of the Phrase

Martin Connor

Because of the magnitude of his musical contributions and the versatility he has displayed on all of his projects, Eminem's oeuvre makes an excellent departure point for a deeper understanding of the strictly musical materials with which rap music is made. One of the fundamental building blocks of rap, as it is for all types of music, is rhythm. However, what separates the rhythms of rap's words from those found in most other types of music, such as folk, is their highly developed complexity. Rather than being random, completely improvised, or even a complicated type of rhythmic swing that makes a music's beats flow together, a rapper's lyrics are delivered in complex rhythmic subdivisions like noctuplets or septuplets. To not recognize or to simplify complexity would be to miss out on much of rap's musical narrative, as we'll see. All of a certain rap's strictly musical characteristics, such as its articulation, fundamental rhythms, indefinite pitch contours, and so on, will now be referred to with the same term that is used in most kinds of music: *melody*.[1] A central part of a particular rap's melody is the nature of its fundamental rhythms, just as the concept of rhythmic swing distinguishes many genres of jazz, or many syncopated rhythms distinguish genres of reggae.

Because many of the terms used in this essay have multiple musical meanings, a note is required. When the word *rap* is used it refers specifically to the musical rhythms of the words that a rapper pronounces over a beat. That is, the term *rap* does not refer to the genre as a whole. Most importantly, *rap* refers to the lyrics and words a rapper writes only insofar as they inform the music of the rap to which I'm referring. That "music of the rap" is separate from even the poetic considerations of academics like Adam Bradley or Andrew DuBois. If a listener conceives of the musical (not poetic) rhythms of rap as being just one part of its melody, the philosophical or aesthetic deficiencies heard in the strictly musical aspects of rap by some commentators can actually turn out to be some of its greatest strengths.

The Phrase in Rap Music

The building block of rap as pure music is the phrase. The term *phrase* refers to many different things in music, but here it will refer to a closed grammatical structure. This closed grammatical structure is most often a sentence. For instance, the first line of Eminem's "My Name Is," when he asks young children what their interests are, is a phrase. This is because it is a sentence with both a subject and a predicate. However, the term *closed grammatical structure* is purposefully used here because phrases in rap can also consist of fragments. This often occurs when a rapper names items on a list. As an example, in the opening of "Brain Damage," Eminem lists the negative effects of a farcical operation being performed on him in order to "fix" his neuroses. While his introduction of this list is a phrase, so are the simple nouns, sans verbs, that come afterward. Evidence of rappers thinking in phrases can be gleaned from a survey of the different manners in which phrases appear, which will then illuminate the different characteristics of Eminem's own phrases.

The existence and importance of phrases can most obviously be seen in the phenomenon of metric transference, which has also been found in the prelude-fugue pairings of Bach's masterpiece *The Well-Tempered Clavier*. Metric transference in Bach will be examined because it will shed light on the musical games that rappers play, and the musically unique way in which they understand rhythm. The thematic and clever connections between each of the twenty-four fugues and preludes in the *WTC* has been studied ever since they were written in the first half of the eighteenth century.

We need the musical concept of a bar, also called a measure, to discuss this music any further. So we don't leave non-musician readers out in the cold: a bar is similar to a minute or hour in that it is the basis of a system of time. But instead of a chronological concept of time, a bar is the basis for a musical concept of time. Just like a minute, bars repeat over and over in a song and always last the same amount of musical time. This flexible unit of time, divorced from exact minute or second considerations, allows some music to be fast and some music to be slow. In the music below, we see the musical length of two bars from the opening of Bach's C minor prelude from the *WTC*. The brackets in these two bars outline the important three-note figure to be looked at:

The notes that concern us are the three ¹⁄₁₆ notes that all happen off the beat in both hands, as are emphasized by the brackets below and above the music. While the bass staff's three-note figure is what will be found in the corresponding fugue's subject, the treble staff's three-note figure is notable for being an inversion of the archetypal three-note figure. The double lines over the black, circular note heads denote the musical duration of the notes as being ¹⁄₁₆ notes. Below is the opening exposition of the corresponding C minor fugue's subject in its first two bars; just notice how the brackets from the music above and the brackets from the music below look similar, with those two lines beneath connecting consecutive notes:

As the brackets show, that same three–¹⁄₁₆-note phrase that was found off the beat in the bass of the C minor prelude occurs no fewer than three times in the following fugue's subject. However, the same three-note phrase found in the fugue now ends on the beat, instead of occurring completely off it, as happened in the prelude. Accordingly, the fugue subject and quasi-accompanying texture in the prelude are both repeated over and over in the whole of each respective composition. So, by preserving its rhythms and melodic outline while transferring its metric position, Bach has transformed the core musical idea in intelligent ways.

The non-musician can envision this by thinking about the verbal accents of different words. Think of the four-syllable word *architecture*, for which one accents the first syllable when it's pronounced: "ARCH-i-tec-ture." The first instance of our three-note motive sounds like those three syllables after the "arch-" syllable, because they're unaccented. Now think of the word *volunteer*, where the accent is on the final syllable. "vol-un-TEER." Bach has musically made the change from the unaccented "-itecture" syllables of "architecture" to the final stress on the last syllable, "-TEER," of "volunteer."

Due to non-durational phonological sounds in language like the glottal stop, rappers don't always have the ability to rap in a flowing, legato manner, as Bach did through his articulations. Additionally, rappers almost never have the organizing principle of definite pitch available to them with which they can outline and denote motifs, as Bach had stepwise melodic seconds to define the fugue subject in the aforementioned C minor fugue. Instead, rappers must rely on the continuation of semantic meaning to craft phrases, which is where the sentences and fragments of before come in. An excellent example of the delicate crafting of a phrase is Busta Rhymes's opening lines from his 2001 song "Holla." The proof and evidence we find in Busta's work will strengthen our understanding of Eminem's musical approach to the phrase and its rhythms.

Busta opens his first verse with three straight phrases of three syllables each. The related, parallel nature of these three phrases is established in three ways, just as Bach had to preserve certain characteristics in order to keep his fugue subject recognizable. These three characteristics are based on Kyle Adams's exhaustive and preeminently useful categorization of what he calls "flow" through a rap's different metrical and articulative character-istics.[2] First, each sentence in question comprises the same, entirely closed grammatical structure. Second, each individual sentence has the same rhythmic profile when notated: a noctuplet ⅛ note, followed by a dotted noctuplet ¹⁄₁₆ note, followed by a noctuplet ⅛ note tied to a noctuplet ¹⁄₃₂ note. (A reader with no musical background should simply conceive of those technical terms as describing three different rhythmic lengths that are repeated.) We can leave out what those particular syllables and their semantic meanings are because, once again, we are interested in only the melody of rap. Finally, these three sentences have parallel rhyme structures.

To see this parallel rhyme structure, we need an easily understandable way to represent this. Consider the rhyme of *pander* with *banter*. Each has two syllables: *pan-der* and *ban-ter*. The first syllable of *pander*, *pan-*, rhymes with the first syllable of *banter*, *ban-*, because they both have the *-ah* vowel sound. We'll consider that *-ah* vowel sound to be part of an A group. These two words also rhyme together on their second syllable: *-der* rhymes with *-ter*, which is an *-er* sound. That *-er* sound will be our B group. If we place these two rhymes inside consecutive sentences in a nonsense rap, such as the line "Talking heads all pander" followed by "They do nothing but ban-ter," then we have our closed grammatical sentences. We'll represent the start and end of those two sentences below with open and closed brackets. Thus, we can represent the relationship between these two lines as follows:

[AB][AB]

The first set of brackets indicates "Talking heads all pander," and the second represents "They do nothing but banter." Thus, we see that the rhymes here have parallel AB rhyme structures.

We can analyze and understand Busta's opening phrases from "Holla" in the same way, by following the landmarks pointed out by Bradley: "Sometimes rap poets devise intricate structures that give logical shape to their creations. Using patterns of rhyme, rhythm, and line, these structures reinforce an individual verse's fusion of form and meaning."[3] The same structures can be considered musically.

Let's examine Busta's first line, beginning "Team select." The initial, identical rhyming vowel sound of the first syllable in each of Busta's three phrases (*-ee*) is represented by the letter A, the rhyming vowel sound on the second syllable of each (*-uh*) is represented by the letter B, and the rhyming vowel sound on the third syllable (*-eh*) is represented by the letter C. Thus, the three sentences can be summarized in this manner:

[ABC][ABC][ABC]

We finally see here that Busta Rhymes has created an archetypal phrase by the nature of its repeated rhythmic profile, its repeated rhyme structure, and its repeated, identical position in a closed grammatical structure. Because these three phrases are all so closely related, they should be thought of as separate instances of the same archetypal phrase. The concept of a phrase is necessary in order to understand what Busta Rhymes does next in his rap on "Holla." This repetition of an established phrase is not in itself remarkable; what is remarkable is the manner in which Busta Rhymes repeats it.

A trained musician may have noticed that the entire length of that phrase's rhythmic profile was of an unbalanced length, because the phrase in question lasts a total of six noctuplet ¹⁄₁₆ notes. That is, if those six total noctuplets are laid in a row, they have still not returned to their original beginning point at the same place with regard to their position in that important musical time unit, the bar.

Because Busta doesn't exactly balance the rhythmic profile into a length of nine or eighteen ¹⁄₁₆-note noctuplets, his repetition of this phrase now starts it in a metrically new place in the measure each time. This is because there are eighteen ¹⁄₁₆-note noctuplets in a bar. In this phrase's first instance, the first syllable falls about midway between the first and second quarters of a bar; in its second iteration, it falls right before the third quarter and is completely syncopated; and in its third iteration, the first syllable lands right after the fourth quarter of the bar. This is shown in the sheet music below:

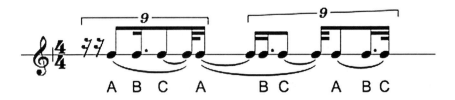

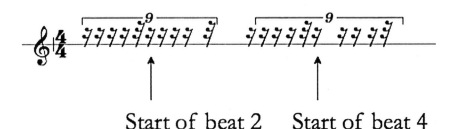

Start of beat 2   Start of beat 4

Thus, Busta has musically transformed the phrase metrically while maintaining its rhyming, grammatical, and durational aspects.

This instance of phrasal metric transference is not an isolated example. This sophisticated technique can be found in Notorious B.I.G.'s 1997 song "Hypnotize" at 0:40, 1:37, and 2:20; Earl Sweatshirt's 2010 song "Earl" at 0:03; André 3000's verse on OutKast's 1998 song "Aquemini" at 1:54; Nas's verse on Busta Rhymes's 2006 song "Don't Get Carried Away" at 1:42; Kendrick Lamar's 2012 song "M.A.A.D City" at 3:30; Common's verse on Kanye West's "Wack Niggaz Part II" at 0:45; Rakim's verse on 1987's "I Ain't No Joke" at 1:00; and still others. This perception of Busta's musical trickery, with its parallels in classical music, is possible only if a listener understands what constitutes a phrase in rap, the importance of those phrases, and how they are used to build musical structures.

The Phrase in Eminem's Music

The importance of the phrase is no less in understanding Eminem's music, especially on the 1999 song "What's the Difference," from Dr. Dre's album *2001*. There, Eminem demonstrates a profound awareness of even the most finely detailed rhythms.[4]

Our process for establishing related phrases will be the same for "What's the Difference" as it was for the metric transference in Busta Rhymes's work. Toward the start of his verse on the song, Eminem rips off a series of six bars that contain just such an archetypal phrase. The rhythmic profile for each of this phrase's six appearances is very similar, as three of the six times it consists of an identical row of three noctuplet ¹⁄₁₆ notes.[5] Each iteration is also in a parallel position in the closed grammatical structure, as each comes at the very end of a sentence.[6] Furthermore, these repetitions display parallel rhyme structures in the same ABC, ABC manner of Busta's rap. And yet, just as Busta Rhymes changed the metric position of the start of each phrase, Eminem similarly transforms the rhythmic profile of his own phrase while maintaining its other essential characteristics in a technique called elastic phrasing.

The appearance of this three-syllable phrase is similar and yet different each time. Each of the six appearances can be categorized according to whether it associates with the third or fourth beat, and whether its rhythms are strictly noctuplet ¹⁄₁₆ notes or not. When it first appears, this three-syllable phrase falls on or extremely near the third beat. It is not three-straight noctuplet ¹⁄₁₆ notes but instead is the total of three straight noctuplet dotted ¹⁄₁₆ notes.[7] The first line is the musical rhythms of Eminem's spoken syllables as represented in traditional Western music notation; the reader should use the second line of notation to orient themselves in the unfamiliar noctuplet groupings. The following phrase happens on the fragment, "told you this":

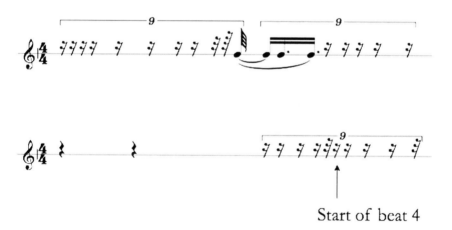

Start of beat 4

(The non-musician can summarize the following discussion and skip the technical jargon by thinking of this three-syllable phrase as lasting different but similar amounts of time each time it appears.)

The slurs in the sheet music above, instead of indicating articulation as in most music, represent a closed grammatical structure—the phrase. A single staff line is used instead of multiple ones to reflect Western notation's inadequate representation of instruments of indefinite pitch like the human voice. Finally, the treble signs, instead of reflecting a rapper's vocal register, instead serves to reinforce rap's nature as pure music, which previous systems of transcription have failed to do both sufficiently and accurately.

When Eminem's three-note phrase appears for the second time, on "know this shit," it falls very near the fourth beat, and comes in uniform noctuplet $\frac{1}{16}$ notes:

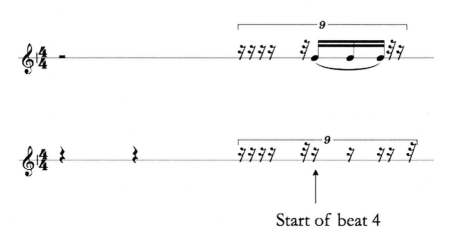

Start of beat 4

When the phrase appears for a third time, on "noticed it," while it is still in its characteristic three $\frac{1}{16}$-note noctuplet form, it now falls right after the onset of the third beat:

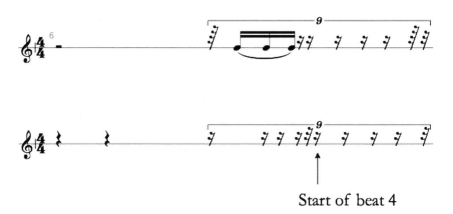

Start of beat 4

In the phrase's fourth appearance, on "blow this bitch," the rhythms again vary across the third beat, as it did during its first appearance, but without straight noctuplet ¹⁄₁₆ notes:

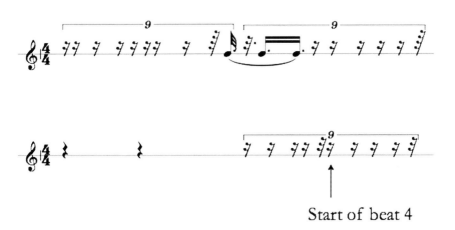

Start of beat 4

In its fifth appearance, the phrase closely mimics the rhythmic characteristics of its second and third appearances, and so further establishes itself as a characteristic, musically important idea in the learned listener's ear. This is on "throat is it."

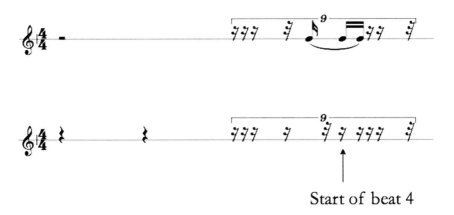

Start of beat 4

In the phrase's sixth appearance, on "ocean is," it falls on the fourth beat, and consists of a noctuplet ¹⁄₈ note, followed by a ¹⁄₁₆ note, followed by the final anceps syllable:

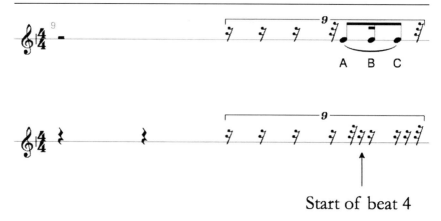

Start of beat 4

Although Eminem slightly and intelligently changes the rhythms that each of the three syllables of the archetypal phrase appears on, he has still maintained their parallel ABC rhyme order and their parallel grammatical position at the end of a sentence. This, and their similar position in the form of the song, informs the listener that they are all related.

In the listener's ear, Eminem has set up the expectation of an unchanging, three-noctuplet ¹⁄₁₆-note phrase through its repetition on three of its six appearances, and on two of its first three. But for the other three appearances, he slightly changes their rhythms to new but related durations. So while the listener expects three noctuplet ¹⁄₁₆-notes, Eminem confirms or denies those expectations throughout this section of music, and this constant surprise and unknowing is part of what drives the song forward musically.

The result is a secret musical game between Eminem and the listener that, if the listener can follow, is great fun to play along with. With a nod and a wink, Eminem subverts an oddly profound moment, as he is apt to do at the most unexpected times elsewhere, with some highly intelligent musical games.[8] We know this is done intentionally, whether it was conscious or not, because each iteration is so closely related to the other, and because this entire section of "What's the Difference" has such a clear, purely musical narrative. Other types of musical narratives include the antecedent and consequent phrases of a period, or a well-led chord progression.

Neither is Eminem's use of elastic phrasing an isolated incident. It can be found later on in "What's the Difference" as well, at the 3:15 mark, in a smaller, more approximate form. For another example, it can be found on Jean Grae's 2011 song "Imagine," where she transforms a five-note phrase over eight bars, starting at the 1:00 mark.

Although such small changes in the rhythms of Eminem's rap might be dismissed by some as mere chance, or even a demonstration of a lack of a sense for rhythm, it cannot be coincidence that Eminem changed these rhythms over an extended period of time in such an intelligent and seemingly preconceived manner. Furthermore, Eminem and Dr. Dre perform the rhythms from "What's the Difference" in live performances exactly the same way as they do in the recorded version.[9] It may be a measure of Eminem's talent that he has managed all of the possible aspects of an MC's style that Adam Krims mentions: "The spilling-over of rhythmic boundaries may involve the syntax and/or the rhymes; it may involve repeated off-beat (or weak beat) accents; or it may involve any other strategy that creates polyrhythms with four-measure groupings of 4/4 time."[10] It is these subtle changes and relationships between phrases that a seasoned rap listener will learn to appreciate.

The Effects of Eminem's Rhythmic Variations

Eminem has slightly transformed the execution of that phrase each time it appears, and this has two main results. The first is to elicit new emotional effects in the listener. Dr. Dre's cynical hesitation on his own repetition of the phrase in its sixth appearance seeks to reinforce his ironic verbal message to Eminem on how to find a proper place to bury Eminem's estranged wife in a future hypothetical murder. Through this elastic phrasing, Eminem also manipulates a listener's expectations, as all great musicians do. Bradley has traced this same manipulation in rap through its poetic aspects.[11]

This infallible feel for the expressive effects of sudden, deliberate changes in rhythm is characteristic of Eminem's rap, and separates him from most other rappers. His use of poetic, suspension-building pregnant pauses is perhaps the most obvious instance of this. At 0:41 on "My Name Is," Eminem introduces a rap from Dr. Dre by lyricizing, "And Dr. Dre said," at which point Dr. Dre enters the song. This otherwise standard line is elevated artistically when Eminem musically repeats the line exactly at 0:31 on "The Real Slim Shady." In sticking with the darker themes of his major label sequel album, as on songs like "Kim," "The Way I Am," and "Stan," Eminem turns that innocent line into a sinister window into his current psyche. After Eminem repeats the line on "The Real Slim Shady," though, Dr. Dre doesn't enter the song. Instead, using a noticeable, awkwardly long pause of about a beat and a half, Eminem informs us that he's killed his best friend and mentor. He further reinforces this surprise by reentering the song on an accented strong beat, and by using quicker rhythms when revealing where Dr. Dre has gone.

Eminem also uses musical rests to great effect elsewhere as well. On the song "Criminal," Eminem directly confronts the race issue that people find it hard to miss when discussing his celebrity. He sets up an external rhyme that the listener continues to anticipate at 2:40 by his repetition of rhymes on "liquor" and "quicker" in musically important places. Eminem then suggests that he's about to rap another rhyme on "quicker" and "liquor" with a racial slur that is unfailingly controversial in all of society. Instead, Eminem leaves that word unsaid, but his insertion of a musical rest allows listeners to repeat the word in their own minds. Eminem understands very well how to set up the listener's expectations and then simultaneously satisfy and deny those expectations.

The noticeable, inhuman breaks in the middle of phrases on "The Way I Am," such at 0:31, communicate his seething anger, through which he is unable to articulate himself clearly. That interpretation is bolstered by the insertion of a deep, angry breath in the background during the pause. The menacing threat to the listener in his imitation of a criminal recently released from prison on "Bad Meets Evil" at 2:48 is deepened by an accelerating rhythmic drive. His complete dismissal of Dr. Dre's suggestion of peace as absurd on "Guilty Conscience" at 2:48 is further strengthened by a deliberate pause. Throughout his entire oeuvre, Eminem displays an understanding of how to affect the listener musically. Perhaps this interpretation of musical phenomena is overly specific, but rap, above all, *is* a thoroughly expressive form. Maybe at one point rap may follow the abstract example of recent contemporary artistic trends like serialism, perhaps through the rapping of nonsense syllables or a greater use of rhymed scatting, but for now, rap remains a primarily communicative art form.[12]

Performance Practice's Influence on Eminem's Rhythms

This kind of finely textured rhythmic game played by Eminem and his colleagues is made possible by the unique manner in which rap music is made. That is, rappers almost never musically notate their rap's rhythms in sheet music before their performance, and they never give musical notation to someone else to perform.[13]

To the classically trained musician, the musical relationship between the beat and the rap may come off as counterintuitive, or even shoddy. For instance, there is little elaborate rhythmic counterpoint or back-and-forth between the rapper and the beat in a kind of rhythmic heterophony.[14] Furthermore, rhythmic mimicking or homophony between the two sources of music in a rap song, as on Eminem's own song "The Way I Am," can come across as thin and strained, just as constant harmonic thirds in classical music is not true polyphony.[15] Here I agree with Justin Williams, who sums this up succinctly in his critique of Adams: "[Adams] argues that rappers 'focused as much on creating rhythmic unity with the underlying track as they did on creating semantic meaning'.... Rather than use the term 'unity,' I would suggest consonance....There may be unity between two or more elements in the recording, but there may also exist a perceivable disunity in other elements such as pitch or density of material."[16] Overall, the relation of the rap's musical aspects to the beat is more ephemeral and ineffable, and it is this lack of blatant or overbearing musical support from the producer to the rapper that makes rappers' rhythmic trickeries possible.

This is due to Eminem's and his producers' lack of formal musical training, which is actually a strength of their music. The complex rhythms that Eminem raps—those dotted $\frac{1}{32}$ noctuplets—could never be accurately performed by an instrumentalist to whom sheet music would be given by a separate composer who conceived of his or her composition far in advance of its eventual performance. This is the process by which most classical music is executed. Thus, rap's melody draws many of its defining features from its performance practice. While straying dangerously close to the genetic fallacy, I'd like to point out that in the previous sentences I am merely referring to phenomena, while hopefully ascribing no supposed, goal-directed agency on any musician's part. I'd like to appeal to Adams's answer to Williams's critiques: "The genetic fallacy, as originally formulated, supposes that 'an actual history of any science, art, or social institution can take the place of a logical analysis of its structure.'... In this context, that would translate to the claim that an analytical method is valid only if it corresponds to the compositional process. This is quite different from the claim that an analytical method can be justified by appeal to the compositional process."[17]

The repetitive nature of some hip-hop beats can now be seen as a necessity and an elegant solution to rap musicians' own lack of voice leading training, or even the question of how to accompany such complicated rhythms. (This should not be taken to imply that hip-hop producers saw this as a problem and went about it consciously.) As Bradley writes on rap's analogous poetic aspects, "The voice gives the beat humanity and variety: the beat gives the rhyme a reason for being and a margin for error.... Rap's dual rhythmic relationship liberates the MC to pursue innovations of syncopation and stress that might otherwise sound chaotic were it not for the reassuring regularity of the beat."[18]

Hip-hop beats that constantly changed the structural elements of their backing music from moment to moment would quickly lose musical meaning in the listener's ear, and so they instead clear out sonic space for rappers to operate in.[19] In his response to Adams, Williams nicely summarizes some of the foundational, binding techniques producers use: "Rap music's layers will more often than not fluctuate through a given song, with sonic additions and subtractions, manipulation of digital samples, and even sharp changes in aspects of the 'basic beat.'"[20] The musical acrobatics performed by producers, then, is how to be most economical with a limited amount of musical material to them. Thus, the gripping musical details of Dr. Dre's 2003 beat "Oh!," on which Obie Trice raps, isn't the complexity of the harmonic voice leading; it's the perfect structural, rhythmic, and melodic proportion with which Dr. Dre balances eight competing instrumental ideas that are each still musically interesting on their own, and which differentiate otherwise repeating sections of the song.[21]

Eminem's Phrasal Approach to Rap Song Structure

The effect of Eminem's sense of phrasing on a song's larger form is groundbreaking as well. Eminem's original approach to the traditional rap song structure is supported by the placement of his rap's phrasings. Once again, Eminem displays an unfailing awareness of the musical tools available to him. This can be seen on the 2004 song "Never Enough," on which 50 Cent and Nate Dogg also appear. On this very short song, Eminem and the producers, Dr. Dre and Mike Elizondo, have structured it so as to place the MCs' rapping skills in the very forefront. The song is short, clocking in at only 2:39, and starts immediately with the rapping verse, without any instrumental intro. Additionally, there are just two choruses, also called hooks, that last only eight bars each, and there is not a single bar during this song that does not have rapping in it. Eminem doubles down on this artistic gamble when he makes his own verse last a full thirty-two bars, which is an unmistakably symbolic number to insiders of the rap community.

This is because sixteen bars is the standard length of a rap verse. In fact, as Paul Edwards notes in *How to Rap*, professional rappers even sometimes refer to a verse as simply "a 16."[22] Any shorter and an MC might display a lack of confidence in their skills; any longer and the rapper quickly risks overstaying their welcome if he or she isn't talented. By extending the phrases in his own verse to twice the normal length and minimizing the comparatively simple sections of a rap song, Eminem musically backs up his verbal message on "Never Enough" that he truly *is* the one of the greatest rappers of all time.

Eminem's awareness of musical structure is further borne out on the

1999 song "Forgot About Dre." This song's particular hook lasts four bars, and first comes after a Dr. Dre rap verse made up of sixteen bars. Although sixteen bars is the standard length of a verse, one can also find verses consisting of just eight bars or less, as on Talib Kweli's 2002 song "Guerrilla Monsoon Rap," OutKast's 2000 song "Gangsta Shit," or The Wu-Tang Clan's 1993 song "Shame on a Nigga."

After the end of the hook's first appearance on "Forgot About Dre," Eminem starts his own verse, at 1:25. But after the first eight bars of Eminem's verse, Dr. Dre inserts a completely new musical idea at 1:54, a distorted guitar riff, in the same place that a hook could typically appear. We also know that this guitar idea is a stand-in for the hook because they both last the same exact amount of musical time on this track: four bars. As Edwards notes, "Choruses can theoretically be of any length, but they are usually four or eight bars long.[23]

During this new kind of hook, Eminem doesn't return to the same rap that he originally delivered in the true hook, as would happen in most other rap songs. Instead, Eminem innovatively continues his verse's rap phrases when the fake hook starts by not dissecting Dr. Dre's supposed reputation, but instead fantasizing over his and Dr. Dre's villainous capers. After this fake hook Eminem continues his normal verse, which lasts a full sixteen bars in total. As a result, the listener hears that Eminem doesn't always have his rap strictly follow the different musical ideas that usually divide separate musical sections from each other. Instead, Eminem expands on this convention by rapping a verse during what would normally have been a hook.

Eminem's variations on the standard verse-hook-verse-hook structure of a rap song is in strong evidence elsewhere as well. For instance, 1999's "Guilty Conscience" is a freestyle with tempoless interludes. "Bad Meets Evil," from 1999, features an exchange of self-contained verses between Eminem and Royce da 5'9" with no intervening hooks.

Indefinite Pitch Melodies in Eminem's Phrases

Along with intelligently varying his phrases' macro-rhythmic and micro-rhythmic characteristics, Eminem varies their melodic characteristics in unmistakable ways as well. Although traditional Western music notation struggles to represent the indefinite pitch of a rapper's voice, a modified MIDI piano roll could do much better. Indefinite pitch refers to the difference between a human voice when it's singing a song like "Happy Birthday," and when it's used to have a normal conversation with a friend, for instance. The pitch from "Happy Birthday" could be called "definite pitch," as opposed to rap's indefinite pitch.

A representation of the indefinite pitch melodies of rap might be more accurate if an MIDI piano roll transcription were to be used. This is because a computer transcription could represent pitch changes smaller than a semi-tone. It would solve at least part of the problem that Krims mentions and that exists for most percussion instruments, which is how Adams treats the rapping voice[24]: "The timbral representation in Western discussion of music are well known; and such limits cannot but hinder some consideration of rap poetics."[25]

I have taken the opening fifteen seconds of a studio-quality a cappella mix of Eminem's first verse at 1:54 on D12's 2001 song "Shit on You" and represented it on a MIDI piano roll with the help of computer software. Colored markers are used to represent velocity, but what is most valuable is the sliding up and down of the lines in melodic intervals that are smaller than semitones, which can't accurately represent a human speaking voice. Although the audio-to-MIDI transformation process is rather imperfect, when the MIDI is overlaid on top of the original audio the well-planned shape of the melodic contour is easier to trace.[26] The logic of Eminem's melodic contours are now more obvious: just as the phrases of an entire melody with definite pitch have certain recognizable contours—an arch, a downward motion, an upward motion—so do Eminem's, according to the start and end of his own phrases.

This description of the creation and release of tension has been used for centuries to assess traditional melodies, like America's national anthem or the "Happy Birthday" tune. Both of those songs go very high in the start of their melodies to build tension and create interest, and then come back down at the end so the tension is released and the songs feel finished. Additionally, some traditional melodic aspects in the melodic contour can be observed: the pitch of Eminem's voice varies over the length of roughly two octaves, from G#2 to F4.[27] One would see that the first three phrases all display a slow downward arc in pitch if he or she were to watch the descending lines, starting at the lyrics "weren't shit."

In the second half of this part of the rap, the pitch of Eminem's rapping voice begins to balance that downward arc by now ascending until the words "me and ..."

Eminem will go on to complete this inverted arc melodic contour at the end of this part of the verse by rising to its highest pitch yet. Once again, we arrive back at the importance of the phrase in understanding the musical journeys rappers lead listeners on.

Summary

Musically, rap is just like any other genre. Its sometimes outlandish trappings—gratuitous verbal themes, criminal behavior, opulent wealth—have long distracted away from its musical, melodic nature. As Krims writes, "So publicly has rap music been debated in terms unrelated to its musical aspects ... that a discussion of rap as music might be a valuable reminder that it is sites of pleasure and artistic production that we are stigmatizing, and experiences of profound investment and artistic engagement."[28] The poetic, sociological, historical, and ethnomusicological discussions from Tricia Rose, Jeff Chang, and others are invaluable. But a complementary, purely musical point of view is necessary to tell rap's whole story.

Appendix: A Note on Transcription

My transcription method of Eminem's rhythms bears further explanation. I have chosen to represent rappers' rhythms exactly as they are performed, taking up Williams on his suggestion: "Rap styles are more varied than the article suggests, and there are a number of ways to update and expand upon Krims's four-genre taxonomy of rap styles.

One way would be to locate instances of expressive microtiming at the sub-syntactical level between songs or artists."[29] I have purposely eschewed the taxonomic approach of Krims. One would never categorize popular or classical music in such specific ways, because their modes of expression are so varied, just as rap's are. Once again, we find another approach that marks rap off as somehow different from other musics. Proof of the accuracy of my transcriptions can be found through overlaying a playback of my transcriptions from "What's the Difference" with the actual audio from the song and seeing their synchronization.[30]

I have received criticism from others who say that rap rhythms are swung or something similar, and should be simplified as jazz notation is into straight rhythms. But to simplify rappers' rhythms into straight notation is impossible without losing all of the meaning of their rhythms. Jazz's swing rhythms, being non–Western, are sometimes simplified into straight notation and given the help of a legend, something like the below:

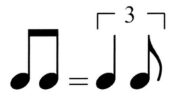

But to do the same for rap would be to lose all of the rap's rhythmic sense. The following straight transcription of Eminem's opening rhythms on "What's the Difference" has no relationship to the actual rhythms, besides containing the same number of notes:

The above would be useful mostly for tracing out where phrases fall in relation to the bar line, but not for representing rhythmic subdivisions. Adams himself notates MF DOOM's "All Caps" and N.W.A.'s "100 Miles and Runnin'" in subdivisions that are all based on the ¹⁄₁₆ note from a 4/4 bar.[31] To use such notation to represent large-scale rhythms, like the beginning and ending of phrases, would be fine. But it could not be used to justify more specific assertions, such as that "These lines are characterized by a 4-against–3 rhythm that appears twice."[32] Besides not landing on the beat, which might be omitted for simplicity's sake, the rhythms do not occur in straightforward quadruplets at all, or even the polyrhythmic groups that Adams chooses. This is the actual notation for the third measure of Dr. Dre's verse from "100 Miles and Runnin'" at 1:31:

To remove distinctions between a noctuplet ¹⁄₁₆ note, a dotted noctuplet ¹⁄₁₆ note, a noctuplet ¹⁄₃₂ note, and so on, would distort the fundamental nature of rap's rhythms as I've described them. It should not be surprising that the music theory world has had to wait for the invention of hyper-accurate computer programs, like Sibelius or Finale, to precisely transcribe such complicated rhythms. I personally could not have begun to learn how to accurately transcribe these rhythms without these programs' playback feature, which I've used to verify their correctness down to the tiniest noctuplet subdivision. The pioneering contributions of Adams, who could never have known where these rhythmic theories would eventually end up, might never have been undertaken in the first place if he had known. As a result, we'd know even less about such a young genre than we do now.

Rappers' rhythms are not swung. They are not a deviation away from the norm of common Western musical practices, and they're not a performer's naturally imperfect interpretation of an ideal composition as represented in sheet music notation, which could otherwise account for these micro-timings in a live performance context. As I hope I've shown, rappers feel all of these very complicated notes, right down to each noctuplet $\frac{1}{64}$ note, exactly as they happen. This can be seen, as was mentioned previously in a note, in the uniform recitation of Eminem's verses in live, non-studio performances. This is another reason why I represent the MC's rhythms exactly.

I've also consciously chosen to always notate rappers' rhythms in noctuplets. Although other tuplets, like septuplets or quintuplets, could notate these rhythms as well, none of those subdivisions have the flexibility or adaptability of noctuplets, which is such that one does not have to go outside of that particular rhythmic subdivision to represent these rhythms. It should be noted that when rappers count their beats as they write their raps, it is highly unlikely that they're counting noctuplets, as a performer might count $\frac{1}{16}$ notes in a quick passage. This is because of the complexity of noctuplets. But for their adaptability and comparative simplicity, I've chosen to divide the usual eight $\frac{1}{16}$ notes in the first half of a 4/4 bar into nine.

Finally, I've chosen to place note heads in the same place as the exact onset of a syllable. The musical durations chosen for each note head are usually selected only to make the music easier to read, and not for a syllable's actual duration in real time.

For all of these reasons, it is my hope that this essay will lead to a more frequent use of exactly accurate sheet music notation in rap's transcription and analysis, and that that use will adhere to the conventions I outlined above on Eminem's sheet music for "What's the Difference."

Chapter Notes

1. I do not use the term *flow*—as Kyle Adams does in his "On the Metrical Techniques of Flow in Rap," or as Justin A Williams does in his "Beats and Flows: A Response To Kyle Adams," and others do—because (1) that term has many different, sometimes contradictory, meanings in the general rap listening community, and (2) it further marks rap as somehow different from other kinds of music, like classical, pop, jazz, and so on. It insinuates that we are left with the next best thing to a melody to talk about when discussing rap. The use of melody further engages the belief that rap is deficient because it does not adhere to Western music's cultivation of complex melody, which is said to reach its zenith in polyphony.

2. Kyle Adams, "On the Metrical Techniques of Flow in Rap Music," *Society for Music Theory* 15.5 (2009): n. pag. [8.] http://www.mtosmt.org/issues/mto.09.15.5/mto. 09.15.5.adams.html.

3. Adam Bradley, *Book of Rhymes: The Poetics of Hip Hop* (New York: BasicCivitas, 2009), xxi.

4. Although both Eminem and Dr. Dre rap in Eminem's the verse that is in question here, Eminem wrote both of their lines, as he did on other songs as well. Examples include "Bad Guys Don't Die," from 1999, and their collaboration "Guilty Conscience" from the same year.

5. For a note on my transcriptions, please see the appendix that follows this essay.

6. Although for brevity's sake I'll refer to this three-note figure as a phrase, in reality each instance constitutes only the very end of a sentence.

7. For each of these examples I've represented the final syllable according to the duration that is most clear, but in reality each is an anceps syllable of undetermined length, being the final syllable in a line.

8. Such as when he comes clean on his addictions at the end of the otherwise jester-ish "I'm Shady" song from 1999.

9. See https://www.youtube.com/watch?v=DsNKkn7p3Sw or https://www.youtube.com/watch?v=dWDKi8E5K1.

10. Adam Krims, *Rap Music and the Poetics of Identity* (Cambridge: Cambridge University Press, 2000), 50.

11. Bradley, xxii.

12. Such rare examples of exclusively sonic rapping can be found on Slum Village's "Fantastic, Pt. 3."

13. Ghostwriting—when a rapper writes lyrics for another rapper to perform—clearly exists in the genre. But when this exchange of musical information occurs, it is done in real time. The ghostwriter raps in front of the ghostwriter, and the latter then simply imitates the ghostwriter's voice on their own.

14. Dr. Dre's "Some L.A. Niggaz," from 1999, is a noticeable exception to this. Rappers Time Bomb, Hittman, Xzibit, Defari, and King Tee all imitate the beat's jarring lack of an impetus on the strongest beat 3—endemic to almost all popular music—in the structure of their rap phrases.

15. Just such a stretching example is 50 Cent's hook on 2004's "How We Do" and his imitation of the synthesized keyboard part in the beat. He saves a possible lack of musical variety by balancing this exact imitation of the beat with free rhythms in the second half of the hook.

16. Justin Williams, "Beats and Flows: A Response to Kyle Adams, Aspects of the Music/Text Relationship in Rap." *Society for Music Theory* 15.2 (2009): n. pag. [9.] Web. http://www.mtosmt.org/issues/mto.09.15.2/mto.09.15.2.williams.html.

17. Kyle Adams, "People's Instinctive Assumptions and the Paths of Narrative: A Response to Justin Williams." *Society for Music Theory* 15.2 (2009): [15]. Web. http://www.mtosmt.org/issues/mto.09.15.2/mto.09.15.2.adams.html.

18. Bradley, 7.

19. An excellent way to trace this repetitive structure can be found in Miyakawa's 2005 book *Flow, Layering, Rupture, and Groove*. See figure 4.3 on page 79 that examines the beat of Digable Planets' "Dial 7 (Axioms of Creamy Spies)" from 1994's *Blowout Comb* album. I've borrowed this typographical method in Jason Thompson's forthcoming article "Cultural Mis/Representation, Musical Signifiers, and Narrative Paradigms in Rap."

20. Williams, 6.

21. See http://www.rapanalysis.com/2011/07/appreciating-rap-music-6-dr-dre-musical.html for more.

22. Paul Edwards, *How to Rap: The Art and Science of The Hip-Hop MC* (Chicago: Chicago Review, 2009), 193.

23. Edwards, 188.

24. Adams, 13.

25. Krims, 53.

26. See https://www.youtube.com/watch?v=Z_GmrwrYQo8&feature=youtu.be for such a video.

27. The MIDI piano roll sheet of music of sorts can be viewed at https://www.youtube.com/watch?v=Z_GmrwrYQo8&list=UULofZ7nhzFqQe-f2OZbZW_Q.

28. Krims, 39.

29. Williams, 18

30. See https://www.youtube.com/watch?v=DKRoRUuxSpo&list=UULofZ7nhzFqQe-f2OZbZW_Q

31. Adams, 23, 31.

32. Adams, 32.

Somewhere in Between:
Eminem's Ambiguities

E Martin Nolan

Given his tendency to provocation, Eminem would seem an easy target for criticism. His lyrics lead directly to issues of homosexual, women's, and minority rights; the meaning of *white trash*, the meaning of blackness; the responsibilities of the public entertainer, the limits of free speech; the value or cost of embodied depravity, the moral consciences of entire generations; and on, and on. Indeed, his work demands, and often receives, an immediate and prominent response. But he can also be a Trojan Horse. Obscured beneath his surface provocations lies a murkiness that lends itself not to certain platitudes but to uncertain ambiguities. This is easily overlooked because listeners can simply construct their own Eminem out of his myriad parts in order to justify whatever argument they would like to prove. Such efforts do more damage than good, however, despite how well intentioned and morally upright the arguments they support might be. This is not only because they ignore the ambiguity of the rapper's provocations but also because they tend to ignore those aspects of his work that would contradict their arguments.

Eminem is not important because he explains, exemplifies, or exposes this or that truth about our society, civilization, etc. He is important because he does something more difficult than that: he confronts us with ambiguity and makes us cope with complexity and misdirection. He does this through an ambitious formal technique as well as through the narratives, arguments, diatribes, and comedy routines that fill his songs. These sources of complexity are dependent on one another. To understand that dependence, we must first know how the form works, then we can examine the content that fills that form and, finally, the ramifications of the final product. His verse in 50 Cent's 2012 single "My Life" exemplifies Eminem's formal craft, so I will start there.

His Formal Achievements

"My Life" sandwiches a roughly minute-long verse by Eminem between two half-minute verses by 50 Cent. 50 Cent's verses are solid, workmanlike efforts. The verses are very similar in structure and content, so for our purposes a look at his first verse will suffice. It reviews his meteoric rise in 2003 and his break from former collaborators Game and Young Buck. After claiming that these rappers are nothing without the support he has now withdrawn, 50 vaguely gestures toward humility—"I'm not perfect"—before pronouncing his own worth—measured in earnings—while also announcing his return to the rap game.

This is all rendered in a well-established rap formality to match the well-established clichés (or tropes if you're being kind). Aside from the last couplet, the end rhymes are almost entirely exact, with the rhyme limited mostly to the final sound of the rhymed foot. Adding to that regularity is the fact that each of the first six lines ends in a monosyllabic short "i" word (e.g., "rich," "bitch"). The seventh and eighth lines interject with a forgettable couplet built on two disconnected clichés (one about lessons "learned" and another about "evil" money "earned"), which at least introduce a new end rhyme. The first eight lines are largely iambic, becoming almost perfectly so as the lines approach their ends, thus adding to the regularity established by the rhyme pattern. Lines nine and ten mark a significant, if brief, formal shift to a run on two internal rhymes describing 50 in a thin glaze of up-from-the-bottom-by-the-bootstraps glory.

The verse ends in nonchalant affirmation of 50's talent and an announcement that this is his "recovery." If the 50-Eminem–50 verse structure of "My Life" did not already invite a comparison between the two rappers, then surely 50's invocation of *Recovery*, Eminem's wildly successful comeback album, does. The comparison is not flattering to 50. Compared to Eminem's verse—which is, to be fair, one of his most formally impressive to date—50's verses seem flat and unimaginative. His verse structure comes off as simple and his content is thoroughly expected.

Eminem's verse is not one of his most thoughtful, intriguing or even disturbing. Like 50's, it is riddled with clichés, although Eminem is also showing off his ability to twist or elaborate on a cliché until it becomes unexpected. Still, it is in its formal achievement that Eminem's verse really stands out. Eminem eases us into his verse. As if aware of the standard nature of the verse that precedes his, he uses the first four lines to establish a formal base from which he will launch the wild excursions to come. The opening content parallels the form: lines one through three describe the speaker in a preparatory mode, sharpening his tools and mulling his lyrical revenge. The form to this point mimics 50 by featuring perfect rhymes fitted neatly onto the repeated final feet. In matching the complexity of 50's first verse, Eminem is effectively taking the formal baton from 50. But Eminem uses the opportunity to near-rhyme the early sounds of the repeated end-feet in addition to the end sounds, creating multisyllabic rhymes where 50 relies on monosyllabic rhymes or entirely repeated phrases. Even in the handoff Eminem is beginning to transcend 50's formal accomplishments.

Both verses are aimed at enemies, but Eminem's are unnamed, probably because the point is not to destroy any particular enemy—not this time at least—but to forge an excuse to unleash lyrical prowess. So the enemy here might as well be identified as the whole rap universe. In the fourth line, Eminem shifts from preparation to attack mode, with spaghetti identified first as a means for storing energy and then as an excuse to use wordplay ("or should I say spaghett-even?") to begin the assault. Lines 3 to 6 form another triplet, this one based on three-syllable cadences and "-ing" endings; but the real action occurs within the lines, with each progressively packing more sound into the interior, until, in the seventh line, Eminem moves the song into new territory: he quickens the pace and packs four additional syllables and at least one extra stress into the line, without disrupting the timing of the end rhyme. Notice how he is beginning to range from the formal base established early while maintaining a connection to it.

In lines 8 to 16 Eminem shows off his range, ability, and control. Depending on how you lineate (always a fraught exercise with a musical, performed literature like rap), line 8 begins either a couplet composed of very long lines, or a quatrain rhyming on the second and fourth lines (I will assume it is a quatrain). The rhythm becomes unhinged, or fluid, here, with the pace quickening between the rhymes—with Eminem still enunciating clearly— and slowing back down near the rhymes, which, again, are perfectly timed despite the complicated route the line takes to get to them. The rhymes here are built on a long "e" sound, which introduces a new sound element to the mix, while the rhythm is varied but contains distinctive feet that echo prominent snatches of rhythm from earlier in the verse, thus reinforcing the verse's overall continuity. This quatrain's elaborate structure matches the elaborate metaphor it describes, in which Eminem's imagined enemies have their vocal chords torn out and connected from their eyes to a source of abundant electricity. This is done so that Eminem can provide lesser rappers with the vision his ability makes possible. This quatrain alone contains more attention to metaphor and imagery, as well as to sound, rhythm and pace, than 50's first and second verses together.

He lets up in lines 12 and 13, before waking the line up with "Fuck letting up" and lowering his voice to a whisper—thus adding yet another feature to his already packed verse—and again quickening his pace in lines 13 to 16, in which he picks up the long "e" rhyme from above before momentarily abandoning rhyme and letting the rhythm free to lead a quick tangent. This segment closes with an interruption similar to that which ends line 13 (these "wakeup calls" act as additional framing devices for the madness happening within the variations of this verse). Lines 17 and 18 work as a variation-by-regularity: this is a straight-ahead couplet that returns the verse to the regularity (it is right on top of the beat) established in 50's verse and Eminem's opening lines, providing a contrast from the variations that dominate the middle of the verse.

This respite does not last long. As soon as the verse regains its formal bearings it takes off again into an interior-rhyme and wordplay-laden couplet in which the rapper's relationship to rap is described as simultaneously forced from without (he is trapped in rap) and self-reinforcing (rapping only makes him more trapped). This is less jarring than the extended metaphor involving vocal chords plugged into electricity. Still, the extended metaphor and dense language in these lines are handled with impressive nimbleness and control, and Eminem does manage to extend the paradox of entrapment through the remainder of the verse, which features a return to the whisper-speedup combination from earlier and an outro that mimics the regular triplet that began the verse.

So, formally we end the verse where we began. Likewise, it is difficult to detect any real change in the speaker, aside from the claim that he "is going psycho again," which is unconvincing, especially in a verse that awkwardly juxtaposes this with more convincing boasting. This is the song's problem in general: the successful rap artist's struggle is not central or convincing but a theme tagged on to give the song the illusion of weight. Despite that, the skill and compositional technique on display in Eminem's verse cannot be ignored, and it could be argued that in this case such excellence alone carries all the meaning the song needs. Still, Eminem's career output provides plenty of opportunities to consider his impressive chops along with more worthy content, as we will see later.

For now, we have found that Eminem's "My Life" verse establishes a strong formal basis, varies widely from that basis while maintaining a strong tie to it, before finally returning to that basis. This is a prodigal verse, and in that it should be familiar to students of formal English verse. Paul Fussell defines "the fixed element in poetry" as "the received or contrived grid or framework of metrical regularity" while "the variable is the action of the rhythm of the language as it departs from this framework."[1] Fussell's definition of "metrical regularity" is more exact than that applicable to the verses of "My Life," but the relationship between fixity and variation that he describes is directly applicable to the song. 50 Cent's verses mostly adhere to the "fixed element" they establish, with a few barely notable variations, like their short runs on interior rhymes.

It is, therefore, in the range of his variations that Eminem sets himself apart from 50 Cent in "My Life." Range of variation, however, is not in and of itself an admirable quality in a rap verse. Rap, like formal poetry, is effective when its variations are restrained by a well-established regularity. T. S. Eliot would go further and insist that a verse of any quality cannot be free of such contact, because "there is no freedom in art."[2] We can further apply Eliot's concept to Eminem's "My Life" verse and claim that the rapper establishes "the ghost of some simple meter" that then "lurks" behind his variations. The ghost meter in rap is usually linked to a consistent beat, and in this case Eminem is always able to return to the regularity established by the beat. It should be noted, though, that unlike the poetry prompting Eliot's formulation, which was seeking freedom from both meter and rhyme, the ghost behind Eminem's meter is also aided heavily by rhyme. But even rhyme, as we have seen, is used loosely and abandoned when necessary in Eminem's verse. Nonetheless, the verse might have gained Eliot's favor in that while it is not consistently patterned, it does not aim for a "absence of pattern."[3]

Still, to rely so heavily on the variations in his verse, Eminem must be able to establish some level of coherence to those variations, or they will become Eliot's dreaded "chaos."[4] Eminem avoids that because he injects in them enough shared patterns to constitute a coherence among the variations themselves. There is the repetition of the whispered, quickened lines, the periodic insertion of the aforementioned "wake up calls," the brief returns to the verse's formal base, etc., all of which hold the variations together as they track the ghost form.

In fact, given the dominant role of Eminem's variations in "My Life," it is not certain that the dominant guide of the verse is an adherence to formal consistency, or if the true base is coherence itself, with consistency playing second fiddle. If this is the case, we should turn for guidance from Fussell to Angus Fletcher, whose *A New Theory of American Poetry* posits that coherence is the dominant base in a great deal of American poetry. For Fletcher, coherence "differs from consistent mechanical conformity" in that it "shares the property of completeness, as distinct from axiomatic consistency."[5] If we look beyond Eminem's formal attributes and consider, as we shall later on, his art as a whole, Fletcher's definition fits: Eminem is nothing if not adverse to "axiomatic consistency," yet his presence remains distinct, complete, and unmistakable.

Regardless, from a formal perspective, a case could be made for either consistency or coherence as the base of Eminem's work. In that, he stands apart from rappers like 50 Cent, Drake (whose catchy hooks about being rich and famous are firmly in 50's tradition), or Kanye West, all of whom are dependent on regularity to keep their verses grounded. That is not to say a rapper cannot be dependent on regularity and produce quality work, as rappers from Chuck D, to Tupac, to Lil Wayne (on subdued tracks like "Nightmares from the Bottom") have proven. It *is* to say that when it comes to the spectrum from consistency to coherence, Eminem is hard to place, that he is somewhere in between, and that he can navigate that spectrum like few others (Lil Wayne on "Let the Beat Build" comes to mind). This leads us back to Eliot's conception of verse, for what I am essentially claiming is that Eminem's verse supports Eliot's claim that "it is this contrast between fixity and flux, this unperceived evasion of monotony, which is the very life of verse."[6]

Slipping Between the Beats like Bird

Considering the role of formal consistency in rap, a number of tempting analogies present themselves. These are taken either from the art forms from which rap has drawn its formal techniques, or to which rap's formal techniques are readily comparable. We have seen the usefulness of Eliot's "freed verse" as a model that escapes rigid notions of formal regularity while not abandoning form altogether. We could also extend Frost's famous analogy of poetry as tennis and claim that Eminem does not get rid of the net but is no a slave to it either. This would be in contrast to a rapper like Q-Tip, who in Ice-T's documentary *Something from Nothing: The Art of Rap* proudly claims to be a "slave to the beat." Q-Tip, indeed, is solidly in rap's consistent camp, varying, with rare smoothness, only slightly from the rhythmical and sound patterns that ground his verses, in which the line's meter closely adheres to the drumbeat. To pick up on that last point, though, it might be beneficial to look outside of literature for a more fruitful comparison.

Rap engulfs music and poetry in a manner rarely found outside of opera. Opera is "an art form that consists of a literary text, a dramatic stage performance, and music [that] should be studied in all its multimedia and 'multimediated' dimensions."[7] The same could easily be said of rap; even leaving videos aside, it is difficult to have any sense of rap's form without considering music. Even in his highly literary, and I'd argue essential, *Book of Rhymes*, Adam Bradley claims that "rap demands that we acknowledge its dual identity as word and song."[8] So it is worth considering a precedent for Eminem's formal stretching in a musical ancestor.

Coleman Hawkins is widely acknowledged as one of the most, if not the most, important early innovators of jazz saxophone. But in a young, quickly evolving musical form (sound familiar?), his innovations were bound to become a norm, or a loosely fixed regularity, that would be accepted and then moved beyond. A 1944 film clip,[9] gives clear evidence of this transition in action (although this transition was already well under way). As Hawkins plays his solo, a young Charlie Parker lounges in the background, periodically laughing in Hawkins's direction. What follows seems to hint at the cause of Parker's laughter, as Parker's solo begins in a flurry of notes that immediately differentiates him from Hawkins. Bird is faster and more agile than his elder, squeezing notes between the patterns already laid out by Hawkins while managing to maintain that pattern's structure. As it turns out, Parker's laughter stems from Hawkins's attempt to mime his solo (the audio was prerecorded),[10] but the viewer's likely initial thought—that Parker's laughter is aimed at the limitations of Hawkins's technique—still contains insight because the difference in Parker's improvisation is so plain to hear.

Andre Hodeir describes Hawkins as possessing a "traditionally balanced, symmetrical kind of phrasing."[11] It would be insulting to Hawkins to compare his technique to a rapper of 50 Cent's caliber, but the difference Hodeir finds between Hawkins and Parker is helpful in making our own comparison. Hodeir describes Bird's difference this way:

> Instead of Hawkins's regular accent on the strong beat and certain pronounced syncopations or of Lester Young's flowing style, Bird's accentuation comes alternately on the beat and between the beats. The astonishingly rich rhythm of his music comes from this alternation, from these continual oppositions.[12]

This description is both reminiscent of Eliot's claim regarding "the very life of verse," and directly applicable to Eminem's achievement. Like Parker, Eminem came to a tradition largely marked by "regular accent[s] on the strong beat," as well as a popular "flowing style."[13] A proper study of Eminem would cover the former characteristic of rap poetics more than it would the latter. But while Eminem may not posses the admirably smooth flow of many of his peers, his jagged, complex, yet tightly contained verses are rarely matched.[14]

Few rappers possess the writing and performative chops to pull off the rhythmical variety on display in Eminem's "My Life" verse, or in any number of Eminem verses (like "No Love" and "You're Never Over" on *Recovery*). To find a rapper on Eminem's par in this regard, listen to his Bad Meets Evil collaboration with Royce 'da 5'9". Royce is not the complete rapper that Eminem is, but unlike most of Eminem's sidemen, he proves he can hang with him. At times, the two are like jazz players trading fours. But a more poignant modern comparison can be drawn from another of Charlie Parker's descendants, the saxophonist Skerik. Like Eminem, Skerik possesses the rare ability to constantly push his solos outward and to constantly surprise, while never losing control or the ability to return to a formal base. Guitarist Charlie Hunter defined Skerik's draw this way: "he's *indefatigable;* he just goes to this place where he can do no wrong as your front man."[15] Skerik's difference is better experienced than explained, but there is one quality that stands out: he has both impressive range *and* the ability to contain that range. The same is true of Eminem and Charlie Parker.

Again echoing Eliot's earlier pronouncement, Hodeir claims that "the variety of formulas [Parker] uses in a single solo makes it possible for him to *avoid all rhythmic monotony*."[16] The word "possible" should be noted— no improviser is capable of avoiding "all rhythmic monotony" all the time— but Bird, Eminem, and Skerik remain exceptional in this regard. Hodeir also claims that "the richness of [Parker's] rhythmic vocabulary," and his playing's occasional "discontinuity" causes "the inexperienced listener [to] often lose the beat in this rhythmic complexity." Yet, "it is all conceived and played with absolute strictness; at the end ... Parker falls right on the first beat."[17] Likewise, listeners can be forgiven if in the midst of lines 10 to 14 of Eminem's verse on "My Life" they lose sight of the relationship between Eminem's words and the formal base made by the beat and the more regular lines. But by line 16 he has, with seeming effortlessness, brought the verse back to its native regularity with unmistakable definitiveness.

It would be enough to end this comparison here, and to simply acknowledge that all these artists have their "instrument completely under control."[18] But Hodeir goes on to note that "regardless of its strength, Parker's kind of individuality cannot do without a climate that is favorable to the manifestation of his message."[19] Hodeir is referring to Parker's ability to surround himself with those able to help him achieve the "polyrhythmic expression" his one-voiced instrument is unable to facilitate on its own, but beyond the very important context of his band, he needed a culture and a form that valued individuality, and to some extent Bird received both.

Billy Taylor, among others, has claimed jazz as "America's Classical Music" because it mimics America's attitude toward individuality: "no other indigenous music reflects so clearly the American ideal of the individual's right to personal freedom of expression."[20] So while Bird was certainly a unique individual, he could never be considered apart from his band or his cultural and historical context. His band and historical context, meanwhile, did impose limitations within which his freedom had to operate. So he was free to a significant extent, but he was not totally free from dependence on the group or society (he was a black man in the early twentieth century, after all).

Yet Parker's particular invocation of individuality *was* different. And if, as Hodeir claims, Bird "accents certain off-beat notes violently"[21] and makes songs in which "the melody and the rhythm are disjointed in a way that verges on the absurd,"[22] then surely this music must intuit some parallel violence or absurdity of meaning. Again, however, Bird did not invent this violence or absurdity, he simply helped bring it into the light by expressing it with an abandon his predecessors lacked (although they paved the way). The parallel to Eminem is again unavoidable, although here it is less neat. Eminem entered a popular rap scene reeling from a violent culture that had just seen two of its greatest stars, among countless others, struck down by the very violence proclaimed in so many of its songs. Yet somehow he managed to push the envelope, to be known as a violently absurd, and absurdly talented, artist in a field stocked to the hilt with those attributes.

As with Bird, we would not know Eminem's particular vision of individuality if it hadn't been for the artistic and formal talents with which he gave it life. Parker, Hodeir writes, "had the courage to challenge aesthetic axioms that were tending to become frozen dogma."[23] In rap terms, Bird was exposing techniques that were "played out." In Fletcher's terms, he was calling out undue "axiomatic consistencies" in the work of his predecessors. Eminem might not put it so politely. The larger point, though, might be that both artists were allowed the freedom to express their difference. Their art, then, says as much about the artists themselves as it does about the nation that offered them a stage.

What He Speaks Within

While that stage allows for a certain freedom within formal constraints, it also demands the transgression of constraints in the name of change and newness. Bird is known today because he "freed jazz of a number of trammels."[24] In doing so he risked displeasing champions of tradition, like Ralph Ellison, who wrote that while "Parker's generation drew much of its immediate fire from their understandable rejection of the traditional entertainer's role," they also "confused artistic quality with questions of personal conduct."[25] Parker was not like Ellison's beloved Louis Armstrong, in whose seemingly cheery music Ellison's Invisible Man could locate a subversive depth encompassing black America's long history and suffering. Armstrong could do this because unlike Parker he assumed a "*make-believe* role of clown,"[26] instead of demanding, "in the name of racial identity, a purity of status which by definition is impossible for the performing artist."[27] Despite

Ellison's misgivings, Bird's antagonistic entertainer stance later became common, for instance in the early electric years of Miles Davis and Bob Dylan, and in punk. Rap would find this stance both natural and lucrative when its stars carved out their place as bestselling anti-establishment tape deck preachers.

Tupac Shakur was of one of rap's most talented and most controversial stars. His work was heavily debated in the public sphere, as well as in congress, and Eminem's eventually garnered similarly widespread scrutiny. At the heart of these debates lies the freedom of speech and the responsibility of the public entertainer. The former gives Eminem the right to transgress social mores with abandon, while the latter exposes him to a sea of potential reactions. But there is a third element in this public drama: the artist's ability to anticipate public reaction. This is what Ellison loved so much in artists like Louis Armstrong: "a clearer idea of the division between their identities as performers and as private individuals."[28] If artists can make this distinction, then they give themselves a chance to manipulate their public personas. Tupac probably knew this better than he is given credit for, and Eminem has mastered his mask, even if he's also fallen prey to the pressures of his role, struggled to keep his public personae from harming his private life, and, finally, come back from the brink of Bird-like self-destruction.

Likewise, Eminem's work stretches from the purposely and strategically wretched, to the honestly suffering, to the redeemed, and back. Reactions to his work are similarly varied,[29] but there has been a particular tendency to react with disgust. I do not claim this to be overbearing, but it is worth noting in particular because it reveals an important, if not ultimately justifiable, critical shortcoming. To be sure, the amount of disgust Eminem's work has received roughly equals the amount of his work that is validly categorized as "wretched." But just as a nation cannot be judged solely on its faults, no part of a complicated artist can be taken in isolation. To do so is to miss the bigger, more relevant picture. To understand Eminem's wretched transgressions, then, we must also understand his better angels. To understand either of those, however, we must first confront the freedom that allows, or forces, him to choose one, the other, or both.

The sociologist Zygmunt Bauman offers a framework to sort that out. In *Freedom*, he claims that "individual freedom cannot and should not be taken for granted, as it appears (and perhaps disappears) together with a particular kind of a society."[30] With that in mind, Bauman argues for the relevance of "the connections between such a free individual and the society of which he is a member."[31] This suggests it takes an Eminem-ready society to make an Eminem. Writing a decade before the rapper's emergence, Bauman identified the societal characteristics that would ultimately facilitate and dictate Eminem's realization of twenty-first-century American freedom in a shift of emphasis from work to consumption: "the individual's drive to self-assertion has been squeezed out from the area of material production. Instead, a wider than ever space has been opened for it at the new 'pioneer frontier,' the rapidly expanding, seemingly limitless, world of consumption."[32]

To an extent, Bauman deeply respects the accomplishment of the "consumer version [of] individual freedom," because unlike the entrepreneurial and work-based model, "it may be exercised without sacrificing the *certainty* that lies at the bottom of spiritual security."[33] The consumerist system achieves this certainty by generating "a kind of society in which the life pattern of free choice and self-assertion can be practiced on a scale unheard of before."[34] The advantage comes in part due to the fact that in the work-based model, society was threatened by the worker who sought pleasure, and who would thus lose discipline, while the consumerist model so encourages self-definition through the pursuit of pleasure that "spending is a duty."[35] In a society that values both self-assertion and material consumption, a self-or-selves-asserting producer of commoditized art like Eminem naturally thrives.

Bauman strains to find a feasible alternative to the consumerist model, aside from "bureaucratically administered oppression,"[36] but doubts remain. For one, if the "social approval of free choices" by others, is, as Bauman claims, a necessity, and if that is available only "together with the identity kits" consumers purchase through the market, then consumerism is a method of social control that is difficult to escape.[37] "It may well be," Bauman writes near the book's conclusion, "that the human drive to freedom will not be satisfied by market-led approaches,"[38] and it could be argued that Eminem's music contains a latent, and sometimes active, political strain that acts against a consumerist ideology (even if this is done through a consumer product and only apparent in his general anger—but more on this later). Barring a social or economic revolution, the popular artist may well be judged by how well he or she copes with the inevitability of consumerism.

Eminem is clearly a product of consumerism. For Bauman, in a consumerist society "everyone has to answer for himself the question 'who am I, how should I live, who do I want to be?'"[39] Eminem could hardly be understood without examining how he has gone about answering those questions. His first three commercial records form a kind of identity map of the rapper's public personae. Carroll Hamilton summarizes the matter succinctly:

> The issue of naming is particularly relevant because, while they are each different, the titles ... are eponymous: *The Slime Shady LP, The Marshall*

Mathers LP, The Eminem Show. The progression from the earlier pseudonym to the later, via the artist's real name, logically culminates in the citation of "Eminem" as the proper name of the celebrity subject that Slim Shady has become; if Slim Shady is white trash, Eminem is a celebrity. Marshall Mathers—as persona if not real identity—occupies a liminal space between the two, through which he manages his twin personas.[40]

Bauman—whose signature book, *Liquid Modernity*, argues that our era is defined by fluidity as opposed to fixity—would very quickly recognize in the above description a creature of the age he has described. Notice that even Marshall Mathers, the legal name of the man, is not endowed with certainty, but with a liminal presence. The ability to name or redefine one's self is by no means new; Whitman's oeuvre is full of self-iterations and Dickinson, in her solitude, was seeking to define her self in all its evolving particularities.

However, with the continual advancement of television, which Bauman points out is a "dramatic mode of communication," we are faced with the fact that "the world split into a multitude of mini-dramas [via the medium of television] has a distinctive mode of existence, but no clear-cut direction."[41] Whitman might have had pretenses to containing multitudes, but it was Eminem's immediate predecessors who first engaged with mediums actually capable of touching those multitudes and it was Eminem and his contemporaries who were left to deal with the further expansion of possibility that is the internet. Of TV—although it also applies to the internet— Bauman writes that "armed with a medium of enormous power, the world of professional communicators and entertainers expands well beyond its once limited, stage-confined territory, appropriating estates previously managed by, say, professional politicians."[42] There is a double challenge presented to the popular entertainer here: he must both take on the ramifications of having a gigantic and highly connected audience, while mapping a media landscape "with no clear-cut direction."

In meeting the latter of those challenges, a natural ally is the self-identifying process, with the self now capable of reverting to directionlessness and picking any of the multitudes of paths available therein. It makes sense, then, that Eminem enacts his dynamic play of identity through mediums—radio, TV, and internet—that allow for maximum freedom of representation. In fact, this fruitful combination of liquid mediums and a changeable self has gone a long way in making Eminem the representative figure he is today. But it is also in the liberty with which Eminem has used this freedom that his harshest critics have found their disquiet.

In *Affirmative Reaction: New Formations of White Masculinity,* for instance, Carroll Hamilton accuses Eminem of manipulating his racial and class identity in order to reap the traditional benefits of the white male. "Eminem's valorization of white trash serves ultimately to enable his escape from it" she writes, because "he transforms white trash into a valedictory identity in order to transcend it."[43] By claiming "white trash" as an identity apart from "white," Hamilton argues, Eminem is able to identify with the oppressed other—in this case black people—while still retaining the benefits of being white. Eminem himself has supported this claim, as when he points out in "White America" that "suburban kids" dig his work at least partially due to his blue eyes.

Hamilton's critique lines up in other ways with Bauman's concept of the entertainer's role in a consumerist society. She claims that Eminem "overcom[es] the inevitability of white trash ... through the production of a traditional narrative of self-sufficiency grounded in the ideologies of possessive individualism [which] result[s] in the acquisition of a compensatory form of celebrity identity."[44] So by banking on the consumerist version of the self-made man myth, Eminem is able to catapult himself from "white trash"—which Hamilton defines as "a class based subject that is so debased as to become racialized"[45]—to the celebrity figure who serves as one of Bauman's "model identities."[46] Eminem's dangerous rhetoric, Hamilton concludes, "should give us pause," because the faults of Eminem are part and parcel of the "the mainstream culture," which "now uses white working poor identities to shore up rather than criticize the excesses of white privilege."[47]

I do not doubt that last point, but Hamilton is not convincing in her claim that Eminem is somehow responsible for this turn of events. Her ability to draw a correlation between her criticism of Eminem and that of "mainstream culture" does not justify her implied claim that the two are directly linked, and Hamilton makes little effort to explicitly draw that link. Instead she presents a slanted argument for Eminem's improper use of his own race—as if he could avoid the consequences of his race—points out that it looks similar to some other troubling patterns in society and suggests this "should give us pause."

In *New Media, Cultural Studies, and Critical Theory After Post-Modernism*, Robert Samuels attacks Eminem as "a strong example of how African American presence represents a source for personal self-promotion and a strategy for self denial."[48] Like Hamilton, Samuels argues that Eminem has identified with the black "other" to his own advantage. Samuels also accuses Eminem of "engag[ing] in the backlash rhetoric of reversed racism" and claims "the people who want to promote tolerance are shown to be intolerant [of Eminem's free speech], while the intolerant [Eminem] have to be tolerated."[49] Samuels bases this on the first three lines of "Cleaning Out My Closet" with no textual context whatsoever provided (Hamilton also fixates on these lines, although she does provide some, but not much, broader context). Still, Samuels's critique contains at least a partial truth, for Eminem *is* a rich celebrity claiming at least some victimhood in that song, even if that is not the overall effect of the song, which is actually focused on the act of moving past victimization (he's *cleaning out* his closet, not filling it up).

However, Hamilton and Samuels do not simply zero in on details of Eminem's songs in order to justify their preconceived theories. They also blow those details up to monumental proportions. To her assumption that whatever goes for Eminem must also go for "mainstream culture" as a whole, Hamilton adds that despite their public dispute Tipper Gore and Lynne Cheney "fail to recognize just how completely [Eminem] typifies the conservative values they embrace." Those values, apparently, can be found in his "capitulation to a conservative mode of possessive individualism."[50] Hamilton also assumes that Eminem "believes the transformations of civil rights have adversely and predominantly affected white men,"[51] while providing little evidence tracing Eminem's actual work directly to any such political or ideological belief. Eminem may be a white man who takes pride in his self-sufficiency, but that in itself does not make him a likely guest on the Rush Limbaugh show.

For his part, Samuels claims Eminem supports the opinion that "since we now live in a post-prejudice society, the only people who still cry racism, sexism, and homophobia are liberal academics" who want to expand the welfare state, presumably for its own sake. Thus, "we are able to cut taxes to the wealthy because in a post-prejudice society social programs helping minorities are no longer needed."[52] So Eminem is also an ideological ally of Paul Ryan and his punishing austerity budgets. Samuels is quick to point out that he is "not arguing that Eminem is part of some large right-wing conspiracy; rather, his rhetoric samples and recirculates the underlying backlash ideology of automodern society."[53] That backlash ideology depends on the reversal of the victimizer and the victimized, meaning that because Eminem falsely claims victimization, when he is actually the victimizer, he is implicitly supporting the larger cultural argument behind Right-wing ideology, which views government aid to the needy as oppression of the well-off, who are assumed to be completely self-made.

By "automodernity," Samuels means to indicate "the seamless combination of individual autonomy with technological automation within a backlash rhetoric"[54] which reacts "against the postmodern desire to promote tolerance for all minority groups,"[55] among other "progressive" targets. We have already established Eminem's "individual autonomy," but his connection to "automation" is less obvious. Samuels finds it in Eminem's "reduction of language to meaningless repetition,"[56] which allows Eminem to skirt the social responsibility implied by his public words. Samuels claims Eminem's "word choices appear to be based more on the identity of sounds and letters than on the semantic value of the terms," thus "reveal[ing] the nonmeaning at the heart of language."[57] This excuse from responsibility allows Eminem to participate in a "new media libertarianism," undergirded by a bogus claim to free speech, that "support[s] a generalized backlash against the welfare state, postmodern social movements, minority rights, and a progressive political culture."

It is absolutely true that the meaning in Eminem's words is *often* sacrificed for the sake of musical advantage, and Eminem does, often, insist on a certain level of meaninglessness, or that he is "just clownin'," in granting himself the freedom to speak the unspeakable. It is also true that Eminem uses "misdirection to hide the true essence of his discourse," but in extending that to argue that that discourse "replicates the rhetoric of premodern traditional hierarchy,"[58] Samuels is taking liberties with the rapper's supposed "meaninglessness" to reach his own theoretical ends (premodern!).

Without a doubt, these critics speak some truth. The problem with both Hamilton's and Samuel's treatments of Eminem is that they limit the scope of their inquiry and thereby create a straw man which they can easily attack. Bauman disapprovingly cites "self-appointed guardians of public morals [who] protest against scenes of violence or sex [and who] assume that the viewers' violent instincts and sexual appetites are boosted by exposer to such images."[59] While the description certainly applies to the Lynne Cheneys and Tipper Gores of the world, Hamilton and Samuels are guilty of a similar moral grandstanding. This is especially apparent when one considers the details of Eminem's art that they leave out.

Consider racial identity: could it not be argued that Eminem complicates our very notions of race? What does it mean, after all, to be black or white? Hamilton correctly claims that Eminem is "a troubling figure … able to work across boundaries of race and class."[60] Here, Hamilton could consider how that ability might disrupt the identification of those boundaries themselves. Instead, she moves on to consider how it reveals "middle class white culture's libidinal investment in American black culture," as if that were the only takeaway from Eminem's racial play. Is not Eminem's acceptance into the rap elite a signal that one need not have black skin to be accepted as a bona fide member of a black-dominated culture? Is this not at least worth considering? Both Hamilton and Samuels suffocate the life of Eminem's work by insisting that it be seen only through the narrow lens they bring to it. This not only discredits their arguments, but it also crowds out the potential for the honest criticism Eminem's insensitivities do deserve.

Who He Speaks For

To find holes in Hamilton's and Samuels's arguments, one need only turn to the work itself. Eminem's "The Way I Am" describes the thoroughly unfixed nature of his media presence. The basic argument is that because he is a mass media phenomenon, lacking a "clear-cut direction," and because this makes his public reception largely beyond his control, Eminem allows that "I am whatever you say I am," suggesting that he accepts that his audience will define him. So in that sense Hamilton and Samuels are acting with Eminem's blessing in making him whatever they would like him to be. But not really. Eminem still has a say in your reaction to him and he can anticipate your reaction (especially if you are gullible). Still, only the audience can have the final say. Realizing he cannot control his audience's reaction, Eminem offers us something that can at least destabilize our preconceptions the way Charlie Parker's best solos did: ambiguity. He is not who he says he is, exactly, but he is not what "you" say he is either; he cannot be the latter because that "you" is necessarily responding to something Eminem did or said to prompt the response.

In "The Way I Am" Eminem gives his ambiguity because that's all he has, all he can give from within the panoply of his virtual and limitless auditorium. This is consistent with one of Eminem's favorite hip-hop invocations, "fuck the world," because if you are to face a potential sea of criticism, it is advantageous to enter it in a "me against the world" headspace. Eminem is also executing an Armstrong-like awareness of the reactions he generates, which allows him to anticipate those reactions. You might argue that Eminem is more like Parker, but the fact is that different eras call for different entertainer masks, and today's includes the antagonism for which Parker was infamous. Eminem knows, as Samuels points out, how to "push cultural buttons."[61] What Samuels does not appreciate is how well Eminem has mastered this cultural guerrilla warfare. Sure, much of Eminem's provocations, especially early in his career, aim directly at drawing attention and increasing record sales, and his struggles with addiction and his withdraw from public life prove he is as much like Bird as he is like Satchmo. But even after his sober comeback Eminem remains a master of public manipulation on par with the early electric Bob Dylan, the meat-dress wearing Lady Gaga, and the greatest current American satirist, Stephen Colbert (based on some of the simplistic responses Eminem generates, one may wonder if his critics also think Colbert is actually a right-wing pundit).

This all comes down to Eminem's ambiguous use of sincerity, a characteristic Hamilton and Samuels acknowledge but fail to grasp the full significance of. It is often easy to detect if Eminem is being sincere, or if he is 'just clownin'—"Cleaning Out My Closet" is sincere, while "My Name Is" is a clown show. The more interesting examples are those that seem to oscillate between the two, like "White America." Hamilton and Samuels both latch on to the song's final line—"I'm just playin' America, you know I love you." Samuels posits the line as yet another example of automodern "nihilism"[62] while Hamilton takes it to mean that all of Eminem's preceding diatribe is just a ploy and that he really sincerely loves America for the "possessive individualism" it allows him.[63] Neither consider that "playin'" might be the most important word in the whole song, if not in Eminem's whole body of work. To play with the listener is to lead the listener astray, and in these critics' case, Eminem has been successful.

Properly read, though, Eminem does more than deceive. Consider "The Real Slim Shady," where we find the usual transgressions, but with a turn near the song's end. Eminem raps that in every person there is a version of Slim Shady "lurkin.'" With that Eminem extends a self-centered song to a universal base. When Eminem performed this song at the MTV Video Music Awards, the army of Eminem lookalikes featured in the music video entered the auditorium, providing further proof that Eminem's aims have never been purely individualistic, but that there has always been a tendency to connect his individualism to "every single person." People will rightly be disgusted by and reject Slim Shady, but the logic of his claim is undeniable. Look under you bootsole, Eminem suggests, and you will find my residue waiting for you.[64] Or as the protagonist in Ralph Ellison's *Invisible Man* would put it: "who knows but that, at the lower frequencies, I speak for you?"[65]

This connection is made in far more Whitmanian terms in "Not Afraid," that most public of personal poems. It was his decision to get clean. "I did it for me," Eminem raps, before admitting he might have done it "subliminally for you." This "you" is the fans, who are addressed throughout the song and whose support "helped see me through." Here's where it gets interesting: after sincerely thanking his supporters, for a second time, and suggesting they might not realize how important they were to his recovery, Eminem allows "believe me you"—a play on "believe you me"—to linger on the end of the line. That he pauses at this phrase before moving on is suggestive. Given the I-you connection forged above, there seems a chance that Eminem means to draw attention on more time to the connection between his "me" and the "you" that supports him. At the same time, it is difficult to imagine a song more neatly fitted to the great American myth of reinvention and second chances. And so one of our era's most prominent individualists created an anthem that argues both for his own renewed individualism, and that we are all in this together.

Elsewhere in *Recovery,* Eminem still reserves the right to be a "sick puppy" and claims he's a "sick pig" even without the swine flu. He remains hard to call, but only when we meet Eminem on the terms dictated by his multiplicity and complexity can we begin to asses his true relevance—the good, the bad and the ugly. We cannot do that unless we come to the work with an open mind and a willingness to invest in ambiguity.

At the Lower Frequencies

As we have seen, Eminem's formal balance between fixity and chaos mimics the ambiguity of his subject matter. I have already compared that balance to T. S. Eliot's concept of "freed verse" as well as to Charlie Parker's technique. Ralph Ellison, for his part, connects Eliot's "new aesthetic for poetry," via the "juxtaposing of earlier styles" to Armstrong's work. All these artists, in turn, mimic the ambiguity of their social and historical milieu. We have also seen how ambiguity gives Eminem's critics the opportunity to cherry pick attributes that they can then attack.

Ellison, too, was unfairly attacked by the literary left. Eric J. Sundquist recounts Larry Neal's 1968 attack on Ellison's *Invisible Man* as representative of the belief that "the experiences of Ellison's protagonist lacked recognizable relevance."[66] Neal would recant this opinion two years later, claiming it represented "one stage, in a long series of attempts … to deal with the fantastic impression that Ellison's work has had on my life."[67] Neal explains that his past opinion rested on "the question of political activism and the black writer."[68] While the Neal of 1968 resented what he viewed as Ellison's evasion of the day's important political questions, the Neal of 1970 appreciated Ellison's contention that "[the novel] is always a public gesture, though not necessarily a political one."[69] Neal attributes this blurring of the public and the political to literary Marxism's belief that "all literature is propaganda, or becomes propaganda when it enters the public sphere."[70] But while Neal eventually backed off that position, he did not do so entirely, claiming that Ellison's separation of the public from the political is only a "half-truth" because "the minute a work of art enters the social sphere, it faces the problem of being perceived on all kinds of levels, from the grossly political to the philosophically sublime."[71]

Like Eminem, Neal understands the value of ambiguity for the artist, who has limited control over his work once it goes public. "Therefore," Neal concludes, "what we might consider is a system of politics and art that is as fluid, as functional, and as expansive as black music."[72] Neal sees in Ellison a potential model for this system, and we can identify the same in Eminem, especially considering his connection to black music. Neal's opening should also be familiar to us: "it is no easy task to fully characterize the nature of Ellison's life and work. He cannot be put into any one bag and conveniently dispensed with. Any attempt to do so merely leads to aesthetic and ideological oversimplifications."[73] That statement's application to Eminem should be obvious by now.

What may not be obvious is the negative criticism Eminem actually deserves. Take Samuels's half-true argument that Eminem evades criticism by claiming lyrical meaninglessness. When Eminem does revert to this strategy, he is essentially claiming trickster status, or that his lyrical transgressions are just the randomized spewing of a sick culture's product. But this is not totally genuine. Echoing Ellison's own denial of the trickster's role in *Invisible Man*, Jason Puskar claims the relevant figure in *Invisible Man* is not the archetypal trickster—like Briar Rabbit in African American folklore, or Coyote in Native American myths—but the joker. Puskar explains that in the African American tradition, "tricksters defy and disrupt the plantation hierarchy from within, but that hierarchy is fundamentally unshakeable. Jokers, however, disrupt a different kind of hierarchy, the aristocracy of kings, queens, and jacks who rule the deck of cards." Puskar goes on:

> Standing in for modern liberal society, the deck of cards acknowledges real power disparities, but it also expects regular power upheavals. More importantly, it makes the joker the most consequential card in the deck, because only the joker can change identities, temporarily usurping and using royal power while leaving the basic power structure intact.[74]

The protagonist in Ellison's *Invisible Man* rose above the role of the trickster when he accepted a level of agency and responsibility denied that figure—when his protagonist learned from Reinhart to "change identities" in order to "usurp power." Eminem, on the other hand, retains a disappointing tendency to revert to a trickster cop-out in an attempt to avoid the social and artistic responsibility inherent in his role as one of the most widely heard and discussed public poets in world history. An innocent example of this is found in "My Life," in which he retreads familiar content that is only saved by the impressive formal achievement of his verse and the sharpness of some of his metaphors and images. *Relapse*, meanwhile, is almost entirely forgettable because of its rampant disregard for basic decency. We can accept the wretchedness of *Relapse* only if we buy that language is meaningless and that Eminem is just a trickster pulling our chain. But that falls apart with a song like "Beautiful," in which the words are clearly meaningful, and poignant. Eminem can have it both ways—he can have Shady pulling chains and Marshall giving us sincerity—and he has, but the balance in *Relapse* is far too much in Shady's favor. Left to his own devices Shady is a trickster, but if Eminem *uses* him for a limited and specific purpose, as he does on *Recovery,* Shady can make Eminem the joker, unsettling our expectations and widening our receptive capacities, while retaining the ability to be sincere.

To claim *Relapse* is regrettable is not a purely moral charge, although it is that; but it is also an aesthetic judgment, and one Eminem himself echoes in "Not Afraid," calling the album and its accents "ehhhh."

The Slim Shady shtick can no longer sustain Eminem's development. Eminem's partially continued reliance on the Shady persona, in play also in his recent collaboration with Royce 'da 5'9", exemplifies a tendency Ellison once observed in jazz: that it is "fecund in its inventiveness, swift and traumatic in its development and terribly wasteful of its resources."[75]

Recovery's development of a more mature, less-shock dependent voice is thus a welcome step. Indeed, *Recovery* marks the beginning of perhaps the most intriguing era of Eminem's career, promising to set a template in which Eminem can still entertain and unsettle with his wit, humor, and sheer skill, while attaining the ability to speak, as it were, from a position of authority and responsibility. Perhaps Eminem can soon join the ranks of his contemporary Black Thought, of The Roots, whose treatment of narrative in the masterful *undun* shows an ability to speak not only from the ambiguity of the raw moment, but to direct that ambiguity from the outside as well. In matching that, Eminem might help pave the way for what Bauman suggests is one possible way out of consumerism's hold: to channel "consumer rivalry" to "the more ambitious end of communal self management (98)." That is, Eminem might move beyond self-definition, and further into the communal-based work he has already gestured toward in *Recovery* and to a limited extent before that, in songs like "Mosh."

That said, one need not be explicitly political to strike politically important notes. In 1930, John Dewey wrote:

> I see little social unrest which is the straining of energy for outlet in action; I find rather the protest against a weakening of vigor and a sapping of energy that emanate from the absence of constructive opportunity; and I see a confusion that is an expression of the inability to find a secure and morally rewarding place in a troubled and tangled economic scene.[76]

That could easily describe the motivation behind the Occupy movement, but also Eminem's body of work so far, which personifies unrest, emanates more from confusion than from specific actionable aims, and describes an economic scene heavily pocked by dead ends. In expressing his own unrest, like Ellison's protagonist, Eminem has expressed that of countless others.

But not explicitly, and not to the degree that he might. A comparison to Ellison's own craft and that of his characters provides a useful gauge for Eminem's progression so far. We can organize the main levels of elocution shared by Ellison and the characters in his novels in the following manner. In *Invisible Man,* Trueblood and the protagonist's grandfather represent the common person on the ground. Louis Armstrong reveals a deep history to the protagonist behind the mask of popular song. Then there is the protagonist himself, an underground writer for now but on the verge of emerging from his subterranean wilderness. Then there is Ellison, the author of *Invisible Man,* a first book, who had explicated the first novel's unsettlement from without. Finally, there is Adam Bradley's assessment that Ellison's never-finished second novel was an attempt at a grand act of "summing up" America.[77] All told, Ellison's explicators, including himself, span the social gamut, from the most common and unseen to the most responsible and visible.

Using Ellison's novel as a template, we can say that at this point in his career, Eminem is his underground-man stage. He was in the world and he was wearing the mask of public performance and then, like *Invisible Man's* protagonist, he escaped into hibernation. *Relapse* was written from his hibernation, when he was "flushing [the drugs] out ("Not Afraid")." *Recovery* was his first peak out from his hole. So for now he's with Ellison's protagonist in beginning to recognize "the absurdity of [the] American character."[78] He is not yet approaching the "summing up" ambitions of the later Ellison, let alone the authorial position held by the Ellison of *Invisible Man* or by *undun's* Black Thought. Then again, Eminem is supposed to have a new album out by the time this essay is published. Who knows what that will reveal.

Chapter Notes

1. Paul Fussell, *Poetic Meter and Form,* rev. ed., (New York: McGraw-Hill, 1979), 32.

2. T. S. Eliot, "Reflections on *Vers Libre*" from *Selected Prose of T. S. Eliot* (New York: Harcourt, 1975), 32.

3. Ibid., 32.

4. Ibid., 36.

5. Angus Fletcher, *A New Theory of American Poetry* (Cambridge, MA: Cambridge University Press, 2004), 226.

6. Ibid., 33.

7. Linda Hutchens, "Interdisciplinary Opera Studies," *PMLA,* Vol. 121, No. 3 (May 2006): 802.

8. Adam Bradley, *Book of Rhymes: The Poetics of Hip Hop* (New York: BasicCivitas, 2009), xvii.

9. "Jammin the Blues,." directed by Gjon Mili (Warner Bros). Released May 5,

1944. Released by Warner Home Video to DVD 2006. http://www.imdb.com/title/tt0036968/?ref_=fn_al_tt_1.

10. "The Charlie Parker Story," BBC 4, directed by Tony Followell. Aired April 19, 2009.

11. Andre Hodeir, "Charlie Parker and the Bop Movement," in *The Andrè Hodier Jazz Reader,* Andre Hodier and Jean-Louis Pautrot, eds., (Ann Arbor: University of Michigan Press, 2006), 64.

12. Hodeir, 61.

13. Might Biggie be rap's Lester Young?

14. Rappers can use their form in so many ways, and any discussion of formal prowess cannot successfully play the fools' game of "who is the best rapper?" For instance, Nas's technique has evolved to utilize silence and space, while his early work is marked by speed and density. Both approaches have their advantages, and Nas has used both well. So in claiming Eminem's work is formally complex, I am not making a value judgment but an observation. A verse can be complex and boring, or it can be sparse and brilliant.

15. http://www.allaboutjazz.com/php/article.php?id=23225#.UYV5Ryt376k.

16. Hodeir, 63 (emphasis mine).

17. Ibid., 62–63.

18. Ibid., 64.

19. Ibid., 65.

20. http://www.billytaylorjazz.com/Jazz.pdf.

21. Hodeir, 62.

22. Ibid., 63.

23. "The Bird is Gone," 127.

24. Ibid.

25. Ralph Ellison, "On Bird, Bird Watching and Jazz," in *Living with Music*, Robert G. O'Meally, ed., (New York: Random House, 2001), 69.

26. Ibid., 71 (emphasis original).

27. Ibid., 69.

28. Ibid., 70.

29. For more on this, see the comment section from "Why 'Love the Way You Lie' Doesn't Redeem Eminem," from the Atlantic blog, in which Eminem is discussed at length and from every angle possible. http://www.theatlantic.com/entertainment/archive/2010/08/why-love-the-way-you-lie-does-not-redeem-eminem/61641/.

30. Zygmunt Bauman, *Freedom* (Minneapolis: University of Minnesota Press, 1988), 7.

31. Ibid., 6.

32. Ibid., 57.

33. Ibid. (emphasis mine).

34. Ibid., 60.

35. Ibid., 76.

36. Ibid., 86.

37. Ibid., 64.

38. Ibid., 98.

39. Ibid., 62.

40. Carroll Hamilton, "'My Skin Is it Starting to Work to My Benefit Now?': Eminem's White Trash Aesthetic" in *Affirmative Reaction: New Formations of White Masculinity* (Durham, NC: Duke University Press, 2011), 111.

41. Bauman, 79.

42. Ibid.

43. Hamilton, 104.

44. Ibid., 109.

45. Ibid., 103.

46. Bauman, 63.

47. Hamilton, 127.

48. Robert Samuels, New Media, Cultural Studies, and Critical Theory After Post-Modernism: Automodernity from Zizek to Laclau (New York: Palgrave Macmillan, 2009), 135.

49. Ibid., 135.

50. Hamilton, 119.

51. Ibid., 101.

52. Samuels, 136.

53. Ibid.

54. Ibid.

55. Ibid., 137.

56. Ibid.

57. Ibid., 140.

58. Ibid., 139.

59. Bauman, 77.

60. Hamilton, 118.

61. Samuels, 137.

62. Ibid., 136.

63. Hamilton, 119.

64. In a *Harper's* interview with John Lofton, a born again Christian, Allen Ginsburg once discussed what Lofton would call "sin" and Ginsburg would call simply "desires." The interview ended this way: "Lofton: Is nothing black-and-white? Ginsberg: Nothing is completely black-and-white. Nothing."

65. Ralph Ellison, *Invisible Man,* Second Vintage International Edition (New York: Random House, 1995), p. 581.

66. Eric J. Sudquist, ed., Cultural Contexts for Ralph Ellison's Invisible Man,13.

67. Larry Neal, "Ralph Ellison's Zoot Suit," in *Ralph Ellison's Invisible Man: A Case Book*, John F. Callahan, ed., (New York: Oxford University Press, 2004), 88.

68. Ibid., 88.

69. Ibid., 106.

70. Ibid., 82.

71. Ibid., 106.

72. Ibid., 107.

73. Ibid., 81.

74. Jason Puskar, "Risking Ralph Ellison," *Daedalus*, volume 138, no. 2 (2009), 84.

75. Quoted in Sundquist, 11.

76. John Dewey, *The Philosophy of John Dewey: Two Volumes in One,* John J. McDermont, ed., (Chicago: University of Chicago Press, 1981), 612.

77. *Ralph Ellison in Progress: From* Invisible Man *to* Three Days before the Shooting (New Haven, CT: Yale University Press, 2010).

78. Ibid., 559.

Eminem 2.0: The Redemptive Subjectivity of Whiteness

JULIUS BAILEY AND DAVID J. LEONARD

Introductory Matters

Art is a form of identity expression within the human experience. To the extent that humanity varies immensely in its social and political dimensions, the art, created by individual subjects who live the individual lives reflected, consequently does also. However, in as much as artistic expressions of individuality can vary, we tend to think of identity art as we do the identity politics that developed in the 1970s. That is, pinning the concept of identity to that of the individual, effectively "black-boxing" the individual as the unit of analysis, pluralism being equated to "multi-individualism." In this paper we will expand on this framework by showing how the realm of intra-individual identity is one of multiplicity: we all have multiple and sometimes competing identities "inside" of us. We will show how this multiplicity "comes out" in artistic expression, and how these many faces of identity art can connect with particular sociocultural conditions. We will do so by examining a very interesting artistic phenomenon, the unexpected success of a multi-identity hip-hop artist who goes by the names of Slim Shady, Marshal Mathers, and Eminem.

In this essay we will explore Eminem's relationship with identity to show how he was able to be accepted by the hip-hop community and be recognized as one of the best rappers of all time. First we will describe the social, cultural, and political context of hip hop in the United States, to "set the stage" for Eminem's feature of becoming the first legitimate and most successful white rapper. Then we will provide a socio-historical account of his musical career. We will then conclude by examining four of his identities in depth to fully understand how these overlapping and mutually inclusive identities work as ways of being that granted Eminem legitimacy and authenticity and eventually worldwide success. The identities will be analyzed in relation to issues of race in America in order to conclude that one of the conditions of being white is that of articulating one's own identity in terms of growth processes. Therefore validating past transgressions as "mistakes" in the framework of maturation, one in which apologizing and moving on is a distinctively white privilege.

Setting the Stage: Mic Check—Can You Hear My Struggles?

Hip hop is an art form born out of blackness; ethno-musically, its roots can be traced to blues and jazz, musical movements pioneered by blacks in the southern parts of the United States. Hip hop's lyrical content mirrors the experience of marginalized voices, often with disregarded humanity. It has been a voice for the "other," and as it has grown and evolved it has been guarded as such, appropriating its "otherness" as part of its political identity. Hip hop has been used as a method of expression for, almost exclusively, young black inner-city men, with very limited access granted to non-black males and females. Thus hip hop has been understood by many scholars and practitioners alike[1] as a response to the alienation and invisibility of the black community—both in terms of media presence and in policy legislation. This alienation has come predominantly from the white–American community: hip hop has focused on several important sociopolitical issues relating to this alienation: some of the most politically charged messages include stories about how the black community's needs are often ignored by white politicians, how they are profiled and (sometimes) beaten by white cops, how they carry a heritage of oppression dating back to white slave owners, and how their material success is often in the hands of white industry leaders. How, then, is one of the all-time bestselling representatives of this art a scrawny bleach-blonde blue-eyed kid from Detroit?

Hip hop as a musical culture is built upon the shared experiences of its constituents, both artists and listeners. There is a certain sort of "black epistemology" from which its members draw and to which they constantly contribute.[2] To be successful in hip hop an artist must demonstrate sincerity and authenticity, a desire to stay "real" and connected with his or her roots. These manifestations of authenticity demonstrate to the other members of the hip-hop community that the person subscribes to a black epistemic phenomenology. The world of hip hop had never been inviting for white rappers, but over time the walls of performative acceptability seem to have become increasingly impenetrable. From the Beastie Boys, Paul Wall, Young Black Teenagers, Snow, 3rd Base, and MC Search to more recent artists Everlast, Macklemore, Mac Miller, MGK, Kreayshawn, Yelawolf, Asher Roth, and Brother Ali, white rappers have found a niche in of hip hop. In a sense, these white rappers have created a space of hybridity where upon white artists emerge within a historically black art form. There is perhaps no better example of the importance of this, and the consequences of duplicity, than the white rapper Vanilla Ice. Born Robert Van Winkle, he achieved incredible success as rapper Vanilla Ice in the late 1980s. In his lyrics he described a difficult youth spent on the streets of Miami, one that earned him respect from black hip-hop artists at the time. His struggles were identified as a commonality between them, despite the racial difference. However a few years after his rap career was trashed after it was revealed that much of his public biography was false. His rise and fall continues to be a glaring warning to would-be white rappers.

There is also the role of white fans within hip hop. White fans can be understood as seeking a touristic experience that authenticates their notions of blackness and whiteness. As such, it can be argued that they have little need for white hip-hop artists to even exist if, as cultural critic Kevin Powell asserts, hip hop functions as a "cultural safari for white people."[3] On the other hand, if hip hop is this imaginary ride of space and place in which one can quickly revert back to themselves once the fantasy is over, wouldn't it be nice for the dream to be reality. What would it be like if I, a white male or female, could be located in actuality and not just imaginarily, within this cultural form? In this case, it is no wonder that white artists are often compelling and profitable, within white social space given white fans' appeal and revolt to hip hop as racial "otherness." After the success and failures of the aforementioned precursors, more white hip-hop artists, led by Eminem have been able to penetrate hip-hop culture? With Dr. Dre by his side, with a performative style, and geographic/class orientation, Eminem was able to break away from the white niche of impersonating or living out a dream of blackness and sustain an authenticity that lies at the core of hip hop.

Eminem: He Is White and He Knows it

Before ever trying to achieve success, Eminem first had to prove himself as a legitimate member of the hip-hop community. Eminem's strategy from the beginning was not to mask his whiteness but to spotlight it, to turn it around on black artists and dare them to act hypocritically. Of course, he did so in a way that reimagined whiteness through a particular vision of white masculinity, one shaped by his geographic kinship with black America.

Eminem's break came in 1997 at the Rap Olympics, during which he warned one of the MCs he was battling not to turn his "facial tissue into a racial issue," that all his "white jokes just backfired," and that he was about to be "beat by a honkey."[4] This event is retold in the semibiographical movie *8 Mile*, in which Rabbit (Eminem) preempts his opponent in a similar way, admitting he is white, trailer trash, broke, and living with his mom. While Rabbit was victorious, Eminem came in second at the Rap Olympics. Interscope label co-founder Jimmy Iovine was impressed, however, and passed a demo along to Dr. Dre.

There is no doubt that Eminem's initial recognition as a legitimate rap artist was due in large part to his association with Dre, who was widely respected for both his solo work and his part in N.W.A., a pioneering California-based gangsta rap group. Eminem's connection to Detroit and his working-class sensibilities further authenticate him as legitimate. He is obviously not black, but his story and his flow rendered him as an alternative white body, "whiteness of different color." Given the commodities trafficked within hip hop, Eminem needed to offer a narrative that highlighted his connection to hip hop and blackness. Eminem, who had cut his teeth by boldly highlighting his difference, was admitted into the hip-hop community by Dre, a respected gatekeeper, one of their own. Eminem now had to defend his authenticity. Using the same tactic as in his early rap battles, he focused on his socioeconomic background.

Hip Hop's Hybridity

Four key separate identities can be found in Eminem's music. The first, and arguably the most popular, is Slim Shady. His behavior is deviant; he is criminal, suicidal, violent, and cartoonish. He has an affinity for sexual violence, domestic violence, drugs, and offending as many people as possible. His maniacal tendencies are both legitimized and enhanced by his juvenile sense of humor. Joking about the above subjects moves him closer to a sociopathic diagnosis. However, it also puts listeners at ease, to an extent, as it seems to leave room for maturation and apology. Because he is changing, because he is dynamic, listeners are able to see his songs about violence or homophobia as a window into a singular moment rather than a glimpse at his soul and morals. The songs and the behavior don't define him as a person but instead are about choices, behavior, and his being at a particular moment. It leaves room for change and growth.

The second identity referenced is Marshall Mathers. He is most often associated with life before commercial success. He is a father, a husband, a son, and a friend. He is aware of his other identities, but himself identifies as a "regular guy." His self-awareness includes a racial awareness, as well as feelings of pain, suffering, and past poverty. Marshall Mathers is the identity rooted in the past.

The third identity is Eminem, the musician and the brand. He is a socially and politically aware lyricist. If Slim Shady is the most provocative of the identities, and Marshall is the most "real," then Eminem is the most interesting and perhaps the most important. This is because Eminem is the performer, and in his music he performs both the Slim Shady and Marshall Mathers personae. He mediates and controls these other identities. In a sense, Slim is the id, Marshall is the super ego, and Eminem is the Ego. The mediation or triangulation of identities is comforting because yet again listeners are told that ultimately Marshall is a good guy, someone who can do good.

The fourth and final identity spans his entire career but has really come into existence in recent years: Eminem 2.0.Focusing on his maturation, evolution, and growth, this persona embodies a story of redemption (whiteness) that has never been available to black artists.

The Four Identities and Their Functions

Satisfying the demand for authenticity is the driving force behind the first half of Eminem's discography. Whereas black artists must "keep it real," presumably along a single axis of the "ghettocentric imagination.[5] Eminem is celebrated for his competing, contradictory, and dynamic identities. Whereas black artists are expected to offer narratives of gangstas, violence, drugs, sex, and urban black masculinity, Eminem is able to offer multiple stories and performative identities. Among these multiple identities, each fulfills the demands of a different social role; while constructing various identities may seem counterintuitive to authenticity, in the end the strategy works for Eminem. His first three albums are an introduction of sorts and are appropriately titled *The Slim Shady LP*, *The Marshall Mathers LP*, and *The Eminem Show*, released in 1999, 2000, and 2002, respectively.

Eminem unleashed Slim Shady with the popular single "My Name Is." In it he describes figuratively hanging himself in his youth and starting to become someone else. The person that walks away from that hanging is Slim Shady, who insults his fans and his mother, dreams of killing his father, drinks and takes drugs, and invites his listeners ("kids") to do the same. The music video for the single is more telling: in it, Eminem parodies his whiteness, presenting himself in normative white characters: a white-haired professor, the entire cast of the *Brady Bunch*, a ventriloquist's dummy, a flasher, an American president, and rocker Marilyn Manson. All the while, a white couple meant to look lower class watches this parade of images on their television.

These creative choices inflate and warp identity by setting up levels of distance between Eminem and the viewer. The first gap is the performance of Slim Shady by Eminem; the second is the performance of white stereotypes by Slim Shady; the third is the fact that those stereotypes are in and of themselves performance (the ventriloquist performs the dummy, actors perform a white family, Marilyn Manson paints himself for concerts); the fourth is the observation of this on the television by the white couple; and the final is our own observation. All the while, the video cuts to Eminem in the uniform and posture of his genre; baggy clothes, crouched, gesturing while rapping. This juxtaposition places his "white person rapping" performance on the same level as all the other performances. By parodying whiteness and "lowering" himself to a spectacle, Eminem takes from his critics their greatest weapon, the ability to claim that he is fake. Critics would claim that he is only dressing the part, that he is not "real." As explained earlier, the hip-hop community then placed, and still does place, a great emphasis on authenticity. Eminem thus demonstrates that we all dress a certain part, that we all distort our identities and are always performing them, in different ways and to different audiences, and that allows him to move the conversation away from his whiteness to show that he is no less skilled than black rappers. In his hit "Role Model" he unashamedly iterates that some folk are sleepin' on his skills by seeing him only as a white rapper.[6] Eminem avoids being labeled as inferior by saying what is on critics' minds first. His self-devaluation, in effect, preempts any attacks. Not only that, he introduces a persona so extreme, so crude, that it acts to shift attention from race to content, as well as showing his would-be critics that he doesn't take himself seriously. The following is a breakdown and description of each of these personae.

The remainder of *The Slim Shady LP* gives the audience biographical clues that help to build the rapper's authenticity. He was bullied as a kid,[7] he is exhausted by his poverty and low pay,[8] and he struggles with being a father.[9] He pays homage to successful white rappers in the past and mocks the unsuccessful ones.[10] As a whole, the listener comes away thinking that Shady is violent, but also that, as a performer, he is something of an underdog, an anti-hero, and misunderstood. The attacks made on Slim Shady only solidified his standing in the hip-hop community. In a 2000 Senate hearing investigating the effect of violence in the media on American youth, Eminem was held up as an example of everything wrong with the entertainment industry.[11] The attacks made on his violent lyrics by those who testified, such as Lynne Cheney, wife of future vice president Dick Cheney, were reminiscent of one of the most infamous clashes between hip hop and "mainstream America." In 1989 the FBI sent an accusatory and shaming letter in response to N.W.A.'s song "Fuck Tha Police" to their record label.[12]

Within the hip-hop community, the press and pressure from law enforcement only increased their popularity and credibility. As with other black artists dominating the hip-hop game, Eminem would sit at the throne of America's culture wars; pundits and culture warriors would cite homophobia, sexism, and violence within his lyrics as evidence of his threat to the morality and cultural well-being of America. He was indicative of a problem within hip hop. Yet his presence within this culture was never akin to his black brothers and sisters. He was representative of the moral failings of hip hop; he wasn't the problem. He embodied the dangers of hip hop yet he was an individual, whereas black artists and blackness came to represent the purported pathologies and dysfunction polluting America's airwaves, streets, and national fabric. Eminem was also a victim in this context. His choices and individual person were on trial; not his body and community, "whiteness comes replete with its assumptions for what to expect of a black body, how dangerous and unruly it is, how unlawful, criminal, and hypersexual it is."[13] By prescribing the black body, white supremacy in America allows white artists like Eminem access to forms of self-creation unavailable to those defined by the color of their skin.

In 2000 Eminem released *The Marshall Mathers LP*, which continues to fill in the details of Eminem's life. It also is a response to the public reception of his first album. This is clearest in the single "The Real Slim Shady." While mocking those in the hip-hop community who imagine him as a racial pioneer, his message to mainstream America is that there is a bit of Slim Shady in each of us. Yet, he's bold enough to say what so many are already saying in private.[14] Maintaining the hip-hop ego by declaring he is the "real" Slim Shady, he also admits that there are millions of others just like him. In this sense, Eminem universalizes his identity, comparing himself to all of his listeners, and indeed all of the people in the USA, further drawing attention away from his whiteness.

At the same time, The *Marshall Mathers LP* continues the pattern of highlighting Eminem's whiteness. He raps that his appearance—his white body—makes his music, his lyrics, and his rap game impossible to miss; he does music that is neither black nor white. Eminem continues to signify his whiteness both with blatant references to the color of his skin as well as using stereotypically "white" pop culture references in his lyrics. The resulting message is clear. Eminem is not out to steal hip hop or to fake blackness; he is a performer, no more and no less. By simultaneously making explicit references to his whiteness, often in a prodding manner, and universalizing himself and his message, Eminem manages to set the tone of the conversation; he claims his music is not "white music," nor "black music," it is simply music, a universal category and thus his value as a rapper ought to be measured only by his skills. His critics cannot argue against this argument because Eminem disarms them even before they can criticize him by reminding them that "white" and "black" are labels that do not hold meaning independent of their context.

The Eminem Show, his third album on a major label, is the last on which he deals extensively with his race, defending himself and his talent. It is also primarily a reflection on his success and what role his race played. He picks up the media's comparison of him to Elvis Presley, who is argued to have appropriated black music and popularized rock 'n' roll, claiming to have appropriated black music selfishly for his own financial gain.[15] In the same track he again responds to his critics, including Mrs. Cheney, who accuse him of being a bad influence on their children. In the next verse, he mentions that his fans' parents, and his biggest critics, "still listen to Elvis," pointing out their hypocrisy.

He begins to describe how he actively constructed his identities. He "took the image of a thug,"[16] and admits on "White America" that it was his whiteness that has led to his success for he maintains if he was black his success wouldn't have been but merely half of what he has garnered.[17] He doesn't pretend to connect only with a black audience but reaches out to other white kids, whose parents are scared because they are "talking black,"[18] while also affirming that he is relatable and acceptable as a spokesperson for suburban youth connection that is only made possible by his whiteness.[19] He admits to having a public persona that, though constructed, people relate to, and he is compelled to describe multiple times that his lyrics shouldn't be taken literally. Finally, in one of the greatest demonstrations of honesty that any celebrity can show, he describes regret in his song "Soldier" by lamenting that his "trapped" status is a sacrifice of his humanity and even suggests that if he had it to do over, he would have chosen a different path than this rap game.[20]

Eminem's Blackness, America's Whiteness

Halfway through his discography it would be prudent to look at the system in which Eminem's lyrics worked. It is too simple to suggest that Eminem is successful because he is good at "acting black." This presumes a singular way of "acting black" and an intransigence of his racial performance. The reality of his performance and personae is much more complicated. Using critical whiteness theory we can explain how Eminem negotiates his identities, how they allowed him access to an exclusive community, and how he has achieved such success. His whiteness, in effect, allows him to move away from the codes of white ethnicity.

Noel Ignatiev defined the white race as "not a biological but a social formation, whose existence depends on its members' willingness to reproduce it through their actions."[21] If whiteness is formed, rather than fixed, then there is possibility for change, for movement. It is "a politics of difference that is subject to the shifting currents of history, power, and culture."[22] These currents, of course, have historically privileged whiteness through systematic oppression. As documented above, Eminem admits to being white, and his association with white ethnicity allows him access to vast cultural capital. Being white, he can push the boundaries further than can minorities. He can experiment with the fluidity of whiteness itself. As a result of his experimentation he has developed his three primary identities.

We can also be confident that Eminem has not completely relinquished his whiteness now that he has achieved success. Ruth Frankenberg describes whiteness as "the production and reproduction of dominance rather than subordination, normativity rather than marginality, and privilege rather than disadvantage."[23] In parodying white stereotypes in his music and videos he perpetuates the extant racial structure. One might argue that it would be impossible to not acknowledge these white signifiers even if a person had, somehow, completely shed their whiteness. After all, a thing is no less real simply because of one person's disbelief. As identities are performed, and embodied, all are real and authentic yet unreal and inauthentic. Eminem acknowledges these things and, importantly, gives them voice. Throughout his albums he will occasionally engage mid-verse in role-play, changing his role and giving voice to his critics or representatives of mainstream America. He has the creative option to simply dis his detractors the way most rappers do: he consciously chooses to include the dialogue. He gives voice to his critics, parroting their criticisms of his lyrics about his mother, misogyny, and drugs.[24] He gives voice to his record label representatives as well and their light censorship of him.[25] On the track "Criminal" he lends his voice to a hypocritical preacher and to "feminist women" who think he's offensive but cute on "The Real Slim Shady."

Acting out identities outside of his own further highlights Eminem's movement within and across boundaries. In his afterword to Henry Giroux's *Public Spaces, Private Lives*, Douglas Kellner describes Giroux's desire for a "'border politics' where individuals cross over and struggle together for democracy and social justice."[26] This, Giroux's alternative to the fetishization of difference, is perhaps the closest whiteness theorists have come to describing the strategy that Eminem employs.

Giroux elaborates that, "[f]or progressive whites 'crossing over does not mean crossing out' or renouncing whiteness as a form or racial identity."[27] Many people would object to describing Eminem in any way "progressive," yet it is clear that Eminem has incorporated border crossing into his schema. Metaphorical crossings align with physical ones in the film *8 Mile*, in which Eminem stars as a version of himself named Rabbit.

The title of the film comes from 8 Mile in Detroit, a road that has long been the delineation of the whiter and wealthier neighborhoods north of the road from the poorer and blacker to the south. Eminem lived north of 8 Mile, confirming racial separation, but he lived with his mother in a run-down trailer, hence the focus on class in his search for authenticity. From his lyrics and the film, it is made clear that he belonged south of 8 Mile, that the reason he lived north of it was flimsy. He was accepted through class connections but applauded because of his minority status; everyone loves an underdog.

Finally, in discussing whiteness and Eminem's identities, we can describe, for lack of a better term, varying degrees of whiteness. Keeping with the image of border crossing, his identities did not all cross and stop at the same point. Slim Shady several times self-describes as imaginary.[28] Elsewhere he asks how he can be white if he doesn't even exist. The archetypal image of the ghost is of something insubstantial, White, fluid, and capable of moving through walls, of crossing otherwise impenetrable boundaries. Being "trapped in a beat" and not existing at all further demonstrates Slim Shady's synthetic nature; he exists only in the music of Eminem, and even then he exists precariously.

If we can describe Slim Shady as having little substance, Marshall Mathers, in contrast, is a solid identity. He is a "regular guy," a father, son, and friend. He is the man who crossed 8 Mile and the one who consciously struggles with his lot in life. "Woe is me," Slim Shady says, referring to Mathers, on the album *Relapse*. He is the one that carries insecurities, including those associated with his whiteness. Eminem, then, is somewhere in the middle. He is the mediator, the one that travels back and forth across the boundary lines of race and class. He represents the musician and makes artistic choices that affect the others. And yet, he raps on *The Eminem Show*, fans don't want Marshall; they want Shady.

Eminem 2.0: A Story of Redemption

The honeymoon period of Eminem's career came to an end after the release of *The Eminem Show*. Following that album, Eminem has matured, to an extent, in addressing life issues and his fame. He has also, however, spiraled into drug addiction, lost critical acclaim, and very nearly ended his career. After *Encore*, a derivative version of *The Eminem Show*, and *Relapse*, a comic-horror resuscitation of the Slim Shady character, it is with his 2010 album *Recovery* he again shows his audience the Eminem who pulled himself up by his bootstraps, and reviving his career he seeks redemption from his audience and his critics.

Recovery chronicles Eminem's growth and maturation. On the first track, "Cold Wind Blows," Shady gives voice to God, who cleanses him of his past sins but warns him against any future ones. Eminem reveals his insecurities on "Talkin' 2 Myself" when he admits he felt so weak and uninspired that he nearly wrote songs going after Lil Wayne and Kanye West. In a rare and humble moment he says, that if he had, he would have been outdone by them, and he knew it.

Recovery is where Eminem's identities begin to blur. It isn't only Marshall Mathers that struggled or Slim Shady that had all the fun. He pulls them together to apologize to his fans, both for his absence and his previous two albums, which he admits were not up to par.[29] One of the clearest signals we get that these identities are shifting is on the appropriately titled track "Going Through Changes," where he admits that he still loves his ex-wife Kim, whom he had vilified, tortured, and killed multiple times in his music. Here, he reclaims Eminem as a new inscription; he pushes aside his class identity and, really, his connection to Detroit, marking his arrival as a white and thus redeemed artist. His focus on universal themes and narratives—maturation, alcoholism, addiction, fatherhood—speaks to this effort to reimagine his own identity and location. In "Not Afraid," he raps about his fears and how he had to overcome them to be a better rapper, man, and person: he got clean for himself, in order to put his life back together. In an interview, he speaks to how his sobriety his changed his rap game, declaring that, "Rap was my drug. It used to get me high and then it stopped getting me high. Then I had to resort to other things to make me feel that ... now rap's getting me high again." His journey, his law breaking, is thus part of the growth and his journey as a hero. He is both redeemable and a source of redemption for us all, especially as religion is imagined as the basis for his purification. In fact, his religiosity is often cited as the turn from the pathological to the inspirational, from the undesirable to the role model, all part of this redemptive process. And because of the power of whiteness, few question the authenticity of Marshall, Slim, Eminem 1.0 or 2.0, since he was always real; he is just growing and maturing all along. As hip hop is imagined as a window into a black reality defined by hyper masculinity, violence, drugs, and sexuality, black artists must fit into this box. white artists, particularly those who can vibe and inhabit these presumed-to-be authentic blacks, are thus able to embody different locations and identities.

Eminem's search for redemption takes two forms. The first is introspection, looking back at his life and his work and attacking both. Second, he makes apologies for rap and himself, seeking to quell some of the genre's infighting and explain his own actions. He is still vulgar (he wouldn't be Eminem otherwise), but we see maturation. The important question: is his search for redemption any more accessible or acceptable because he is white? Does his difficult childhood excuse him? And does this suggest that the "angry white man" is only a transient identity, a step in any young white man's maturation process, while silently cementing the "angry black man" as "born this way?"

The Redemptive Space Reserved for Whiteness: Second Chances in the World of Privilege

State legislatures and the federal government have spent the last three decades drafting policies that preclude second chances to formerly incarcerated Americans, who have disproportionately been African Americans. "The United States imprisons a larger percentage of its black population than South Africa did at the height of apartheid."[30] By stigmatizing those imprisoned, thus limiting their chance at reentry to society, we create a new "undercaste," one that is largely defined by race by our country's white-supremacist value system. This relegation to a seemingly legitimated position of inferiority, cleverly concealed as an issue of class in our believed meritocratic system, creates a more nuanced version of the Jim Crow framework, as described by Michelle Alexander: "So long as large numbers of African Americans continue to be arrested and labeled drug criminals, they will continue to be relegated to a permanent second-class status upon their release, no matter how much (or how little) time they spend behind bars. The system of mass incarceration is based on the prison label, not prison time."[31] By legally denying access to public housing or public assistance, thus preventing the once incarcerated from becoming barbers, teachers, or sometimes even entry-level employees, black bodies are imagined as unredeemable and therefore undesirable.

This plays out in terms of suspensions and expulsions in America's schools within the criminal justice system's sentencing practices. According to studies conducted on sentencing procedures, researchers have found that "Black defendants convicted of harming white victims suffer harsher penalties than blacks who commit crimes against other blacks or white defendants who harm whites." The study also shows that harsher sentences favor youth and the unemployed. Young unemployed blacks, to extrapolate, are the most severely punished group in the United States. It so happens that young blacks listen to a lot of hip hop, and for social reasons that extend beyond this paper, more young blacks are unemployed than their white counterparts.

We, as a system, are more willing to forgive whites, to give whites a second chance, to give them the benefit of the doubt, and/or to empathize with them. With the ability to existentially create and control one's essence and its perception by others, white people manifest their privilege even in their ability to be separated from any kind of a priori valuation. There is an evident space in our country for redemption for the white male. It is considerably smaller for the black male, who is faced with a fixed preexisting essence that limits his ability to be redeemed. As George Yancy writes, "one might say that blackness functions metaphorically as original sin. There is not anything as such that a black body needs *to do* in order to be found blameworthy."[32] We have seen this recently in 2012 with the endless coverage of mass shootings (and the limited coverage of violence in Chicago and Detroit). The media narrative surrounding mass shootings (forty-four of the sixty-two mass shooters since 1982 have been white, with only one of those female) has in many ways sought to understand and explain the unexplainable. While seeking answers as to "why," a question not asked when involving youth of color. The media works to redeem and humanize these white men. As Leonard wrote about the mass shooting in Newtown, Connecticut:

> The most recent shooting in Newtown highlights whiteness and the ways it has been rendered invisible after every mass shooting. Described as a "nerd," who "still wears a pocket protector," Adam Lanza has been re-imagined as a character straight out of *The Revenge of the Nerds* series and not a cold-blood killer. He carried a brief case, not a gun; he read *The Catcher in the Rye* and *Of Mice and Men*, not *Guns and Ammo*; he wore button down polos, not fatigues. His life was not extraordinary but was that of an average kid. From the reading list to the sartorial choices we have been sold a Normal Rockwell painting. The Associated Press painted a picture of Adam that imaged him as a character ripped out of a *Brady Bunch* script: "He was an honors student who lived in a prosperous neighborhood with his mother, a well-liked woman who enjoyed hosting dice games and decorating the house for the holidays."[33]

The narrative afforded to Adam Lanza is one of redemption and understanding; while Eminem 2.0 is all about chronicling the path to redemption, one that is accessible because of his whiteness, each and every one of his personae is about our insatiable desire to understand why "he"—a white male from Detroit—thinks and acts "that way." The spectacle that is Eminem rests with outsider status, his presumed incongruity with the blackness, the pathology, the criminality, and the danger of hip hop. His early career was all about explaining how he, whiteness and all, was "this way." His recent work is about how he is no longer like "that." In each instance, we believe and accept, reading him through the lens of whiteness.

The implications of second (and third) chances, much less the ability to Eminem to change and still be real at every step of his journey, are evident outside the music industry. Widening the scope of redemption from the music industry to race relations on a national scale, the justice system is where to best mine for trends in forgiveness and empathy. How many articles about Michael Vick and Kobe Bryant[34] references their past encounters with the criminal justice? In other words, whereas Eminem's past is imagined as a point of departure, a dock in the horizon from which he has departed, the past is never the past for African Americans. The past is the present and the future. Compared to blackness, which is consistently imagined as "a problematic sign and ontological position"[35] and a "dystopic structure or delinquent body,"[36] whiteness is a universal passage that affords acceptance and redemption. It is no wonder that blacks *without* felony convictions are less likely to be hired than white applicants *with* felony convictions.[37] The fact that Eminem not only made multiple comebacks, but also marked this transformation (and his past problems) as part of his marketable identity is a testament to the power and profitability that come from that being white in America. Beyond Eminem's own brushes of the law, he has also been subject to much objection and criticism; unlike African Americans, he has been allowed to grow from those experiences to move beyond the behavior and artistry that defined him as a twenty-something rapper.

Therefore we can understand white privilege as twofold: first there is the capacity to have multiple identities, as Eminem does. The fact that Eminem can disengage from his whiteness, at least temporarily, to be able to reflect back on it critically through parody is itself an enactment of the privilege afforded by whiteness. It is as if being white is a primary condition onto which other more "cultural" positions can be mapped temporally, in this case the sub-culture of hip hop. There then is an ability to assimilate the cultural markers and signs of "the other" legitimately, and the whole process is framed as one of cultural understanding and dialogue. However this process is not a dialogue. The flow of cultural appropriation goes one way mostly, from the oppressed to the oppressor. In other words even in the small cases where blacks are able to appropriate white culture, they never fully transcend their blackness.

The second enactment of white privilege present is how Eminem is able to utilize these many identities to frame his career as one maturation process. In this framework, previous experiences are seen to lead into the present, and linearly accumulate wisdom and life lessons, which are then manifested in the person's present judgment. Therefore Eminem 2.0 is an identity that encompasses all of the previous ones, Slim Shady, Marshall Mathers, and Eminem, or at least all the lessons learned from them. With the theme of redemption so present in the later stages of his career, Eminem 2.0 is able to articulate his previous judgment mistakes, moral transgressions, and moments of fault as leading up to the present, wiser version of himself. This privilege of self-creation is one which most black males are denied; the privilege to change or to be seen as changed is also denied to black males. In this framework, apologizing for the past provides validation: He "made a mistake" only; there is nothing inherently wrong with him. For example, when the BP Deepwater Horizon Oil spill took place in 2010, the then-CEO of BP, Tony Hayward, was publicly criticized for saying "I'm sorry." It is as if white males in American can get away with anything if only they show remorse for their past actions. The much-litigated violence within hip hop is not defined by whiteness; whiteness is not defined by violence but by innocence, and therefore redemption is always available when participating in an art form that is imagined as dangerous throughout the American landscape. The satirical show *South Park* made fun of Hayward extensively for his moment of apology in their episode " Coon 2: Hindsight."[38] Similarly, Eminem 2.0 is the embodiment of remorse in Eminem's identity space. Eminem 2.0 is able to reflect on the immaturity of Slim Shady, on the crassness of Eminem, on the irritability of Marshall Mathers, and is able to neatly wrap up these lessons in marketable commodities. As we can see, then, Eminem's success as a rapper cannot be easily disassociated from his whiteness. Eminem's career trajectory as a rapper has been defined by his ability to express vastly differing realities within his verses, as well as his ability to frame these realities as belonging to an overall process of maturation and of moral redemption. Both of these, as we have seen, are indeed privileges granted almost exclusively to white males in America.

Chapter Notes

1. Jeff Chang, *Total Chaos: The Art and Aesthetics of Hip-Hop* (New York: Basic Civitas, 2007); Todd Boyd, *Am I Black Enough for You?: Popular Culture from the 'Hood and Beyond* (Bloomington: University of Indiana Press, 1997).

2. P. J. Olson and B. Shobe, (2008), "White Rappers and Black Epistemology," *The Journal of Popular Culture* (41): 996.

3. Kevin Powell in Allison Samuels, "Minstrels in Baggy Jeans," *Newsweek*, May 4, 2003.

4. Eminem, "Eminem—Rap Olympics Battle," http://www.youtube.com/watch?v=dKHOkSr2FmA (April 24, 2013).

5. S. Craig Watkins, *Representing: Hip Hop Culture and the Production of Black Cinema* (Chicago: University of Chicago Press, 1998).

6. Eminem, "Role Model,"*The Slim Shady LP*, 1999, Aftermath.

7. Eminem, "Brain Damage," *The Slim Shady LP*, 1999, Aftermath.

8. Eminem, "If I Had," *The Slim Shady LP*, 1999, Aftermath.

9. Eminem, "Rock Bottom," *The Slim Shady LP*, 1999, Aftermath.

10. Eminem, "Cum on Everybody," *The Slim Shady LP*, 1999, Aftermath; and Eminem, "Role Model," *The Slim Shady LP*, 1999, Aftermath.

11. Robert Mancini, "Eminem Targeted at Senate Hearing," *MTV*, 13 September 2000, http://www.mtv.com/news/articles/1428579/eminem-targeted-at-senate-hearing.jhtml (April 24, 2013).

12. Steve Hochman, "Comptom Rappers Versus the Letter of the Law: FBI Claims Song by N.W.A. Advocates Violence on Police," *Los Angeles Times*, October 5, 1989, http://articles.latimes.com/1989–10–05/entertainment/ca–1046_1_law-enforcement (April 24, 2013)

13. George Yancy,*Black Bodies, White Gazes: The Continuing Significance of Race* (Lanham, MD: Rowman and Littlefield, 2008), 3.

14. Eminem, "The Real Slim Shady," *The Marshall Mathers LP*, 2000, Aftermath.

15. Eminem, "Without Me," *The Eminem Show*, 2002, Aftermath.

16. Eminem, "Soldier," *The Eminem Show*, 2002, Aftermath.

17. Eminem, "White America," *The Eminem Show*, 2002, Aftermath.

18. Eminem, "Sing For the Moment," *The Eminem Show*, 2002, Aftermath.

19. Eminem, "White America," *The Eminem Show*, 2002, Aftermath.

20. Eminem, "Say Goodbye to Hollywood," *The Eminem Show*, 2002, Aftermath.

21. Noel Ignatiev, (2003), "Whiteness and Class Struggle," *Historical Materialism*, 11(4) 227–235.

22. Henry A. Giroux, (1997), "Rewriting the Discourse of Racial Identity: Towards a Pedagogy and Politics of Whiteness," *Harvard Educational Review*, 67(2):285–320.

23. Ruth Frankenberg,*White Women, Race Matters: The Social Construction of Whiteness*(Minneapolis: University of Minnesota Press, 1993), 239.

24. Eminem, "Kill You," *The Marshall Mathers LP*, 2000, Aftermath.

25. Eminem, "I'm Back," *The Marshall Mathers LP*, 2000, Aftermath.

26. Douglas Kellner, "Afterword," in Henry A. Giroux, *Public Spaces, Private Lives: Democracy Beyond 9/11* (Maryland: Rowman and Littlefield, 2003), 158.

27. Henry A. Giroux "White Noise: Toward a Pedagogy of Whiteness" in Kostas Myrsiades and Linda Myrsiades, eds., *Race-ing Representation: Voice, History, and Sexuality* (Maryland: Rowman and Littlefield, 1997), 71.

28. Eminem, "Bad Meets Evil," *The Slim Shady LP*, 1999, Aftermath.

29. Eminem, "Talkin' 2 Myself," *Recovery*, 2010, Aftermath.

30. Michelle Alexander,*The New Jim Crow: Mass Incarceration in the Age of Colorblindness* (Perseus, Kindle Edition, 2012), 6.

31. Ibid.,14.

32. George Yancy, *Black Bodies, White Gazes: The Continuing Significance of Race* (Lanham, MD. Rowman and Littlefield, 2008), 5.

33. David Leonard (2013), "The Unbearable Invisibility of White Masculinity: Innocence In the Age of White Male Mass Shootings," http://gawker.com/5973485/the-unbearable-invisibility-of-white-masculinity-innocence-in-the-age-of-white-male-mass-shootings.

34. David J. Leonard and C. Richard King, (2011), "Lack of Black Opps: Kobe Bryant and the Difficult Path of Redemption," *Journal of Sport and Social Issues*, 35(2):209–223.

35. Rhonda Williams, "Living at the Crossroads: Exploration in Race, Nationality, Sexuality, and Gender" in Wahneema Lubiano, ed., *The House that Race Built* (New York: Vintage Books, 1998), 140.

36. Ronald Jackson,Scripting the Black Masculine Body: Identity, Discourse, and Racial Politics in Popular Media (New York: State University of New York Press, 2006), 55.

37. DevahPraeger, *Marked: Race, Crime, and Finding Work in an Era of Mass Incarceration* (Chicago: University of Chicago Press, 2009; Paul Von Zielbauer, "Race a Factor in Job Offers for Ex-Convicts," *The New York Times*, June 17, 1995), retrieved October 8, 2008 from http://www.nytimes.com/2005/06/17/nyregion/17felons.html?_r= 1&oref=slogin.

38. http://www.southparkstudios.com/clips/360436/were-sorry.

The Farther Reaches
of Human Proficiency

Steve Bramucci

When I was in college, I was profoundly affected by Abraham Maslow's *The Farther Reaches of Human Nature*. Maslow's spot in history seems to be limited (for the non-psychologist) to diagrams of the "Hierarchy of Needs" contained in Psych 101 texts, but in *The Farther Reaches of Human Nature* he extends the definition of "self-actualization" that we know from the apex of the diagram's pyramid to describe people who are living life as one extended peak-experience. In short, it's used to identify people who maximize what it means to be fully human. Of the peak experience, Maslow writes: "One main characteristic ... is just this total fascination with the matter-in-hand, this getting lost in the present, this detachment from time and place."[1]

Maslow is describing people who have turned the act of living into a transcendent art. As a nineteen-year-old, having just returned to school after a dropping out for a semester to hitchhike cross-country, talk of peak-experiences and self-actualization flattened me. I felt like he was speaking directly to the *On the Road*-inspired, everything-now impulsive joys I was swimming in at the time. The whole notion of striving toward an incandescent version of self, toward a set of higher values, found me at the perfect time and quickly became part of my own spiritual belief pattern.

None of which has anything to do with Eminem—besides the fact that by listening nonstop to the rapper around the same time I discovered Maslow, I perhaps bound the two together in my brain.

The version of Eminem that Marshal Mathers III has presented to the public sounds nothing like one of Maslow's self-actualizers, who have reached the highest plateaus of what it means to be human, typified by virtues that he shares in various books (e.g., "their sense of humor is philosophical rather than hostile"; "they identify with mankind").

But this idea of striving to meet some unknown "farthest reach" of potential—that sounds a *lot* like Eminem's rapping. By the time the *Marshall Mathers LP* dropped in 2000 (if not before), it was clear that we were dealing with a rapper who was striving toward the transcendent. The song "Stan," which appears on that album, is a journey into full character creation and narrative point-of-view shifting that was brand new to fans of mainstream rap. More than that, Eminem was digging into "his stuff"—insecurities, fears, and private pain. In the process, he was smashing the mic, burning the building to the ground, and pissing on the ashes. Lyrically speaking, that is.

Point being, when working at optimum levels[2] Eminem is fiercely intent on bringing his considerable reservoirs of skill to bear, crafting verses that push deep into the frontier of what it means to be an exceptional MC. In *The Farther Reaches of Human Nature*, Maslow says of self-actualizers: "They are devoted, working at something, something which is very precious to them—some calling or vocation in the old sense, the priestly sense."[3] The quote perfectly describes Eminem's approach to rap. He is in the business of exploring the farthest reaches of human proficiency (which we can define as the sum of skill + talent)—looking at rap as both an art and a craft. He's way out at the frontier, clearing a path for the Kendrick Lamars of the world. He studies words, breaks down syllables, twirls them on his finger, and recombines them in surprising ways. When he slips, he knows as much and isn't afraid to point it out, as on "Talkin' 2 Myself," when he raps that *Encore* was produced on drugs, *Relapse* while detoxing.

As a result, his peers recognize him as a self-actualizer. They know how good he is. Lupe Fiasco once said mid-concert: "I can't fuck with Eminem, but I got everybody else covered"[4]—a high-magnitude compliment in a bravado-heavy industry. It's a sentiment that's been echoed in one form or another by virtually every member of the living rap pantheon.

This absolute commitment to the art and desire to destroy every verse that he puts his name on[5] isn't just what makes Eminem a true artist, it's what, for this particular writer, makes him listenable at all.

Zing!

Allow me to clarify. I am a liberal-minded person raised in a liberal household, in a liberal neighborhood, in a liberal city. Humanistic, inclusive values were spoon-fed to me with my mashed carrots. When my cousin and I started listening compulsively to Eminem on family vacations, our aunts and uncles found it absolutely horrifying. Being the sort of family that discusses such things over dinner, we were often put on the spot to defend what could only be described as admiration-headed-toward-complete-hero-worship of a guy who sang (with regularity) about murdering his wife. I wish

I remembered how we tried to explain the hold that Eminem's music[6] had on us. I'm sure we fell back on tired arguments like "no generation understands the next generation's music" and "he's sharing his genuine experience." To which I'm sure our family, made up of psychologists and teachers, took turns tearing us to shreds until there was little left of these two cocky teen boys but a few empty bottles of hair bleach and two sets of baggy clothes. They whupped us (in that Pacific-Northwest-liberal crumbled-our-best-arguments-over-grilled-salmon sort of way).

A few years later, as my realm of experience widened and I made friends in the gay and lesbian community, this love of Eminem was called into question once more. The general sentiment being "you're too enlightened to like this stuff." Once again, I careened back against anyone who challenged me with half-baked rebuttals. And once again, I can only imagine that I lost.

Because, like any argument defending bigoted, hateful speech, it's flawed at its core. It's bound up in a quagmire of hypocrisy—the same jester who makes his living off of words is telling us that words don't matter. But we know words matter and, in truth, so does Eminem. If words matter, if words *mean*, then mean words matter too.[7]

The fact is that Eminem's early albums saw him killing his wife (twice explicitly in extended role-plays, a few more times in subtler mid-verse references), bashing gays, beating women, and committing a host of other ugly crimes that aren't commonly associated with Maslow's values. Justice, right action, and benevolence are all mentioned as qualities that typify Maslow's self-actualizers—content-wise, Eminem's discography reveals a sparsely stocked pantry when it comes to such things.

Sure, the crimes Eminem raps about are made up crimes upon humanity (Zadie Smith once deftly pointed out that for the attention Eminem got about violence, he carried out almost none of it)—but the fact is: words lead to thoughts, which lead to prevailing beliefs, which lead to actions. Words have power even in the clumsiest hands; when wielded by someone with the prowess of Eminem, words can slice to the bone.

Does Eminem know this?

When his use of the word "faggot" was criticized, Eminem explained to the website *NY Rock* that he didn't mean it as an attack on homosexuals, he meant it as "taking away your manhood. You're a sissy. You're a coward."[8] Which is apparently the only worse argument than whatever my cousin and I were coming up with to defend him. Clearly, Eminem was identifying "gay" with being *less than*. But somehow he was trying to redefine the meaning. Without the aid of a backing beat, the argument fell flat. Changing a word's meaning isn't that easy and Eminem knows it—which is why he never says the N-word on wax.[9] He obviously realizes that certain words hold a charge and can't be said, even by someone who wants to be excused as a prankster.

Even more thoughtful arguments—like the fact that Eminem often uses aggressive speech in intentionally ironic or provocative ways, or that Marshall Mathers III's worst diatribes are spoken through his various avatars (Eminem, Slim Shady) or characters like Stan and Ken Keniff—are broken down easily, specifically because of Eminem's refusal to distance himself from the thoughts he puts on record. To this point, the *NY Rock* interview actually weakened all of these arguments. Why couldn't Em have just dismissed every single lyric he ever wrote as fiction? Why didn't he just say: "assume every word I've ever said is spoken by a character?" Then he could have been off scot-free under the precedent set down by masterworks like *Lolita*: "It's not wrong if it's a character!"

Had he chosen to hide behind the veils of persona and character, we as an audience would have been intellectually obligated to separate man and artist. The problem is, this argument doesn't work for Eminem. It's too detached, and Em, in the Tupac tradition, has made a point to never be emotionally detached about a single verse that he spits. The prevailing thought on Tupac is that he *felt* everything he said when he was creating it. No matter how contradictory it was with his other philosophies (compare lyrics of "Keep Your Head Up" to "Wonda Why the Call U Bitch"), in the moment he was writing or spitting a verse Tupac felt it down to his bones. This is perhaps where Pac's influence on Eminem is most acute: the emotional urgency of every line."[10] Pac went real thug plenty of times, and stood behind his thug talk in score of interviews. The *NY Rock* interview proved the same for Eminem: he wouldn't hide behind his characters—which had the result of making his content seem that much more toxic.

And with that, I have officially become one of the content-focused nags that Eminem mocks on record. In "The Way I Am," for example, he mocks listeners who can't hear past lyrics. And I'll cop to that, as old and uncool as saying so makes me feel. But alas—

I still like to listen to his music, quite often in fact. At the gym, in the car, when I'm cleaning my apartment—I rap along, editing out the words (or songs) that I find over-the-top offensive. And, ten-plus years after the Eminem cultural zeitgeist, I think I'm ready to say why I tolerate his content and continue listening: he's too proficient at rapping for someone who loves rap to ignore.[11] He's too good to throw out because of his content alone. To bring it back to Maslow: though Marshal Mathers III doesn't represent himself on record as self-actualized, he has certainly fully actualized his talent. He is indeed pushing into the "farther reaches."

Which is what I really set out to write about in the first place.

INTERLUDE:

We have now entered into the tricky land of tastes, which are, as we all know, variable. It's not my contention that Eminem is the best rapper ever. That is too vague and too broad. The canopy of "rap" is not as wide spreading as the canopy of "art," but it's still far too big to declare a "best." Rap, like literature, is full of genres and sub-genres and evolves too quickly to crown a grand champion.

BUT:

In all of art, if criticism is to have any place in the world at all, there must be some sort of absolute value. Maybe not for the artist's entire body of work, but at least for a certain skill set. Example: If I say that Hemingway is the best writer ever, you'd dismiss me. But if I say: "Hemingway knew how to construct clear, evocative, declarative sentences as well as any writer we've had in the past hundred years," my point deserves thoughtful consideration.

So let me apply that level of specificity to Eminem: "When he decides to spit heat—which I'll define as the act of compiling a verse that dances along the razor's edge of contained vs. uncontained rage—there is no one in today's current hip-hop landscape who can rhyme with as much dexterity, cleverness and unarguable skill."

That is as close to undebatable as I can imagine getting, but it's all still just one man's humble opinion. And might be heavily affected by the fact that Eminem's rise to prominence came during my teenage years, when I was just discovering the intensity of what music could make me feel, or (as the editor of this book pointed out in conversation) the fact that we are both white. But as long as we're talking about taste, I'll say that Eminem isn't my favorite rapper (Chali 2na), my favorite rap philosopher (Talib), or my favorite on-mic persona (Tupac). Hell, Eminem isn't even my favorite white rapper. Being from the Pacific Northwest and having a very similar well of experience, I have fallen under the spell of Macklemore's humanistic content and in-love-with-the-world vibe.

BUT:

If my life depended on me picking a single rapper to write a single verse that showed verbal-gymnastics, a complexity of rhyme and the ability to be razor-clever without ever losing the thread of the verse's central thesis—I would pick Eminem.

100 times out of 100.

Who wouldn't?

END INTERLUDE.

To illustrate just how proficient Eminem is, let's look at rhyme scheme. Rap started with a simple: A, A, B, B, C, C couplets.

"Took a walk last week, I went to the store, (A)

Dude acted like I'd never been there before. (A)
Went to the fridge to grab some milk, (B)
Thought 'I'll go vegan'—Almond Silk!" (B)

As the art form evolved, rappers quickly adopted internal rhyme (rhyme that occurs within the line before the final rhyming word): B, B, A, C, C, A

"It was a treat to move my feet, shuffle right to the store," (B,B, A)
Bought milk (Almond Silk!) and took a left out the door." (C, C, A)

Now allow me to chart out the rhyme scheme for Eminem's verse from the song "No Love." Sadly, the lyrics permission people can't allow me to include the entire verse—but a glance at the video or a read through on RapGenius.com is probably well warranted. The verse is 90 seconds long, I'll chart out four lines:

Starting with that adrenaline phrase let's look at the rhyme scheme:
A, A, B-C-D
E, E, B-C-D
EF, EF, EF, C-D
C, GH, GH, C-D

This is all done in the space of a few lines—Eminem rockets forward and back, turning flips and pirouettes, without ever taking the time to catch his breath. He reaches back to pick up rhyme-threads that the listener assumed he'd left behind. It's breathtaking.

In Zadie Smith's piece "The Zen of Eminem," she quotes the song "Square Dance" at length. Her essay ends with a challenge to the various haters: can you do what Em makes look so easy in "Square Dance"? Can you rhyme like that? Can you? And it certainly is an excellent verse. But it's also filled with a lot of gibberish words. Which is to say: it's good Em, but not the best he can spit. Smith's whole thesis is "look how good this guy is"—and yet that verse never came up once in the dozens of fan-polls and hip-hop-head chat rooms speculating on the rapper's best bars (this is a topic that people apparently love to argue over) that I uncovered while preparing this essay. No devoted fan I've spoken with has ever even mentioned it as among Em's best verses. That's not to say the gauntlet that Smith lays down to readers is wrong—it's still 100 percent right. It's just a little bit like challenging a young playwright to risk comparing their work to *Titus Andronicus* rather than going full bore and dropping *Julius Caesar* on them. Smith told people (correctly): "Look at this, you can't do this!" and she did it using a B+ verse at best.

A better verse to investigate might be Eminem's portion of the Jay-Z song "Renegade." Em's portion of the song is so famous, that it has actually been used as a knock against Jay-Z in his battles with other rappers (famously, in Nas's "Ether.") The verse serves up a smorgasbord of literary techniques:

alliteration, onomatopoeia, internal rhyme ... it's staggering when added together. But the true brilliance comes in the irony of the verse's climatic (but not final) thrust when Em points out the irony of the media's fascination with him while riding the beat so tight that every single syllable seems to be hermetically sealed to the bassline.

Allow me one last attempt to fully encapsulate Eminem's level of mastery:

In recent albums Eminem's content has faced another challenge. Not because of what he's saying this time, but because of the words he uses. Rappers are notoriously falling victim to rhyme repetition (both in their own catalogs and across the hip-hop community). The perfect example of this is any verse that uses "cry, dry, eye" as rhyming words—the three words are so horrendously overused that any verse containing them automatically feels stale and lazy (it already did when Snoop used it all those years ago). As if to avoid such redundancy, Eminem has increasingly made use of complex food references in his verses. Just a cursory examination reveals nods to condiments (a great mustard-mustered riff in "You're Never Over"), desserts (a play on words about roasting marshmallows in "No Love") and Mac & Cheese (a layered, extended metaphor in "I'm on Everything"). Each reference is purposeful and hits on two levels. It's as if Em is playing the magician, letting his hands be bound over and over and over then shedding the ropes in a matter of seconds and appealing to the crowd with a shrug—"I'm sorry, I'm that good."

He is that good.

He really is. And acumen like Eminem's makes audiences incredibly tolerant.[12] Perhaps one day, Eminem will be as tolerant of others as we're willing to be of him. Perhaps he'll start chasing Maslow's higher values and head toward self-actualization. Perhaps he'll be the one-time rogue who somehow finds a way to use his power for good.

Or perhaps not.

I don't know.

What I *do* know is that Eminem is going to war with words, linking rhymes in a way that is unique and creative and wickedly clever. He is approaching the absolute value of MCing excellence. He way out in the wild territory of what it means to be exceptional, slicing through the spiky brambles and thick vines that block his path. He is deep in the farthest reaches, twisting, spiraling, cavorting lyrically in a way that no one else can.

And so, despite my own objections, I listen. I ignore songs like "Kim" and favor songs like "Mockingbird." I close my eyes, I zone—and keep coming away amazed.

Chapter Notes

1. Abraham H. Maslow, *The Farther Reaches of Human Nature* (New York: Penguin Compass, 1971), 60.

2. The biggest exceptions here seem to directly correspond with Eminem's well-documented periods of heavy drug use, though a close listen to his various mix tapes and dis songs, reveals that rushing certain concepts to market has also, on occasion, hurt Em's standard of quality.

3. Maslow, 42.

4. Old Dominion Homecoming, 2009, http://www.youtube.com/watch?feature=player_embedded&v=zkFCUYlsG9M.

5. "I'm Back," The Marshall Mathers LP.

6. With Em, unlike other writers I admire (Hemingway, Fitzgerald), his art really was the only piece that ever captivated my attention. I could tell you Hemingway's favorite drink and list his most passionate affairs, but know very little about Eminem's personal life. Perhaps that's because the version that he presents on wax is so very interesting, real and raw all on its own, it doesn't need to be tabloidized.

7. I'm not saying for even a moment that the work should have been banned or commercially limited somehow. I'm only saying that it's hard for anyone who describes themselves as non-misogynistic, and non-homophobic (and on the path toward self-actualization) to say: "As a matter of taste, this suits me just right."

8. Gabriella, "Interview with Eminem: It's Lonely at the Top," *NY Rock* (http://www.nyrock.com/interviews/2001/eminem_int.asp).

9. Not exactly true, Eminem can be on early bootlegs calling best friend Proof "my nig" but occurrences like this disappeared when he hit the mainstream. In "Criminal," Eminem plays with this by leading listeners to believe that a certain rhyme will end with the N-word, then he leaves the rhyming word off completely.

10. "Square Dance," *The Eminem Show*.

11. There is a precedent for this type of permissiveness with regards to mega-skilled artists. Film director Roman Polanski gave a thirteen-year-old girl Quaaludes and forcibly sodomized her, but *Chinatown*, *Rosemary's Baby*, and *The Pianist* have yet to be removed from the canon. As recently as three years ago, he had a cadre of Oscar-winning Hollywood stars petitioning for all charges to be dropped. As horrifying as it sounds, letting Eminem slide for hate-speech is far, far, far more reasonable.

12. Roman Polanski would never have gotten the pass that he got from Hollywood if instead of *Chinatown* his resume was made up of only the *Scary Movie* franchise. That is an ironclad fact. Likewise, Eminem wouldn't be nearly so successful with the same content and the flow of a less precise rapper, like Diddy (which is why Diddy's content has always had to be much more neutral).

The White Negro Gone Mad:
Race and Pathology in Eminem's
Construction of Slim Shady

Miles White

In his penetrating essay "Eminem: The New White Negro," Carl Hancock Rux[1] characterizes the platinum blonde/platinum-selling rapper as an outcast minstrel rebel superstar icon of the outlaw reborn as a postmodern pop culture hip-hop badass. More or less. Rux calls attention to the extremes Eminem has gone to in order to transform himself not simply into the new post–Elvis, late-millennium, white-meat Other doing racialized vaudevillian slapstick, a wigged out incarnation of what Ice Cube might call "The Wigga Ya Love to Hate"—a white cat doing a hopped-up machismo Black Like Me drag so viciously surreal that when he broke on the scene America was not sure whether to hate him or buy up all his records, so naturally (given the intense ambivalence of American attitudes around bad boys and racial carnivalesque) it did both. Rux's analysis notwithstanding, I think it is possible to examine Eminem more deeply in the context of his most controversial put-on and alter egoistic creation Slim Shady, the Monster Mack Daddy who conflates previous incarnations of the black male as Boogey Man into a single serving. But before we get to that, we must consider this: In many ways, hip-hop music and culture since the 1980s have brought issues of gender and race to the forefront of popular culture studies. Yet scholarly studies have largely failed to fully investigate the ways in which hardcore styles of hip hop in particular have recast ideas about masculinity and the performance of the body, and how these have both come to be informed by a dominating racial subtext that is at once obvious yet seemingly invisible. The performance practices of contemporary mainstream rap music privileges hypersexual and spectacularized representations of the black male body that have subsequently come to be performed by social actors of other races—but this is not your great-great-granddaddy's T. D. Rice Jump Jim Crow shtick; this takes playing the Other to a whole 'nother level. Yet much of the scholarship in this musical culture has not fully addressed how representations of black masculinity engaged as performance art in global popular media have perpetuated pejorative racial feelings and attitudes that demonize young black males even while such representations have become increasingly appropriated by others as totems of "authentic" masculine performance.[2]

In a genre with no shortage of contradictions it is also somewhat ironic that the victims of demonization are also the primary perpetuators of these representations. Nonetheless, contemporary hard and hardcore styles of hip-hop performance and the culture of masculinity that surrounds them have reformulated and helped to articulate new models of self and identity for many young males over the last quarter century. Objectified, fetishized, and commodified representations of black males and the performances of masculinity associated with them have been appropriated in any number of global geographical locations using the same language of codes, signs, and gestures that have exerted a defining influence on young male constructions of identity in the United States. This obscures the fact that the gender constructions and expressions of masculinity popularized in hip hop with the arrival of Run-D.M.C. in the early 1980s are not *naturalized* any more than any gender performance is somehow natural in itself. James Messerschmidt argues in his book *Flesh and Blood* that "men and women construct varieties of gender through specific embodied practices"[3] that replicate and perpetuate certain kinds of "hegemonic masculinities" as dominant forms of masculine gender practices in a given social milieu. Hegemonic masculinities, he suggests, are "culturally honored, glorified, and extolled at the symbolic level and through embodied practice, and constitute social structural dominance over women as well as over other men."[4] Hegemonic masculinities are constructed in relation to other kinds of masculinities including subordinated masculinities, oppositional masculinities, and complicit masculinities, for instance, and represent different strategies to the practice of masculine gender performance. These gender practices are not all equal, however, "because certain forms have more influence than others in particular settings."[5] What this opens up is the possibility of yet another kind of masculine performance based on racial tropes.

Hardcore hip-hop performance by African American youth, on the one hand, reinscribes the black male as the historical "Bad Nigger" figure, who John W. Roberts describes in his book *From Trickster to Badman: The Black Folk Hero in Slavery and Freedom* as a lawless man feared by blacks and whites alike during American slavery since he exerted his power by resisting all social and moral control. The kind of man regarded as a Bad Nigger tended to be viewed as a threat not only by whites but by other blacks as well since he acted in his own self-interest. Antebellum slaves who were labeled Bad Niggers did not simply provoke confrontation with whites by disregarding the rules of their masters but "were also as likely to unleash their fury and violence on their defenseless fellow sufferers" as on their masters.[6] Black slaves may have relished the defiance and the rebellious exploits of such men but did not celebrate them as heroic figures even though they stood up to white authority; such men refused "to accept the values of the black community as binding on them,"[7] and their rebelliousness tended not to be in service to their community. After emancipation, "Whites continued to view almost any black person who challenged their authority or right to define black behavior and social roles" as a Bad Nigger type who could be socially sanctioned or killed.[8] A number of black heroic figures emerged in the late nineteenth century, Roberts points out, who became catalysts for black heroic creation as a necessary step toward community building, but are more properly referred to by the term Badman.[9] This type of figure tended to exert a positive influence on the world around him because his interests and law-breaking were more often than not in service to a community under siege by racial oppression. Roberts accuses folklorists of having erroneously and "consistently painted a portrait of this figure [the heroic Badman] as a champion of violence, directed primarily at the black community"[10] rather than as a man of good works. Consequently, this portrayal of the black folkloric Badman "as a source of unrelieved violence in the black community"[11] has marked him as a source of fear "and not a model of emulative behavior adaptable to real-life situations"[12] or as a normative expression of black heroic ideals. What this has led to is confusion between the redemptive rebelliousness of the Badman and the anti-heroic Bad Nigger. It is a mistake, Roberts argues, to use the terms Badman and Bad Nigger interchangeably or as synonyms for a black male character type unlikely to be differentiated between by whites.

In the styles of hard (think Run-D.M.C., LL Cool J, and Public Enemy) and hardcore (think Schoolly D, Ice-T, and N.W.A.) rap performance and that emerged in the 1980s, the politicized black radical and militant of the 1960s gave way to the depoliticized nihilism of the gangbanger and the thug. Furthermore, the urge toward a ghettocentric authenticity posited on inner city street culture helped to elevate the Bad Nigger, in the guise of the Badman, as an iconic figure in rap music performance. The term "bad" has always more or less suggested an empowered and liberatory masculine performance in black folklore, and men labeled bad certainly skirted both sides of the law. In late twentieth century hip-hop culture however, it also reflected an aggrieved masculinity (read this as pissed off) and an increasing disengagement with mainstream society, its norms, and mores by young black males—real social outsiders and outlaws who found their Post-Civil Rights Era Asses marginalized, disenfranchised and abandoned to America's impoverished neighborhoods and drug-infested ghettos. The New School rap performer aspired to a heroic badness by embracing an antiheroic niggerhood. Run-D.M.C. were Badmen from the jump-off—with songs like "It's Like That" and "Proud to Be Black" engaging issues around race and class while "King of Rock" and "Walk This Way" bumrushed the Rock 'n' Roll Ivory Tower with hard beats and the B-Boy Lean. Public Enemy were Badmen with Nat Turnerish uppityness and black nationalist rhetoric that back talked white hegemony like they were channeling Malcolm × before the *Hajj*. Thrown in the mix was LL Cool J, one of the earliest rappers to spectacularize the black male body by ripping off his shirt to show off a powerful, muscled physique as he took on the aggressive persona of a rhetorical prize fighter. In the introduction to his 1987 song "I'm Bad" he also dramatized himself as a criminal and a fugitive in conflict with society in general and the law enforcement community in particular, a motif that would become integral to rap music's thug-masculinist meta-narrative over the next decades. Greg Dimitriadis recalls that it was LL Cool J who "began to wed aggression against dominant society … with an often racialized masculinity."[13] "I'm Bad" was critically important in establishing a new type of pop culture social actor defined by aggressive masculine performance, race, social deviance, class and geographic location, inasmuch as the rules of the new *keeping it real* game meant that credibility was everything, that credibility depended on authenticity, and that authenticity was bestowed on the mean streets of the black inner city. The implication of these factors all coming together, writes Dimitriadis,

> is that being (metaphorically, of course) aggressive, violent, and "bad" would make one "authentically" black. L.L. Cool J's image is thus tied into a kind of racialized macho posturing. Indeed, he embraced these ideals in full force, often posing shirtless to show off his muscular figure and often boasting of his boxing prowess. His second album, *Bigger and Deffer,* sports a photo of him working out on a heavy bag, complete with thick gold chains and Kango hat. This image—the violent and aggressive young black male—would lodge itself in the collective psyche of America and its perception of rap music, drawing as it did on decades of affectively invested, dominant cultural discourses and ideologies.[14]

The West Coast rap group N.W.A. (Niggaz with Attitude) became the poster boys for Bad Nigger shenanigans when they kicked the 1988 album *Straight Outta Compton,* which set in motion a sea change in American popular music and culture that found white adolescent males fascinated by young black men weaving narratives of ghetto violence and shootouts with cops told in the most graphic of language. N.W.A. introduced a style of hardcore rap that would reintroduce into popular culture historical representations of black males as the hypermasculine brutes and hypersexual bucks turned street-hardened gangbangers and drug dealers, told in ghetto narratives involving casual black-on-black violence, drug trafficking, misogyny, and gunplay. These were bad men for sure. Bad because they were dangerous, because they had guns and were shooting up the place, but not because they were redemptive expressions of black rage. They were abhorred not only by liberal whites but by middle class blacks as well because they gleefully assaulted the values of both. N.W.A. bore no resemblance to the Badman of African American folklore but played instead to the trope of the Bad Nigger re-contextualized within inner-city street gang culture and its ethos of masculine behavior translated into performance art rendered in the register of the real. That this model of masculine performance was eventually appropriated in the construction of self by many adolescent white males was predictable given the history of such appropriations in popular culture. White consumers of this edgier style of rap music adopted models of powerful black male performance even if (*especially* if) those models were based on deviance and criminality. In *Nobrow: The Culture of Marketing, the Market¬ing of Culture*, John Seabrook acts out the seduction of the black sociopath for young middle-class white males in the 1990s. He is walking down the street in New York City listening to the Notorious B.I.G.'s 1994 song "Ready to Die," wearing "a black nylon convict-style cap, a fashion I picked up from the homeys in the rap videos."[15] Later, riding the subway, empowered by his own bad ass imagery and Biggie's powerful music, he imagines himself a menacing figure who lets "the gangsta style play down into my whiteboy identity, thinking to myself, 'Man you are the illest, you are sitting here on this subway and none of these people are going to FUCK with you, and if they do FUCK with you, you are going to FUCK them up. What's MY muthafuckin' name?'"[16]

The performance of black masculinity by whites and other youth who participate in hardcore hip hop also recalibrate another recurring trope in American culture, that of the White Negro, given perhaps its most graphic explication by Norman Mailer in his 1957 essay "The White Negro: Superficial Reflections on the Hipster," which celebrates the pleasures of opting out of whiteness and acting out behind the mask of blackness. Mailer's white hipster represents "a new breed of adventurers, urban adventurers who drifted out at night looking for action with a black man's code to fit their facts."[17] In Mailer's hipster manifesto, the Negro male satisfies himself in the worst of perversion, promiscuity, pimpery, drug addiction, rape, razor-slash, bottle-break, what-have-you, the Negro discovered and elaborated a morality of the bottom, an ethical differentiation between the good and the bad in every human activity from the go-getter pimp (as opposed to the lazy one) to the relatively dependable pusher or prostitute.[18]

The White Negro, writes historian and literary critic Louis Menand, "is built up from the proposition that American Negroes by virtue of their alienation from mainstream American society, are natural existentialists who not only have better orgasms but who also appreciate the cathartic effects of physical violence."[19] The aim of the White Negro and hipster has always been the imitation of the Bad Nigger in order to, as Mailer writes, be "with it." What this has ultimately evolved into is a politics of racialized masculine desire in which it is no longer desirable to merely be *with it* but *to be it,* so that it is no longer necessarily the case, as Menard writes, that "the sort of gender roles central to Mailer's imagination have disappeared from the repertoire of contemporary identity."[20] If Mailer's writing seems to enact a panic about masculinity and its fate, as Menand suggests, then he might well be pleased with the way things have turned out, since White Negroism has become de rigueur for the performance of maleness among legions of adolescents in post-hip hop America, and the Bad Nigger has become its most defining trope.

Against this background we are able to locate Eminem and his alter ego Slim Shady, whose performance of the White Negro hellcat hipster is executed with adroit musicality and lyrical brilliance but informed by malevolent themes including murder, misogyny, homophobia, extreme cruelty and torture. Eminem nods to the notorious pimp and hustler Iceberg Slim, a man celebrated and imitated by contemporary hustlers, gangstas and many in the rap game, in constructing the moniker for his evil twin, but chooses to appropriate the last name rather than play on the well-used first name picked up on by Ice-T, Ice Cube, Vanilla Ice, Kid Frost, Ice Berg, and others. In Shady, we have a figure who is a walking synonym for everything the name implies—suspicious, shifty, suspect, devious, dodgy, dubious, fishy, underhanded, and morally ambiguous—meaning he is capable of damn near anything. But Slim Shady did not stumble upon the horrific by happenstance. He was built for it. In the Detroit-based rap collective D12, Eminem, the only white member in the group, experimented with horrific and ghoulish material that incorporated the violent realism of Hollywood slasher films and the hip-hop underground cult of horrorcore.[21] Shady became his pissed off social miscreant Zip Coon with a chip on his shoulder and a sadomasochistic mean streak.

Eminem's background growing up surrounded by family dysfunction in economically depressed neighborhoods where he forged friendships with black males allowed him to credibly negotiate discourses around blackness, masculinity, social marginalization, and inner city desolation in a way that Vanilla Ice, for example, could not. But if he grew up rough, Eminem also understood the implications of hip hop's hardcore aesthetic and its move toward themes of aggression, pathology, deviance, criminal behavior, explicit language, and violence.

Slim Shady was his solution to the dilemma of acting out the Bad Nigger as social outlaw in a manner that was for him in some way more authentic if only because he was able to draw from his own life experiences. Consequently, Eminem did not portray himself as a gangbanger or street thug, but as a victim of childhood abuse, deprivation, and perhaps depravity, unable to cope with the emotionally damaged women in his life, self-medicating himself with prodigious amounts of booze and drugs and acting out revenge fantasies against everybody who had hurt him. Slim Shady enacts then, the victim turned perpetrator, an abused child as adult abuser capable of sadistic scenarios of cruelty, transgression, and violation because maybe this is what he knows best, or at least knows well. In taking his personal torments to egregious extremes however, Shady offers not simply a Bad Nigger, but a sociopathic composite (as the term "wigger" suggests), a simulacra based on darkly pejorative presuppositions around the black male in the American racial imagination. Like N.W.A., Eminem makes himself out to be "bad" by raising holy hell, running through the crowd pulling everybody's britches down. He is a provocateur for sure, but there is nothing redemptive in his behavior because, other than his running cronies, he does not see himself as part of a community whose values he shares. Instead, Eminem's Bad Wigger, bilked and 'bused, doesn't see that he owes anybody jack so everybody becomes a target of his sociopathic mayhem, even if it means he must humiliate, torture, rape and murder. Eminem follows the Beastie Boys, Vanilla Ice, and other white performers who have appropriated the Bad Nigger trope in the move to come off as hardcore—all "take their cues from a savage model"[22] of the black male as rapist, murderer, criminal, and social deviant taken to the extreme—he is Norman Mailer's alienated white hipster turned Alfred Hitchcock's Norman Bates, a mentally disturbed loser gone stark raving mad. As Run writes:

> Niggaz may talk bad about bitches and they baby's mama—Eminem brutally murders his. Niggaz may have issues regarding absent fathers or dysfunctional mothers—Eminem comically exposes their dysfunctions, and hangs his mother's pussy high up on a wall for all the world to see. Niggaz may be misogynist, may boast of sexual superiority and sexual indiscretions with a multitude of women, may commonly relegate women to just

another piece of ass prime for the taking status—but Eminem drugs the bitch, fucks the bitch, moves on to the next bitch.[23]

Eminem's 1999 *The Slim Shady LP* brings together cartoonish representations of the brute taken past the reprehensible to the repulsive. On the album track "Just Don't Give a Fuck" he plays with tropes of addiction and multiple personalities and a summoning up of internalized demons as Shady traverses themes of extreme violence, drug use, despair, bestiality, and derangement—he declares himself a half man, half animal whose litany of decadence includes doing acid, smack, coke, and smoking crack. The song "97 Bonnie and Clyde" depicts a macabre scene in which he has stuffed his murdered wife's corpse into the trunk of his car and dumps it off a pier while his young daughter assists him. In "Guilty Conscience" Shady eggs on three desperate men to commit a series of heinous crimes—an underage girl is drugged and raped; a betrayed husband shotguns his cheating wife and her lover in bed. West Coast rap producer Dr. Dre, who has produced most of Eminem's work and who appears in this song, has always brought a racial value to the music that in vernacular parlance might be expressed in terms of a "ghetto pass" that bolstered Eminem's street credibility much the same way that Def Jam opened up the streets to the acceptance of the Beastie Boys. Dr. Dre was the perfect foil for Eminem's transgressive shenanigans given his credentials as a member of N.W.A., the group that single-handedly took gangsta rap's malevolent metanarrative and transformed it from a style into a genre. If Dr. Dre threw down the gauntlet, Eminem was all too eager to pick it up where N.W.A. left off and take it further—balls out lunacy, mad dog antics, and the kind of potty mouth lyricism guaranteed to get an official PMRC[24] panic alert stamped on the front of every album.

On the 2000 album *The Marshall Mathers LP*, Eminem again plays with multiple personalities and horrific themes of rape and murder in songs such as "Kill You" (where he acts out the rape of his estranged mother) and "Kim" (in which he murders his ex-wife by slitting her throat). In live performance, he often underscored references to horror/slasher films like *The Texas Chainsaw Massacre, Psycho, Halloween* and *Scream* by appearing with such affectations as a hockey mask and a chainsaw. During the 2000 "Up In Smoke" tour he infamously drew out a large knife and repeatedly stabbed a life-sized effigy of his baby's mama. For his 2002 record *The Eminem Show*, Eminem displays a much broader diversity of thematic material that puts some distance between Eminem the entertainer and Slim Shady the monster. After the somewhat retrospective album *Encore* in 2004, he retired from performing for several years, during which time he underwent drug rehabilitation. It appeared that Eminem was sending a message that he was rethinking himself and the nature of his music, and that he might kill off the homicidal Shady—in a skit at the end of *Encore,* Shady is heard being shot. In 2009, however, Eminem came back with bloodlust and vengeance when he released *Relapse,* a record that contains perhaps his most horrific scenarios of drug-induced violence and schizophrenic brutality. The record opens with a nightmare in which Slim Shady is revived (in slasher films the killer is always dispatched in the end only to recover for a final bloody encore) before launching into the ghoulish "3 a.m.," narrated by a psycho-pathic, drug-crazed serial killer who enjoys the slashing, slicing, and gash-ing he inflicts on his victims. On the song "Insane" Shady recounts being sodomized by his stepfather and describes sexual acts of astonishing lewd-ness. Eminem may never be able to kill off Slim Shady for good because he apparently needs this nefarious character in order to perform the ventril-oquistical Zip Coonish exorcism of his inner demons, knowing that in the end he can always protest: the black guy did it.

Eminem and his success in the popular mainstream with white ado-lescent youth illustrates how the complexities of racial discourse and inter-action in post-hip hop America are more contradictory than those of the past because they occur in a "post-racist"[25] environment. By this, Richard Thompson Ford does not mean to suggest that racism is a thing of the past but that it implies a new stage of racial behavior in which certain ideas and practices remain pervasive. The post-racist consumer of hardcore hip hop unabashedly indulges the stereotypes of the black thug, the pimp, the drug dealer, the crack whore, and the hustler, "free to be explicitly and crudely bigoted because he does so with tongue planted firmly in cheek."[26] It is, as he suggests, racism without racists since there may be no racist intent *per se* in such representations, but the acting out of reductionist racial fantasies merely becomes "the continuation of racism by other means."[27] It is racism by other means when it perpetuates racist stereotypes in the American racial imagination around black people in much the same way as nineteenth-century minstrelsy performance framed pejorative representational prac-tices regarding African Americans in popular culture for the next hundred years, or in the way that *The Birth of A Nation* was accepted at face value by many whites and gave rise to a resurgence of the Klu Klux Klan in the American South in the early 1920s. While there may have been no racist intent *per se* in either of these cultural projects, both had real and lasting implications on racial attitudes in American culture. This was no less true of 1950s rock 'n' roll in that, while it certainly had a transforming affect on American culture and mainstreamed African American rhythm and blues, it nonetheless foregrounded white grown-up fears of race mixing, miscegenation, and desegregation such that contemporary rock itself can be seen as founded on a distancing racial subterfuge that continues to trouble the bifurcated ways in which Americans categorize and consume popular music.

What has shifted since 1950s rock 'n' roll and the racial attitudes that it exposed is the ways in which the cultural and political currency of the black body has accrued in value over time so that the racial exchange rate of mainstream whiteness continues to lose interest. White hip-hop performers and consumers now aspire to an authenticity that, rather than attempting to obscure racial subtexts and the hijacking of black subjectivity, covets, foregrounds, and celebrates them. In the hip-hop generation, performing the black body, whether on the stage or in the street, has become the litmus test for a new cultural ideal of authenticity around masculinity. The "Afro-Americanization of White youth"[28] has seen white kids adopt the sartorial style, language, and often the speech patterns of inner-city black youth, appropriating the affective gestures of blackness as the performance of the everyday even if it often amounts to parody and racial hooliganism. It is this territory that Eminem works through his tricked out racial trickster figure, although the irony of the carnivalesque in which he is engaged is not lost on him. On songs like "Without Me" he is able to draw a line between his own white Negroism and that of Elvis and understand why they both succeeded in expanding the white audience for music styles dominated by black males. Both Elvis and Eminem are products of their times but in many ways are inverse to each other. Where Elvis's racial masquerade was a more implicit performance of the black male body in which he was only permitted to flirt with the idea of danger, deviance, and blackness, Eminem transverses and transgresses racial boundaries with an incendiary aplomb and a lunatic's gleeful enthusiasm.

Eminem's popular legacy however, will probably not be as durable as that of Elvis. Slim Shady will ultimately be his undoing if only because by largely basing his appeal on prurient voyeurism and the morality of a bottom feeder, he has painted himself into a fairly small niche that is not likely to age well over time, at least as music. The thing is, Eminem is certainly capable of more mature and challenging work , and he has already given us impressive examples of it in songs like "Stan" or like "White America," like "Lose Yourself" or "Renegade," and "Like Toy Soldiers." But people who go to see Eminem aren't going to hear him do songs like that, and he knows it. They go to see him rip a chainsaw and mutilate an anatomically correct blow-up doll of his ex-wife—sophomoric antics that put the butter on his bread and make the next day's headlines. The price of the ticket is this: unless Eminem comes up with a final act of artistic reinvention, at the end of the day it is Slim Shady who will define his legacy (he knows that, too), and his most enduring material will remain songs like "My Name Is," "'97 Bonnie & Clyde," "Kim," "Guilty Conscience," and "Kill You." In fifty years, nobody will be rapping his rhymes, and he will likely be looked back upon as nothing more than a passing curiosity when his time is done.

Chapter Notes

1. In Greg Tate, ed., *Everything but the Burden: What White People Are Taking from Black Culture* (New York: Broadway, 2003).

2. Selected sections of this essay were previously published in my book *From Jim Crow to Jay-Z: Race, Rap and the Performance of Masculinity* (Urbana: University of Illinois Press, 2011).

3. James W. Messerschmidt, *Flesh and Blood: Adolescent Gender Diversity and Violence* (Lanham: Rowman and Littlefield, 2004), 44.

4. Ibid., 43.

5. Ibid.

6. John W. Roberts, *From Trickster to Bad Man: The Black Folk Hero in Slavery and Freedom* (Philadelphia: University of Pennsylvania Press, 1989), 176.

7. Ibid., 176.

8. Ibid., 177.

9. Ibid., 173.

10. Ibid.

11. Ibid., 174.

12. Ibid.

13. Greg Dimitriadis, Performing Identity / Performing Culture: Hip Hop as Text, Pedagogy and Lived Practice (New York: Peter Lang, 2001), 24.

14. Ibid.

15. Seabrook, p. 3

16. Seabrook, p. 4.

17. Norman Mailer, *Advertisements for Myself* (Cambridge: Harvard University Press, 1992), 341.

18. Ibid. 348.

19. Louis Menand, *American Studies* (New York: Farrar, Straus and Giroux, 2002), 149.

20. Ibid., 155.

21. Horrorcore is a subgenre of hardcore hip hop that indulges macabre themes such as homicide, rape, and torture taken from horror and slasher films but that also borrows from heavy metal rock and bands such as Black Sabbath and Judas Priest, whose material often includes dark themes around death and the occult.

22. Rux, 25.

23. Ibid., 28.

24. The Parents Music Resource Center, formed in 1985, won a battle to have the Recording Industry Association of America put "Parental Advisory" labels on albums that contained content deemed objectionable or unsuitable for minors. The PMRC no longer exists.

25. Richard Thompson Ford, *The Race Card: How Bluffing About Bias Makes Race Relations Worse* (New York: Farrar, Straus and Giroux, 2008), 335.

26. Ibid., 25.

27. Ibid., 337.

28. Cornel West, *Race Matters* (New York: Vintage, 1994), 121.

Neither Black nor White:
Poor White Trash

Sylvie Laurent

Who, really, is the person who goes by the name of Eminem? The willingness to multiply personae (Marshall Mathers, Slim Shady, Rabbit, and above all Eminem) and thus emanate "mythicized versions" of himself[1] makes this a puzzling question. His identities, self-narrated and fictionalized, are multiple, de-centered, unsettled, and undergoing constant reinvention. Yet there is a common thread to his narratives that lies in his denouncing of the intractability of American racism and classism. A singer of rhapsodies as well as a rapper, Eminem is indeed the contemporary and popular bard of the "Poor White Trash," a racial representation used in his music as an allegory for class.[2]

From the former slave Frederick Douglass, who exchanged bread for literacy with the poor white kids, to Harlem writer Ralph Ellison, who escaped the South because of mean whites, poor white trash is, to the black eye, the embodiment of white degeneracy. Zora Neale Hurston illustrates this process magnificently in her novel *Mules and Men*. In chapter V, the character Joe Wiley's storytelling of slave John includes this exposition: "'Bout' this time John seen a white couple come in but they looked so trashy he figgered they was piney woods crackers, so he told'em to g'wan out in the kitchen and git some barbecue and likker and to stay out there where they belong. So he went to callin figgers agin."[3] But if blacks have despised this nemesis, the derogatory label was used and popularized by the white southern elite who expressed their assumptions about poor whites' unworthiness and degeneracy and sought to conjure their fear that such degradation would jeopardize white supremacy. But, as Annalee Newitz and Matt Wray put it in their book *White Trash, Race and Class in America*, "it is not just a classist slur, it's also a racial epithet that marks out certain kind of whites as a breed apart, a dysgenic race unto themselves."[4]

Bufoonery, abjection, shamelessness, and racial in-betweenness characterize those poor whites labeled as such. Denigrated, the poor white trash live on the margins—culturally and socially. It is also because they are perceived as garish parodies of whites who reclaim their whiteness that white trash stereotypes are often considered dangerous to social order. By their filthy destitution and their sometime noisy discourse of social demands, they force "whiteness" to emerge from its invisibility. Eminem plays regularly with these notions in his work, complicating them through his mixture of parody and representation. A social Frankenstein, he disrupts the white middle class, but also encapsulates their anxiety over the threat of social and racial pollution. Precisely, Eminem is a social hybrid and wishes to be a cultural threat.

Arguably, as do other artists, he incarnates the resentful poor white male and represents the American proletariat so often absent from popular discourse. He appears to be following in the footsteps of Elvis Presley or Bruce Springsteen in this respect: the universal voice of those whites who, as he raps himself in "The Real Slim Shady," act like him, talk like him, and are like him. Neither his nihilism nor his anger are new, but he is unique insofar as is the discursive mode he chooses to express his frustration and rage. A white man, he chooses rap over rock, Kurt Cobain's wails and Springsteen's resigned melodies. Interestingly enough, the white-trash characters, in response to the accusation of social and racial breeding with black people have sometimes interiorized this idea and invent themselves as symbolic mulattos. Eminem embraces the suspicion bred by the white-trash mixed identity. By speaking hip hop, he refuses assimilation into a culture of white power and privilege. His irony is meant as social subversion; his voice exists "through a mask darkly."[5]

In this essay I will argue that as a stigmatized figure of the poor white trash, Eminem transgresses the racial boundaries and uses the middle class's social prejudice as a means to debunk American taxonomies. Creolized by class hatred, Eminem embraces the stigma to return it. His self-proclaimed white-trash identity has been constructed on the premises that white trash is a naming practice that thrives on picturesque racial and social stereotypes. Thereupon, he has dramatized his "tainted blood" and "racial unworthiness" through parodic self-portraiture. Furthermore, by displaying an odd, clownish, inappropriate, unsettling whiteness, his public persona allows him to redefine the concept of authenticity in the highly dramatized racial theater of hip hop. Thus, if blackface minstrelsy is seen as one of hip hop's *intertexts* the "white trash" figure transcends this middle-class inspired representation by giving it a sense of transitiveness. With Eminem, blacks can laugh at the white-trash pantomime. The grotesque of the poor white trash is somehow the inversion of the racial process sustaining the minstrelsy.

The audacity of this rapper from Detroit is that he dares to heroize this transgression, his "darkened whiteness"[6] being fully embraced. With a self-proclaimed white-trash identity, a vaudevillian grotesqueness, and the black voice of hip hop, he stands for and embodies interracial camaraderie. His is therefore a subversive wake-up call for an America stuck in a Civil War-era racial ideology where poor whites are inherently closer to rich whites than to poor blacks. In 1935, W. E. B Du Bois calls their racial privilege a "symbolic wage"[7] that poor whites racially earn for not being blacks. In 1964, Bob Dylan puts it beautifully in his song "Only a Pawn in Their Game" when he has a southern politician foment racial antagonism among poor whites.

The Universe of Social Isolation

Eminem's American epic (we can hardly isolate his life from his work) takes us into the universe of trailer parks, social frontiers, into the imaginary "wilderness" and the brutal reality of drug addiction and broken families. His work illustrates a brutal realism. The stages of his chaotic existence are transmitted to us through his music and film with the obvious intention of negating the distance between artist and object. Eminem's life and art are raw, alienating to him and to some extent to his spectators. This "V-Effect"[8] is accentuated by the naturalist dramatization of the environment, oppressive and inspiring all at once. Eminem thus breaks down the fourth wall by mythologizing the urban universe. Detroit is described as a run-down, crime-filled city, stained by graffiti and decay that give it the appearance of a war zone. In such a desolate place, no poor white trash can escape their destiny.

The symbolic spatial organization of Detroit is essential to the self-identity forged by Eminem, that of an individual on the margins. The poorest neighborhoods of Detroit inhabited by the poor whites (one of whom was Eminem) and the nearby black communities, are locations marked by a certain sense of insecurity, not only material but temporal as well. Like exiles' provisional encampments, these neighborhoods give the impression of being no more than stopovers on the path of an interrupted migration. If the black families come from the old South, the poor white trash also evoke an American "elsewhere." Paul Clemens, a writer from Detroit, describes in his autobiography, *Made in Detroit: A South of 8 Mile Memoir,* the neighborhood of his childhood friend Kurt, an area populated by hillbillies who arrived from Appalachia wearing traditional overalls and speaking with mountain accents. These poor white neighborhoods of Detroit and the faces of their inhabitants extemporaneously evoke for Clemens the sharecroppers of James Agee's *Let Us Now Praise Famous Men*.

The final stage of this cultural and spatial marginalization is reached when houses are no longer stone or wood but rather substitute accommodations, mere semblances of neighborhoods. The trailer thus remains the emblem of social exclusion. It is the universe of Eminem's origins, that which he wishes to escape but defines him interminably; in the song "Lose Yourself," the trailer is presented as the place of creation as well as damnation: despite his talent, the rapper is broke and he's got to get out of the trailer park.[9] It is part of Eminem's daily life, the earliest symbolic space of confinement and imprisonment. The trailer is in some ways the matrix from which he developed. But even more than that, it is the metaphor for the social inferno of the poor whites who have no hope of social ascension.

Eminem grew up between his mother's trailer and the refuge of his grandmother's shack, rarely leaving the scorned area of the trailer park. The singer evokes his childhood in the despised neighborhood of Warren: "Across 8 Mile back over there is Warren, which is the low-income white families. We lived over there in a park; people think there're all trailers, but some of 'em are just low-income housing parks.... Some redneck lived over there.... They were the only other white people."[10]

It is noteworthy that Eminem describes "rednecks" as other whites distinct from himself; he is absolutely white trash, but not exactly an ordinary poor white. The territory is still sectioned in this way—gorges of black ghettos that incarnate the terrifying *terra incognita* imagined by the urban middle class. The working-class areas of Detroit still separate blacks and whites, but the spatial segregation is more profound than the racial frontier; poor children, black and white, roam around together in malls reserved for the upper crust.

The symbolic spatial organization of Detroit is essential to the identity that is forged by the individual on the margins, as Eminem narrates on, for example, "Yellow Brick Road." This song calls up several other authors' ideas and imagery. On the one hand, one finds the theme of the perpetual displacement of a poor white who belongs neither with the whites nor the blacks and who must settle on an intermediate space. Excluded from the wealthy neighborhoods and the center of social conformity—the Bel-Air Shopping Centre—he is sent back to the "bad side"; his lyrics (especially in the first verse) express the daily life of a poor white excluded from a society of consumption that rejects him a priori. The use of the present indicative tense nicely shows the permanence of the stigmatizing regard given the artist, even now that he has found fame and fortune. The irony of this discrepancy between Eminem's success and his irreducible image of a "bad poor" person is emphasized in the final verse by the image of the "good old notorious oh well known tracks." Detroit's no-longer-used railroad tracks are very well known by Detroiters. Furthermore, they symbolize the fantasy of escape to one's destiny. The train tracks and its hobo mythology, made famous by Woody Guthrie's "This Train Is Bound for Glory"[11] during the 1940s, are known by the educated rich as well as by Eminem.

They are also linked with a sad urban reality: they got the better of the Mississippi steamboats of Mark Twain's era and later got the better of exhausted cities: since 1950, Detroit has lost half of its population. Eminem's mother herself left Detroit to return to the South. In Eminem's Detroit, the South is a reference to elsewhere. Like Huck Finn and T. S. Eliot, all of his mother's family comes from Missouri. Born in Kansas City, he still retains the imagination of a southerner. This imagination has given poor whites and all those who are socially maladjusted the desire to depart for the dreamed of "elsewhere" represented by the North. And the train tracks, the modern version of Huck's and Jim's small boat, permit one to reach the fantastical promised liberty of the large, fascinating city. Before being abandoned, Detroit attracted the fringes of society. Eminem carries the double burden of the frustration of stifled flight and the painful culture of the exiled. For Eminem, migrating means crossing not the Mason-Dixon line but rather 8 Mile Road.

Paul Clemens reports that the poor whites living along the terrible arterial feel like the last of the Mohicans or General Custer, isolated and threatened. For them, it is an impassible fortification that isolates them from the rest of the world: "8 mile Road was *the wall* and they lived with their back against it."[12] The allusion to James Fenimore Cooper's novel is useful.[13] It reveals the force of community confrontation, even in the unlikely mixed neighborhoods. The black ghettos are the new "wilderness," the somber forest in which Eminem/Hawkeye finds his true identity. Central Detroit's population is nearly eighty percent poor blacks,[14] and is also home to the most visible American social plagues, such as daily crime and race riots, on incomparable scale. For Eminem, belonging to this side of the frontier is therefore a sign of his "mixing" or an initial "passing." If we rely on the representation given in the film *8 Mile*, the road of the same name holds Rabbit/Eminem on the side of African American marginality. He must thus reinvent this axis, regenerating it in order to make a bridge between these areas that permit him to cross over to the ideal of white masculinity while at the same time dramatizing his "black" roots.[15]

In reclaiming the frontier, Eminem chooses to remain between the black world and the white world that he rejects because of its social hostility. Indeed, the greatest discomfort here is that which emerges from the confrontation with the middle class. The "they" that traditionally designates the well off takes in this case the audacious form of "you," as Eminem directly addresses those who both disparage him and (as his performative tone attests) listen to his songs. He thus presents himself as the bad social conscience of America: given how poor he was just a couple of year ago, he never knew he'd have the new houses and cars we aspire to.[16]

The film recounting a fictionalized version of the artist's life takes the name *8 Mile* because the artist was born on the poor, therefore black, side, and traversing the street acts as a metonym of his existence, as he describes in the third verse of the song "8 Mile," wherein he's walking Detroit's border, which is the certificate of authenticity he must have.

Crossing 8 Mile ultimately signifies the emergence from poverty and from marginality in order to find success and potentially finally become rich. Yet, what is most remarkable is the permanence of the white-trash conscience, despite fame and fortune. Eminem never ceases to think like Marshall Mathers and speak as if he still lives in a trailer: he remains tired of being poor and white trash, tired of returning pop bottles for money.[17]

Spokesman for the Silent Majority

Detroit plays a critical role in Eminem's working-class narrative, particularly with regard to racial resentment and rhetorical boundary constructions such as poor white trash. As John Hartigan points out in *Toward a Cultural Analysis of White People,* whiteness in deindustrialized Detroit is less a normative condition than a sense of being an endangered minority in a black metropolis that "remains charged mythic ground, symbolizing for whites in the nation at large both the unsalvageable refuse of the underclass left in the wake of ... post-industrial economy, and the shambles wrought by black civic self-rule."[18] The singer brings about a symbolic, social shift that consists of slipping from the white-trash identity to one that is more general, that of the angry white working man. Lyrics addressing his biographical encounter with dead-end jobs and social resentment are to be understood in that regard. Examples appear in "Rock Bottom" and other songs on *The Slim Shady LP* in particular.

In *8 Mile*, playing an automobile factory worker, Eminem identifies (like Bruce Springsteen) with the white working class. The automobile factories of Detroit were theaters of racial competition between workers. The bitterness of white workers confronted with the slow death of their industry created not only a reemergence of class-consciousness but also a realization of racial "inculpability," what Michael Eric Dyson calls "negative culpability."[19] Because of this, fired white workers were seen as victims themselves. Eminem belonged to the modern working class, that of the precarious service sector and unskilled labor; he worked, temporarily, as a dishwasher and kitchen assistant at the restaurant Gilbert's Lodge,[20] as he recounts on "If I Had."

In 2002, in a still infamous appearance at the MTV Video Music Awards, Eminem was accompanied on stage by several dozen young men dressed like him. He illustrated and modernized in this appearance Michael Novak's well-known concept of "unmeltable ethnics" with great social relevance.[21] As Anthony Bozza summarizes in his biography, "Eminem spoke of situations many of his fans shared—broken homes, dead-end jobs, drug overindulgence—while exploring taboo emotions many could not face—parental hate, gender hate, self loathing."[22] Eminem also sings to bring to light the social paradox of poor whites: they are simultaneously marginalized outcasts, excluded from official society, and representative of the real America, massive in number and muzzled by bourgeois conventions.

Taking Slim Shady as his *nom de guerre*, Eminem seems to be bringing this America out of the darkness. He thus asserts the demographic force of this aggravated nation, resurrecting the subject of the silenced minority from the Nixon era. The nation has discovered those resentful whites of the post-civil right era, some of them being named "white Ethnics," who wish they could go back to the good old days of their supremacy. This trope of the "white backlash" of the angry white male took a sanitized yet relevant form in the 1990s youth. Mathers grasped it, understanding the dialectics of—as president Obama would put it in Philadephia in 2007—"back anger" and "white resentment".[23] The bitterness was passed on from one generation to another. Eminem thus claims to be the spokesperson for a white disaffected youth: he leaves it to himself in "Fight Music" to first internalize a generation's rage and then save kids from parents who could not raise them. He claims that those who speak like him, dress like him, and swear and curse at society like him number at least one million.[24] His clones form a rebellious army who rise up against a detested white America, an image once again articulated on "White America."

He conveys, on songs like this, without hesitation the homophobic insecurities of the bitter white man. The traditional hierarchy in which the poor white affirms his power is founded on race and masculine power. Feminism and homosexuality contradict this semblance of social harmony. The sexual and racial norms are what remain when class is voluntarily silenced.[25] Eminem develops a homophobic rhetoric that aims to ridicule effeminate men who try to seduce him (e.g., "My Name Is") or who are imaginary interlocutors. He repeats the insult "faggot" while sarcastically calling attention to the "queer" world of disguise, clowning, and makeup (e.g., "Marshall Mathers"). He emphasizes here his recovered virility and his sudden social conformity. This condemnation of the painted mask and the bizarre is made more illogical considering that the singer is evolving in this very same universe. Moreover, he responds to the supposed eccentricities of homosexuals with his own verbal peculiarity in songs such as "Criminal" and "My Dad's Gone Crazy."

Hatred of liberals appears in the ambiguous relationship between Eminem and Bill Clinton during the former's first successful years. One cannot help but be amused by the confrontation of two contemporary icons of white trash. Toni Morrison set up the Democratic president as the first "black president," his "black skin" symbolized by his being a poor white. The analogy of black/white trash is complete with Morrison's description of Bill Clinton: "single-parent household, born poor, working class, saxophone-playing, McDonald-and-junk-food-loving boy from Arkansas."[26] Others, particularly John Shelton Reed, have previously analyzed the form of this poor white, southern identity that goes by the name "Bubba."[27] Some have challenged this identity construction that they see as false and meant only to create "intraethnic demonization."[28] The rapper also seems to perceive the limits of this type of media-friendly figure and the contradictions of the educated man who currently belongs to the elite and the general order. In his music video for "The Real Slim Shady," Eminem dresses up as a crude double of Clinton in a scene that parodies the president's affair with Monica Lewinsky. Eminem does this to remind Clinton of who he really is and to empathize with him, while laughing at him at the same time for the public disgrace of which he is the object. The rapper thus does not treat his other white trash gently, reproaching him for his hypocritical preaching of the moral order—of the bourgeois—when his true nature, that of poor white trash, predisposes him to bodily excess and rule breaking. These transgressions are symbolized by fellatio, a hidden act that the two men have both made public. The occurrences of "suck" and "dick" are innumerable and the allusions to Clinton are recurrent (e.g., "Marshall Mathers"[29]). He criticizes the hypocrisy of those, like Hillary Clinton, who condemn the rapper for his verbal obscenities (e.g., "Role Model"[30]).

Having embodied the average American, Eminem readopts white-trash characteristics: a marginalized person who rejects order and conventions, a victim of the self-righteous majority who consider him to be the ideal scapegoat for social issues, notions he dramatizes on songs like "Cleaning Out My Closet." Like blacks, those for whom Eminem speaks are spatially regulated to the margins. They are no longer accused of menacing

society as a whole, as many consider them a disorganized group (and as the
black community now supposedly has a monopoly on being a threat to
society). Rather, they are accused of taking pleasure in embarrassing society.
"These people" shame "good people" by the plagues they inflict upon themselves. Eminem exposes his scars, in particular that of a "wounded whiteness."[31] They damage America's reputation with their scars.

Eminem's Eugenics

The construction of a biological white underclass by early century
eugenicists as an ideological symptom of white deviance and interracial
breeding is key to the "white trash myth."[32] Eminem obviously gives cre-
dence to the theory of genetic inferiority and appropriates the intraracial
class hatred felt by the middle class through those they accuse of being
social parasites. His social degeneration is thus inherited, not only through
the trailer and the city that "trashes," but through blood as well. In reading
Eminem's lyrics, one immediately notices that the "genealogization" of the
white-trash fate is carried to the end by the singer who accuses his own
mother of every wrong, in particular of having transmitted to him this dou-
bled social identity of an all-consuming loathing.

His use of the biological terminology ("bad seeds") complies with the
stigmatizing and "trashing" vernacular of the poor whites from their southern roots. In this sense, his appropriation of the hatred of a class displaced
from its homeland permits him to shift his self-hatred and its suicidal consequences toward that which is seen as a social enigma by the well-to-do
(just as they see Eminem as an enigma himself). His personal sufferance is
a heritage, a burden. To the question "Who is to blame?"—Eminem responds
without hesitation that his mother is responsible for this biological condemnation to the white-trash condition: it is her drug use that resulted in
his disfigurement and insanity.[33]

Eminem's attacks on his mother and on his girlfriend/wife/ex-wife
Kim are in line with the fear of the white race degeneration, for which
women were blamed.[34] Indeed, the fear of the white middle class—like that
of the "trash" patriarchs—is that "their" women cross the "color line" and
mix with the riffraff of the black side In 1930s-era Chicago, a "trashy"
woman was exactly that. In Detroit in the 1970s, the analogy remains the
same. "Bitch" can be read as the combination of female and "trash." Paul
Clemens illustrates the fate of the word in the poor neighborhoods of
Detroit where it appears as a declension of social, slanderous remarks: "'You
know what follows white trash, don't you?' you could hear people asking
each other across front porches. We did. Bitch."[35]

From Doubling to Compagnonnage

The acting out of Eminem's white-trash identity sustains a fierce derisive discourse. He appropriates the conventions of the minstrel aesthetics to reverse them: as for a cakewalk, he pokes fun at the whites who act like blacks while comforting them by displaying his whiteness. His minstrelish performances of whiteness is exemplified in his interpretation of the song "Jimmy Crack Corn," a blackface song thought to have been composed in 1846 by Daniel Decatur Emmet, who may have borrowed it from a black musician.[36] G. Taylor sets up a very stimulating comparison between this racial incertitude of the speaker/Eminem and the character of Jim Crow, as performed by the comedian Daddy Rice, as both men possess a "double identity." Eminem is white, but he addresses white America in the same way that Jim Crow had addressed "O white folks, white folks" ... the popular art form addresses a more larger (and socially more diverse) audience than academic monographs on the subject; ill all ... cases, the vocatives defines that audience is white, but simultaneously defines the speaker as non-white."[37] Of course, poor whites were historically frequently bigoted and racist, masking their own racial indetermination. But authors like Eminem created a reversal of racial stigmatization, reflecting it onto themselves and breaking with the discourse on white privilege. If the rapper made the southern discourse of "good blood" his own, he did not use it to separate "black blood" from "white blood" as do white supremacists.[38] He proclaims his tainted whiteness and transposes racial anxieties onto himself by fashioning himself as the "bad white" or "white beast" willing to kill and terrorize "white America." Metaphorically, creolizing whiteness is indeed killing it.

The rapper is the grotesque fusion of these two constructs (oneself and the other) in the respect that he openly curses his biology—and in doing so declares himself a poor white—while simultaneously adopting black cultural codes, blurring the cultural and pigmentary frontier. The poor white trash is more than ever an agent of subversion.

But the name is still insufficient to signify the strange creature of mixed identity. A term that stems from the impromptu encounter of two defamatory qualifications "nigger" and "white trash" is used in by the middle class: "wigger" or "wigga." This modern form of "white nigger" appeared at the end of the '70s and carried a less insulting connotation, designating whites who were keen on black culture.[39] But for the most part, its use was aimed to denigrate the identity confusion of these whites. It is important to specify that, in the same way that the first occurrences of the term "white trash" around 1830 were among black speakers, the word "wigger" was also probably born from "black speech."[40] The semantic reversal of the term as well as its generalization in the public sphere are exactly coincident with Eminem's success. The rapper so personifies this concept that for some he is even an uber-wigger. Just as he did with the term "trash," Eminem criticizes those who use the term "wigger" while salvaging his own threatened identity: he does speak with an accent, but whites cannot thereby dismiss him and what he's saying.[41]

The wigger who celebrates the blacks' splinter culture expresses his hate of his own culture, that of the white middle class and its conventions that he claims are profoundly "foreign": "At the center of the wigger's role is a critique of white culture.... They are trying to remake themselves into aliens in that atmosphere, and hence showing its power to alienate."[42]

Eminem is therefore, like the most humble black families of his neighborhood, subject to the shame of poverty. He voluntarily integrates himself into the gestures of the blacks with whom he shares the misery and denigration of "good people." Thus his songs tend to erase the racial differential in the name of a common history. He is in a way a comparable figure to George Johnson in Alex Haley's *Roots*.

This poor white comes to live on a plantation, with the slaves, becoming their brother while also using the white masters by acting as the supremacist and the foreman. To the blacks, he initially appears to be a miserable, pitiful lout, "some scrawny po' white boy," drawn out of the woods by hunger. Then, it is to the powerful whites that he appears to be "trash" when asking the landowner to let him work in the fields: "I was born and raised in the fields. I'll work harder'n your niggers." His goal is, in reality, to relieve the black workers. It is because this equivalence is inconceivable to the "plantocracy" that he is hired as a (supposedly racist) foreman, and that this deception manages to work.

George Johnson, friend of the destitute, is from then on called "Ol' George." His adoption by the slaves, unlikely and subversive, finds its origins in the common will to laugh at the powerful, to play the trickster with the master. This African American folkloric practical joker uses laughter to reverse the order of servitude. After having taught George how to be the foreman, how to mimic his viciousness and violence—"You got to learn how to growl an' cuss' an' soun' real mean, to make massa feel like you ain't too easy an' got us goin'"—the blacks and the poor white fraternize in this pretence of a supremacist society, sharing meals and daily work, language and above all social revolt against an order that holds them in comparable contempt: "But Ol' George, too, was treated as one of 'them'—shunned socially, kept waiting in stores till all the other white customers had been taken care of."

Eminem tells a similar story, in which he is judged like his black friends by concerned salespeople in the stores of Detroit's commercial center. One such tale is related on "Yellow Brick Road." He is from the black side, dark and damned by the America of the powerful. It is this aspect that fundamentally distinguishes Eminem from other white rappers such as the Beastie Boys, the imposter Vanilla Ice,[43] or more recently Macklemore, all of whom were middle class. He subverts the equation; he is perceived as and describes himself as black although his skin is white. In a scene from *8 Mile* Eminem's mother is in her trailer watching the film *Imitation of Life* when Rabbit returns from a rap battle. This very film recounts a story of "passing," emphasizing that the discursive identity of the battler forces him to "pass" from the other side of the racial frontier, enforcing his social singularity.[44]

Eminem, poor demeaned white and "mercurial man,"[45] roams the streets thinking of himself as a black, "white-washed negro" as was said about Ishmael in *Moby-Dick*[46] identifying with rather than imitating his "others" and his black doubles, idols idealized by adolescents but always in a mocking way. He does not "act black," attempting to usurp an identity and social codes that the color of his skin does not allow. He never forgets that he is implacably white. He thus refuses to utter the word "nigger," widely used by other rappers.[47] Eminem's unique talent is to recreate a chain of signifiers in the tradition of African American folklore in order to deliver on top of his demanding tone a series of *topoi* of his condition that are evocative in terms of the denigrations themselves as well as representing those who always saw themselves as distanced "others" and guarding them from this social and cultural damnation.

The ambiguous mutually identified relationship that bonds the part-black white-trash character to the black "other" does not exactly correspond to the definition of genuine friendship. I would classify it as companionship (in French, a "*companion de route*" is one with whom one shares ideological and political views). There is a common undesired destiny between blacks and white-trash characters that goes further than spontaneous distrust, the romantic minstrel-like wish to be the other, or the fallacious negation of racial tensions.

Like the populist Tom Watson in his time, Eminem designates the white middle-class person as someone who condemns poor whites and blacks to the same social and cultural marginality. "Them" thus designates the guilty whites whose hands and words have forged the racism referenced by the African American poet Robert Hayden in "speech."[48]

The figure of the double, simultaneously black brother and mirror, is thus central to Eminem's dramatic identity. His best friend Proof, killed in March 2006 in Detroit, was the rapper's first black double. But it is with Dr. Dre that the concept of a pair came into being in terms of rhetoric. Marshall

Mathers and Dr. Dre (who produces much of Eminem's work) are both presented in a quite unique manner: if the poor white is the ill one, the fallen and the savage, then his black double is the practitioner, the wise and the middle class. There are numerous examples of the patient and the doctor (Dre), the psychotic and the therapist (e.g., "If I Get Locked Up Tonight").

Generally speaking, Dre is the moderator, the one who calms and tames the enraged poor white. It is he who attempts to calm Slim when he explodes on "Guilty Conscience." The relationship between the two men is characterized by the moral influence of the reasonable Dr. Dre, acceptable figure of the middle class (he is a "doctor"), over savage Eminem. Eminem is the white savage speaking and acting like poor white trash from the South; Dre the civilized one who calls for moderation and level headedness.

The urge to immerse oneself in the world of the "black other" is not new. We can identify the rapper with the hipsters of the Beat Generation, for example, specifically regarding the question of social identity. The Beats wanted to abandon their white skin and middle-class origins and swap them for black identity. But their "cultural capital" is irreducible and their voluntary degradation is contrary to the aspirations of the black community.[49] They therefore do not have the "common vocation" shared by the poor white trash and the black social climber.

This subtle hierarchy between the two men is expressed by Eminem's reverence of his mentor's environment and the gratitude he shows him. This pushes even the rapper to reveal the theme of the usurper, the white who, as Elvis was once accused, had unduly profited from black talent. He concedes that if he were black he wouldn't have sold nearly as many records,[50] and that like Elvis he's using black music for personal gain.[51]

Eminem's ambition is two-sided: to sing the "common vocation" of the "deromanticized" blacks and the white trash without denying the existence of the privilege that America has accorded to whites. The use of dialogue with a black partner enables this dialectic. It allows the exchange of racial masks in order to prove the equivalence between the black and the fallen white. In a duet with the black rapper Sticky Fingaz titled "If I Was White," Eminem asks what his black friend would be if he were white. Sticky Fingaz also has the chance to question the possible "tonality" of his white skin, clear as that of a member of high society or ambiguous like that of a "redneck." He is interrupted in the middle of his inquiry by a sarcastic and teasing Eminem, who knows what the conversion from black to white produces: Sticky Fingaz wonders whether he would be a redneck, a skinhead, a prep, or high class—Eminem answers for him: white trash. More than just a provocative quip, this phrase once more reveals the fundamental racial impurity of the "trash" figure who cannot be considered fully white as well as showing that Eminem himself knows that he is not really a member of the dominant race.

Eminem thus occupies a delicate racial position in the sense that he refuses to present himself as privileged; he is "trash," but he must recognize that the color of his skin has historically conferred a symbolic influence over those he considers his brothers. His absolute refusal to use the word "nigger" reflects this uneasiness. To utter this word as blacks do would be to reveal himself as racist since no one can forget that his skin is the same as that of the former persecutors. He thus does not say the "N-word," rather proclaiming himself "trash." In this way, he presents himself as a marginalized white who carries the weight of his visible membership to the dominant group while blurring the identifications by exiling himself from his race of origin. He is thus akin to one of the albinos who used to be put on display at county fairs: "a freak and a demon."[52]

A White Trash Voice?

Eminem, the trickster who acts as a double of the villain, certainly takes after both the white tall tale[53] extravagances and the imaginary "black" discursive.[54] His language reveals this hybrid identity. His predilection for pastiche, irony, derision, costume, and farcical undressing situates him in a black–American tradition, evoking vaudeville and more generally the African American "voice." This taste for "making fun" is even for the linguist Hermese E. Roberts one of the essential dimensions of "black speech." Eminem defines his musical and discursive mixing in these terms: " Talking black, brainwashed from rock and rap."[55]

In Eminem's works, the word "motherfucker" is a keyword. However, he turns the insult against himself. He publically and furiously insults his own mother, unheard of in any African American tradition but common enough to the white-trash identity. But his high color eloquence does not correspond in any way to poor whites' taste for silent rumination. He thus re-invents a "po' white speech." The question of the existence of a "poor white speech" is a difficult one. It is clear that Eminem uses "black speech" to tip the themes of the black claim of identity toward the expression of the white-trash conscience. This admixture is found in the language of southern whites, whether it be Erskine Caldwell or Faulkner using a mixed southern dialect or in the country music of the novelist Dorothy Allison. Mark Twain gave in his day a brilliant version of such a vernacular, particularly through his Tall Tale telling characters:

> Whoo-oop ! I'm the old original iron-jawed, brass-mounted, copper-bellied corpse maker from the wilds of Arkansaw!- Look at me! I'm the man they

call Sudden Death and General Desolation! Sired by a hurricane, dam'd by an earthquake, half brother of the cholera, nearly related to the small pox on the mother's side! Look at me![56]

But it is without a doubt Huck Finn's speech that corresponds most closely to the discursive mixing of Eminem's oeuvre. Although materially enriched by treasure, Huck is a poor white, subjected to the tyranny of a violent, racist, alcoholic father who even deliriously attempts one night to murder his son with a knife. The body of this father who incarnates the odious decline of whites, is in miserable shape, not only because, as a corpse, it floats on the river's surface but also since when Huck is confronted with the body he describes its skin as "not like another man's white, but a white to make a body sick, a white to make a body flesh crawl-a tree-toad-white, a fish belly white"[57]

Two "interracial" readings emphasizing the theme of the mask allow us to read the linked rhetoric between the white and the black in Huck Finn. Eric Lott highlights the influence "blackface" shows in Twain's works and particularly the moment in which Huck claims to know that in reality Jim is "white inside."[58] But the influence of the racial role-playing in Twain's work seems to go in a direction pertinent to our study. The other hypothesis claims that in effect Huck, the poor white, speaks a dialect directly influenced by "black speech," which would then make him Eminem's indirect ancestor. Shelley Fisher Fishkin, in his analysis *Was Huck Black? Mark Twain and African-American Voices*[59] suggests that Huck's verbal cadences, syntax, and dialectical diction as well as his role as an explorer make him a figure of the black "voice," for which Jimmy, Twain's young black friend of his youth, would be the model. She identifies the linguistic structure and language[60] register of the poor white as stemming from the speech of the poor blacks. Above all, she identifies Huck's African American "signifying" that is also found in the work of the Detroit rapper, marked by irreverent laughter.[61] She defines Huck as the "trickster" who must survive in a world dominated by whites. In this sense as well, Huck and Eminem mirror each other. Where the first shouts, "They're after us!" the second sings that he could be one of America's kids.[62] Poor whites and blacks are thus together, at the very least for a moment of common contestation of the world order.

Between asserting his existential unease and his impassioned social conscience, Eminem reveals his explicit racial hybridization. His "black speech" that is applied to social stereotypes that vilify the "bad poor person," and the integration of his brutal view of his circumstances together succeed in the articulation of the racializing of poor white trash. It is the monster that America does not want to see but can laugh at and claim to fear. Eminem often claims to be "brainwashed" like a degraded creature. A "generation

Frankenstein," born of modern racial "mixing," led by Eminem, frightens conservative America.

Conclusion

His pursuit of recognition reveals the weight of the social taboo in the United States that ignores class and favors a racial interpretation of society. If Eminem can be understood as "a walking spectacle" and if his personal theater is so extravagant, it is perhaps because it is necessary in order to reveal the class structure and subvert racial univocity. Like other authors who have succeeded financially but remain prisoners of their roots, Eminem is obsessed with his formative years that were racked by hunger to succeed and self-hatred. He still searches the streets of Detroit for the source of this anger that acted as his driving force. The "black other" serves his companion throughout this perpetual and inevitable distancing from and return to his roots. As an "underserving poor," a not-quite-white villain, he grasps the pain, frustration, anger, and self-doubt many blacks have felt. America's youth identifies with him. Eminem's whiteface is clearly intended as a self-parody: a divided self allows him to mock the white in him as the trickster used to poke fun at the white man; he performs a work of racial self-recognition and self-consciousness as though the doubtful color of his skin stands paradoxically as a token of legitimacy, enabling him to "accompany" blacks in their cultural voicing.

Far from unrestrained romanticism, the poor white invents in this case a new relationship with the double—a relationship, as I have attempted to show in this analysis, marked by the commonalities of destiny and amity: Eminem doesn't make black or white music, he makes fight music.[63]

Chapter Notes

1. Eric King Watts writes, "The Detroit native is so fixated on his image that he has manufactured a handful of personae, including a 'mythicized version' of Marshall Mathers, subjecting each to a spectacular performance for public derision and adulation," in "Border Patrolling and Passing in Eminem's *8 Mile*" in *Critical Studies in Media Communication* 22.3 (August 2005): 187.

2. Annalee Newitz and Matt Wray, *White Trash, Race and Class in America* (New York: Routledge, 1996).

3. Zora Neale Hurston, *Mules and Men* (New York: Harper Perennial, 1990), 82.

4. Annalee Newitz and Matt Wray, *White Trash, Race and Class in America* (New York: Routledge, 1996). http://www.amazon.fr/dp/0415916925/ref=rdr_ext_tmb

5. Richard Middleton, *Voicing the Popular: On the Subjects of Popular Music* (New York: Routledge, 2006), 37.

6. In "Border Patrolling and Passing in Eminem's *8 Mile*" Eric King Watts writes,

"The complex relationship between race and class allows white folks to be represented as 'discursively black' and potentially white.... Following the logic, if characterized as poor white trash, whiteness is darkened; it can be whitened by characterizing as heroic its passing over his race/class boundary."

7. Analyzing the outcome of the Reconstruction, Du Bois underscores the "political success of the doctrine of racial separation, which overthrew Reconstruction by uniting the planter and the poor white.... It must be remembered, that the white group of laborers, while they received a low wage, were compensated in part by a sort of public and psychological wage," *Black Reconstruction in America 1860–1880* (New York: Atheneum, 1992), 700.

8. "V" signifies *verfremsdungeffekt* and is generally used to qualify the dramatic conventions corresponding to the theater of Berthold Brecht.

9. It hardly makes sense to have lyrics analyzed without a single reference to the lyrics themselves. Please see the third verse in "Lose Yourself." Eminem's lyrics are freely available and easily accessible online.

10. Quoted in Anthony Bozza, *Whatever You Say I Am: The Life and Times of Eminem* (New York: Crown, 2003), 119.

11. As a figure of the "Okie" fleeing the misery of the West by train for the promised success in the cities, Guthrie addressed a popular and industrial population, condemning worker exploitation and the brutal, racist society.

12. Paul Clemens, Made in Detroit: A South of 8 Mile Memoir (New York: Doubleday, 2005), 14, my emphasis.

13. Recounting his childhood in the '80s, he explains that the white children of his elementary school dressed like Indians, with ponchos and war paint, in order to signal their "racial existence."

14. Bozza specifies: "Of the 76 percent in the city, nearly half of those African American are under the age of eighteen, living in impoverished homes, compared to just 10 percent of kids in the same straits in the suburbs. The degree of racial and economic division is as close as a major American city gets to the kind of class imbalance found in Third World countries," 213.

15. Jackson Katts, "Advertising and the Construction of Violent White Masculinity: From BMWs to Bud Light," in Gail Dines & Jean M. Humez, eds., *Gender, Race, and Class in Media: A Critical Reader* (Thousand Oaks, CA: Sage, 2003).

16. "Who Knew," The Marshall Mathers LP.

17. "If I Had ...," *The Slim Shady LP.*

18. John Hartigan, Jr., *Odd Tribes: Toward a Cultural Analysis of White People* (Durham, NC: Duke University Press, 2005), 229.

19. "Many poor workers invested their surplus-valued whiteness into a fund of psychic protection against the perverse, impure meaning of whiteness. They drew from their value-added whiteness to not only boost their self-esteem but to assert their relative racial superiority by means oh what may be termed a negative inculpability: poor whites derived pleasure and some cultural benefit by not being the nigger." Michael Eric Dyson, "Giving Whiteness a Black Eye: Excavating White Identities, Ideologies and Institutions," *Open Mike: Reflections on Philosophy, Race, Sex, Culture and Religion* (New York: Basic Civitas, 2003), 105.

20. Anthony Bozza, Whatever You Say I Am: The Life and Times of Eminem (New York: Three Rivers, 2004).

21. Michael Novak, The Rise of the Unmeltable Ethnics: Politics and Culture in the Seventies (New York: Macmillan, 1975).

22. Bozza, 31.

23. "Just as black anger often proved counterproductive, so have these white resentments distracted attention from the real culprits of the middle class squeeze ..." in Barack Obama, "A More Perfect Union," March 18, 2008.

24. "The Real Slim Shady," *The Marshall Mathers LP.*

25. Richard Goldstein, music critic of *Village Voice* adds: "When Eminem says he is indifferent to women and hates them (Homosexuals, SIC), and ejects any sign of femininity from his personality and projects everything he hates about himself about women, that is a macho value, which makes him an alpha male," cited in Bozza, 247.

26. Toni Morrison, "Talk of the Town: Comment," *The New Yorker*, October 5, 1998.

27. John Shelton Reed, 1001 Things Everyone Should Know About the South (New York: Doublday, 1996).

28. Dyson writes: "Interestingly enough, Bill Clinton figures as a key subject and subtext of such conversations. For many, Clinton is our first nation's "Bubba," our country Trailer trash executive, our nation's Poor White President. It tells on our bigoted cultural beliefs and social prejudices that Clinton ... an Oxford University and Yale University Law School Graduate and president of the U.S.—could be construed as a poor white trash, cracker citizen. The study of whiteness prods us to examine the means by which a highly intelligent man and gifted politician is transmuted into "Bubba" for the purpose of intraethnic demonization," *Open Mike*, 111.

29. "Marshall Mathers," *The Marshall Mathers LP.*

30. "Role Model," The Slim Shady LP.

31. Eric King Watts, "Border Patrolling and Passing in Eminem's *8 Mile*," 193.

32. Nicole Hahn Rafter, *White Trash: The Eugenic Family Studies, 1877–1919* (Boston: Northeastern University Press, 1988).

33. "Criminal," The Marshall Mathers LP.

34. Anna Stubblefield, "'Beyond the Pale': Tainted Whiteness, Cognitive Disability, and Eugenic Sterilization," *Hypatia*, Vol. 22, No. 2 (Spring 2007): 162–181.

35. Clemens, *Made in Detroit*, 181.

36. William E. Studwell, *The Americana Song Reader* (New York: Haworth Press, Inc, 1997), 53.

37. Ibid., 346.

38. Roebuck and Hickson claim: "Being white is not sufficient for being somebody, but it is a necessary first attribute to such a status. Fearful, insecure, narrow-minded, dependant, hostile, rigid, and envious, the redneck adopts the racial dimension as a master identity in his self-concept, that is, he is a white man. In line with the Southern emphasis on blood ("good seed," "bad seed," "weak seed," "good stock") the redneck perceives the cultural differences between himself and blacks (in music, dancing preferences, speech patterns, body language, body tonus, style of walking, sexual and marital patterns, and alleged black indifference to achievement goals) as biologically based." Julian B. Roebuck & Mark Hickson, *The Southern Redneck: A Phenomenological Class Study* (New York: Praeger, 1982), 90.

39. Geneva Smitherman, *Talkin and Testifyin: The Language of Black America* (Detroit: Wayne State University Press, 1986), 298.

40. "The word 'whigger,' a contraction of 'white nigger' probably originated in the early 1970s in urban African American speech; it resembles other ironic black compounds- like witch (white bitch) and whitianity (white christianity)—that whittle down white to a prefix," Gary Taylor, *Buying Whiteness: Race, Culture, and Identity from Columbus to Hip-Hop* (New York: Palgrave Macmillan, 2004), 342.

41. "The Way I Am," The Marshall Mathers LP.

42. Crispin Sartwell, *Act Like You Know: African-American Autobiography and White Identity* (Chicago: University of Chicago Press, 1998), 149.

43. Vanilla Ice invented a hoodlum childhood for himself. Perceived as an impostor, he nonetheless appealed to a white audience seduced by his impersonation of the "cool white guy." See Harris Daniel "Coolness: The Psychology of Coolness," *American Scholar* September 22, 1999.

44. "White passing narratives center the individual passer as social maverick" Gayle Wald, *Crossing the Line: Racial Passing in Twentieth Century U.S. Literature and Culture* (Durham, NC: Duke University Press, 2000),196.

45. Watts, 196.

46. Non only is Ishmael being called a whitewashed Negro but Melville attempts, through Queekeg and Ishmael's friendship, to deconstruct the very notion of race. "Posing a mixed race marriage between himself and Queekeg, Ishmael upsets epidermal expectations immediately with the claim that a white man is not anything more dignified than a white washed Negro." Bridget T. Heneghan, *Whitewashing America: Material Culture and Race in the Antebellum Imagination* (Jackson: University of Mississippi Press, 2003), 145.

47. Randall Kennedy emphasizes the significance of this forbidden discourse in the definition of the rapper's distance regarding identity and race: "Eminem has assumed many of the distinctive mannerisms of his black rap colleagues, making himself into a 'brother' in many ways—in his music, his diction, his gait, his clothes, his associations. He refuses to say, however, any version of a word that his black hip-hop colleagues employ constantly as a matter of course; the nonchalance with which he tosses around epithets such as bitch and faggot does not extend to nigger. 'That word,' he insists, 'is not even in my vocabulary.'" Randall Kennedy, *Nigger: The Strange Career of a Troublesome Word* (New York: Pantheon, 2002), 40–41.

48. Robert Hayden, "Speech," *Heart-Shape in the Dust* (Detroit Falcon, 1940).

49. Gary T. Marx makes this analysis: "Both are initially identified with the values they reject- Negroes as a result of their skin color and frequently lower-class background and Beats as a result of their skin color rand middle class background. In their attempt to avoid identification with their presumed past, both may go out of their way to show that they are in fact opposite. Negroes will show how middle class they are and Beats what white Negroes they are. What Negroes embrace wholeheartedly beats reject just as furiously. The hipster behavior patterns which Beats embrace and go out of their way to be identified with are the very behavior patterns that middle class Negroes strongly reject. They have switched drummers and in so doing both may be hearing the beat not quite right, resulting the misconception by Beats of what it really means to be Negro." Gary T. Marx, "The White Negro and the Negro White," *Phylon*, Summer 1967, vol. 28, no. 2; cited on mit.edu.

50. "White America," *The Eminem Show*.

51. "Without Me," The Eminem Show.

52. Charles D. Martin, *The White African American Body: A Cultural and Literary Exploration* (New Brunswick, NJ: Rutgers University Press, 2002), 4.

53. Davy Crockett struts about in these terms in his 1834 autobiography: "I'm that same Davy Crockett, fresh from the backwoods, half horse, half alligator, a little touched with the snapping turtle; can wade the Mississippi, leap the Ohio, ride a streak of lightning, slip without a scratch down a honey locust, can whip my weight in wildcats." "Tall Tale," *Columbia Encyclopedia* 2004, Encyclopedia.com.

54. Black is written here between quotation marks because it is used in the contexts of African American folklore as well as the racial stereotypes of white society.

55. "Sing for the Moment," *The Eminem Show*.

56. Mark Twain, Life on the Mississippi River.

57. Mark Twain, Thomas Cooley, ed., *The Adventures of Huckleberry Finn* (New York, London: Norton Critical Edition, 1999), 31.

58. "Despite Twain's self-consciousness, though, the evidence suggest we take Huck's admiring remark about Jim in chapter 40 ... that he 'knowed' Jim was 'white inside'—as the crowning statement on the centrality of blackface's contradictions to Twain's imagination. The remark is a perfect specimen of the imperial psychological orientation Homi Bhabha calls 'ambivalence' ... Twain ... returned over and over to the actual practice and literary trope of blackface, which hedges by imagining the Other as black only in exterior, still white inside." Eric Lott, "Mr Clemens and Jim Crow: Twain, Race, and Blackface," in *The Cambridge Companion to Mark Twain*, Forrest G. Robinson, ed., (Cambridge: Cambridge University Press, 1995).

59. Fisher Fishkin, *Was Huck Black? Mark Twain and African-American Voices* (New York: Oxford University Press, 1993).

60. She particularly emphasizes the notion of "colloquial style."

61. Fisher Fisckin stresses that "The 'text' on which Twain is signifying is the subtext of these character remarks: it is the familiar assumption that their kind alone are superior beings with special claims to empathy and privilege as embodiment of 'civilization.' Twain acidic treatment of bigoted white folks in Huckleberry Finn may well reflect some of his early exposure to African American satirical social critic, to the practice Lawrence Levine calls 'laughing at the man.'" Fisckin, 62–64.

62. "White America," *The Eminem Show*.

63. "Who Knew," The Marshall Mathers LP.

Appendix.
He Is Whatever We Say He Is:
On Eminem, Fame and
Hip-Hop Aesthetics

KYLE "GUANTE" TRAN MYHRE

Cast:
- Hater Jones, 21, hater
- Professor Uplift, 56, Black Studies professor
- Colin Pennyworth, 27, hipster music journalist
- Stanley Johnson, 19, Eminem fan
- Eddie Kay, 22, hip-hop head

Scene:
Cafeteria at a community college—late afternoon, nearly all of the lunch traffic has passed; Professor Uplift and Colin Pennyworth walk by, glancing over to a lunch table at a freestyle cypher in progress.

Hater Jones: (*beatboxing*)

Eddie Kay: (*rapping, in progress*) ... you know the spit stay vicious, the kid is, flippin' by the minute / g'd up like G-Dep spittin' "let's get it."

Stanley Johnson: (*rapping*) Yeah, let's get it, you better call the medics / I leave your abdomen sliced open with intestines / fallin' out, callin' out all these fake lames / usin' your appendix as a hand grenade ... (*sees Uplift and Pennyworth and stops*) You wanna join the cypher?

Colin Pennyworth: (*laughs*) No, no. I was just interviewing the professor here for an article I'm writing about hip hop. He said he sees you three in here almost every day and thinks you might be good interview subjects too.

191

Eddie Kay: Oh yeah? What's the article about?

Colin Pennyworth: It's mostly about the record industry, and how people aren't really buying CDs anymore. The timely element is that it'll be published right around the time Eminem's new album drops, and I'm kind of using that as a lens through which we can—

Hater Jones: (*loudly interrupting*) Ayo, does the universe really need another article about Eminem?

Professor Uplift: (*chuckles*)

Colin Pennyworth: Why do you say that?

Stanley Johnson: Because he's a *hater*, that's why.

Hater Jones: Naw, naw. I'm just the only one left who can see that the emperor ain't got no clothes on. I just see through the shtick. I'm not gonna say he's not talented, but I *am* gonna say he started out as overrated and devolved into audio vomit faster than a crappy Yelawolf double-time verse; he's been coasting ever since "Lose Yourself" dropped. Now he's all weird voices and melodramatic pop bullshit, and I just cannot fathom why people keep buying his records and writing articles about him.

Stanley Johnson: (*rolls eyes*) Maybe it's because he's the best songwriter in hip hop? Maybe it's because he writes songs that show his actual emotions and isn't just talking about bitches and cars and money? Maybe it's because he's a flat-out better rapper than anyone else ever? Maybe it's because the level of thought he puts into—

Professor Uplift: Or maybe it's because he's white? Let's not ignore the elephant in the room here.

Stanley Johnson: So why isn't Cage world famous? Or Eyedea? Or Asher Roth? Race has nothing to do with it.

Eddie Kay: Whoa there, fam. Of course race has something to do with it. But in his defense, you also can't deny Em's pure technical ability. I mean, artists like Pharaohe Monch and Tech N9ne and them have been doing microphone acrobatics for years, but there's not really anyone out there who sounds like Em, who makes it look so effortless. Even on his later stuff, which I agree has its problems, he's out-rhyming the devil in there, just mad syllable chains and mind-blowing flow patterns and all that.

Professor Uplift: But you said it yourself—other artists, black artists, have been doing what he does for years. He jumps in with his own amateur take on something someone else built and is propped up as the messiah. He sells a whitewashed version of black culture to white children, and in the process becomes the most celebrated and successful hip-hop artist in history. The Elvis comparison may be an easy one, but it's only easy because it's so accurate.

Hater Jones: Exactly. Eminem makes music for white trash pre-teens who think fart jokes are hilarious and drugs are edgy. It's some lowest-common-denominator shit, and that will always make you famous in America.

Stanley Johnson: (*scoffs*) Did either of you ever even listen to "Stan," or "Cleanin' Out My Closet," or "Hailie's Song," or "Love the Way You Lie," or—

Hater Jones (*interrupting*): Oh you mean the song where he got Rihanna to sing a hook about refusing to leave an abusive relationship? Yeah, that's deep, man.

Stanley Johnson: It *is* deep. The song is about breaking the cycle, about how hard it is to—

Hater Jones: He's just chasing clicks, homie. Trying to remain relevant because everybody knows his skills just ain't there no more. Maybe that's why he SHOUTS all his LYRICS now—he's getting desperate, on some "I'M NOT AFRAID"—

Eddie Kay: (*laughing*) What about you, Mr. Music Writer? What do you think about Eminem?

Colin Pennyworth: I don't know. I guess for me, it's about angles. You can always find something to say about him. Yeah, you can write about the novelty of a white rapper, but you can also write about the Dr. Dre cosign, or the shockingly offensive lyrics, or the untouchable skillset, or all the high-profile beefs. For a music writer, he's really the gift that keeps on giving.

Eddie Kay: And that's the problem for me. Like I said, I like Em; I think he has crazy talent. But who out there is actually writing about talent? Y'all pick up some narrative or angle and run with it, but no one seems to care about the actual music any more.

Hater Jones: Exactly. It's funny that Em beefed with Canibus, because if Eminem were black, he'd *be* Canibus. Another technically proficient weirdo underground rapper. "But he's white, and Dr. Dre likes him, so here's your GOAT," says the media.

Professor Uplift: Here's your goat?

Eddie Kay: Greatest of All Time. And for the record, I think he's in the conversation, extracurriculars aside. Just on pure skills alone. Top ten at least, maybe cracking the top five—

Stanley Johnson: Man, he *is* the conversation. Who else is even on that same plane of existence? You can really name five MCs better than Em?

(*all at once*):

Eddie Kay: Rakim, Jay, Big L, Big Pun, Nas.

Hater Jones: Jay, Biggie, Pac, KRS, Andre from Outkast.

Professor Uplift: Chuck D, Rakim, Tupac, KRS-One, Nas.

Stanley Johnson: You're all crazy. Ain't none of them seeing Em, bar for bar.

Colin Pennyworth: As someone who isn't as well versed in rap, I'm inclined to agree. Just to my ears, he's doing something that's wildly different. Listening to some of these old-school guys these days is like watching a black-and-white TV after visiting the IMAX theater.

Professor Uplift: But there it is. "As someone who isn't as well-versed in rap." You're Mathers's target audience. He appropriates black culture, performs his rhymes without the polyrhythmic "swing" of his more culturally attuned peers, subverts and ridicules black masculinity, and all but spits on hip hop's history as a tool of uplift for black and brown peoples, all while—

Eddie Kay: Hey, hey now. A tool of uplift? You ever actually listen to the lyrics to "Rapper's Delight?" Or any old-school shit beyond "The Message" and "The Breaks?" My dad is from NY and he has a box full of tapes from that era; I've listened to them all. Rap used to be about having fun and showing off your skills. Sure, the existence of the art itself may have been implicitly political and may have served as a tool of uplift, but I think it's a misrepresentation of history to imply that this was all some conscious master plan. In that sense, I think Em is paying homage to the culture's origins, even if I don't agree with his sexism or homophobia or shock-for-shock's-sake lyrics, he's killing it with the flows. He's showcasing his talent. He's having fun making words rhyme, and I respect that.

Hater Jones: But is that enough? I mean, it rips me up inside to admit this, but yeah, the kid can spit. But so can Myka 9. So can Pharaohe. So can Gift of Gab. So can a million other MCs none of us have ever heard of. Em may have talent, but he's never been famous because of his talent, let's be honest.

Colin Pennyworth: So why is he so famous?

Hater Jones: Because people like you keep shoving him down our throats instead of writing about any of the million other talented MCs in this country.

Colin Pennyworth: (*taken aback*) … but, I mean, I'm just giving our readers what they want. He's famous because people like him—that's what talent is, right? Making music that people like? It's not like we've picked some nerdy underdog white backpacker super-scientifical MC to get everyone to jump on *his* bandwagon. It's not my fault he's white, and even my black friends think….

Eddie Kay: (*interrupting*) Okay, okay, we get it, relax. Let me answer your question another way. Let's think back to when the *Slim Shady LP* dropped. It was 1999, post–Telecommunications Act, when mainstream hip hop was at its most hedonistically blinged-out and capitalistic and underground hip hop was at its most grimy and challenging. You got Nelly, Ja Rule, DMX, and Jay-Z on one side, and then you got the Roots, Mos Def, Company Flow, and dead prez on the other. And then you turn on the TV and it's the video for "My Name Is." And this shit just didn't make any sense. It didn't really belong anywhere. This wasn't just a white guy rapping. It wasn't just a white guy rapping well. It wasn't just a white guy rapping well with Dr. Dre in his video. That song was *weird*. To this day, "My Name Is" is a weird-ass song that doesn't sound like anything else out there. It got play on alternative rock stations—

Professor Uplift: (*coughing*) WHITENESS!

Eddie Kay: Yeah, you're right, but it's not *just* about whiteness. In the same way that it's not *just* about talent. Either of those things may be the main ingredient in a given context, but you can't make chili with nothing but beans. That song—and that album—blew up because of its novelty. And I mean novelty not like a gimmick, like "look at this whiteboy with the funny voice rapping about crazy shit," but as in something novel, something new and different and, for a lot of people, refreshing. And yeah, he can spit too, which doesn't hurt.

Hater Jones: It just doesn't seem fair to me that he gets so much attention for being quote-unquote "novel." Like I said, lots of rappers are talented. And lots of rappers are novel. These days, lots of rappers are white. Maybe it's because he's all three, I don't know; right place at the right time with the right skin tone kind of thing. It's still some bullshit. I get that he has some talent, but how people can just look right past his godawful beat selection, laughably wack singing hooks, emo-ass lyrics, tough-guy posturing, and all that misogyny and homophobia.

Professor Uplift: You know, I hate to be the old man saying the same thing over and over, but that's textbook white privilege. In this culture, white celebrities are readily forgiven for all but the worst offenses. We look the other way. A white athlete, musician, actor or politician can do everything wrong and still succeed. The world is set up for them to succeed. Mathers may be talented, I don't know. I don't think he is at all. But like Mr. Jones pointed out—that talent has its limits, yet public praise for it seemingly does not.

Stanley Johnson: *But he's the best rapper ever!* That's basically an objective *fact!*

Eddie Kay: (*laughing*) Objective? How is that an objective fact?

Stanley Johnson: Look. It's math. You can break down any MC into some combination of flows, content, songwriting, voice, and relevance. You guys do it all the time. It's why Boots Riley is objectively better than Waka Flocka. Waka may be more relevant, but loses out in all the other categories.

Hater Jones: I mean, voice would be a tossup.

Stanley Johnson: Sure, whatever. But when you look at Eminem, he gets a ten out of ten in all five categories. He's an omega-level MC. The only one, too. You just can't argue with that.

Professor Uplift: Dear boy, I think I could argue with that. Your categories themselves are subjective, and furthermore, it seems to me that one category missing from your framework is cultural foundation. Is it not true that artists, especially artists representing—indeed embodying—the white supremacist-capitalist-hetero-patriarchy, should be held accountable to the culture from which they purloin their very livelihoods?

Stanley Johnson: (*thinks for a moment*) You just don't like him because he's white! You teach a class on hip hop and you don't even listen to any hip hop after 1995!

Professor Uplift: And you only like him because he is white! You weren't even born in 1995 and know nothing about the culture's history!

Hater Jones: (*to Pennyworth*) See what it's like to try to have a critical conversation about this dude?

Eddie Kay: (*laughs*) And that's key, y'all. I feel like most people aren't interesting in having any kind of critical conversation. It's either Em is the GOAT and beyond reproach or Em is an overrated culture vulture. But hip hop has never been that simple. He's both. He's neither. On some Zen shit, you have to hold both realities in your mind at the same time. If you want to really talk about Eminem—or hip hop in general for that matter—you have to grapple with complexities, you have to engage in the kind of dialogue that maybe doesn't fit into a one-line thesis statement, or a 300-word album review, or a punch line. Instead of asking pointless, abstract questions like "Do white people belong in hip hop?" let's ask "What is the responsibility of white people in hip hop to the culture?" Instead of asking "Is Eminem the best ever?" let's have more conversations about hip-hop aesthetics and what makes someone "good" or "bad." Instead of writing another pretentious-ass sociology paper with a long-ass title bifurcated by a colon, let's try to, I don't know, actually listen to the music, go to some local rap shows, and develop a real relationship with the culture. In the end, I don't even care about Eminem; but if he can be a gateway for people to start to really understand hip hop as the vibrant, growing, beautiful culture that it is, let's have that conversation. Let's keep it moving.

Colin Pennyworth: … Right. Sooooo, back to my article, what do you guys think about Macklemore?

Hater Jones, Stanley Johnson, Eddie Kay: (*simultaneously*) We gotta get to class.

About the Contributors

Aaron **Apps** holds an MFA in poetry from the University of Minnesota and is pursuing a PhD in English literature at Brown University. His first book of poetry, *Compos(t) Mentis,* was published by Blazevox in 2012. His work has appeared or is forthcoming in *LIT, Denver Quarterly, Verse, Los Angeles Review, Pleiades, Caliban, PANK, Caketrain, Sleepingfish, Spork*, and elsewhere. He is coediting *An Anthology of Posthuman Poetry* with Feng Sun Chen.

Julius **Bailey** is an associate professor at Wittenberg University in the Department of Philosophy. He is a philosopher, cultural critic, social theorist, and diversity lecturer, whose interests range from Russian literature to hip-hop culture. His publications include *Jay-Z: Essays on Hip Hop's Philosopher King* (McFarland, 2011); *Imani: Amplifying Whispers from the Cave: A Vision of Community in the 21st Century* (University of Illinois, 1998) and many articles on hip-hop pedagogy and social justice.

Steve **Bramucci** writes for *Huffington Post, Outside, Orange County Register Magazine,* and various other print and online outlets. His work has been collected in humor and travel anthologies. He tweets about travel, food, and hip hop from the handle @stevebram.

Martin **Connor,** a graduate of Duke University with a music degree of high distinction, has contributed to college courses, research papers, and musicological conferences and has composed musical works that have had multiple public performances. He is working on a book, *Check Out My Melody: How to Listen to Rap Music,* chapters of which can be read at *www.RapAnalysis.com.* He lives in Philadelphia.

Darin **Flynn** is an assistant professor of linguistics at the University of Calgary. His research and teaching cover phonology, sociolinguistics, and endangered language documentation and revitalization. His previous work in hip-hop linguistics includes "Negation in African American Vernacular English," in Yoko Iyeiri, ed., *Aspects of English Negation* (John Benjamins, 2005).

Ben **Hoerster** graduated from New York University with a Master's in Social Work and is a child and family therapist in Portland, Oregon. His Twitter handle is @BennerH.

Sylvie **Laurent** is a cultural historian and W.E.B. Du Bois fellow at Harvard University. She teaches American civilization and African American studies at Sciences-Po in Paris and has published two books, the latest being *Poor White Trash: The Unbearable Poverty of the American White* (Presses de La Sorbonne, 2011).

David J. **Leonard** is an associate professor and chair in the Department of Critical Culture, Gender and Race Studies at Washington State University, Pullman. He is the author of *After Artest: Race and the Assault on Blackness* (SUNY Press, 2012) and *Screens Fade to Black: Contemporary African American Cinema* (Praeger, 2006) and the coeditor of *Commodified and Criminalized: New Racism and African Americans in Contemporary Sports* (Rowman and Littlefield, 2011).

Kyle "Guante" Tran **Myhre** is a rapper, two-time National Poetry Slam champion, activist, and educator based in Minneapolis, Minnesota. See www.guante.info for more of his writing, music, and poetry.

E Martin **Nolan** is a poet and nonfiction writer. He received an MA in creative writing from the University of Toronto and is a poetry and blog editor at the *Puritan Magazine*, where he also publishes interviews and reviews. His essays and poems have appeared in the *Detroit Free Press, The Toronto Review of Books, The Toronto Quarterly,* and *Contemporary Verse 2.* He teaches at the University of Toronto.

Scott F. **Parker** is the author of *Running After Prefontaine: A Memoir* (Inside the Curtain Press, 2011) and the poetry collection *Revisited: Notes on Bob Dylan* (North Star Press, 2012). He is the editor of *Conversations with Ken Kesey* (University Press of Mississippi, 2014) and coeditor of *Coffee—Philosophy for Everyone: Grounds for Debate* (with Michael W. Austin, Wiley-Blackwell, 2011).

Gilbert B. **Rodman** is an associate professor of communication studies at the University of Minnesota. He is the author of *Elvis After Elvis* (Routledge, 1996), coeditor of *Race and Cyberspace* (Routledge, 2000), and editor of *The Race and Media Reader* (Routledge, 2013). He is also the founder and manager of CULTSTUD-L (an international listserv devoted to cultural studies) and the chair of the Association for Cultural Studies.

Miles **White** is the author of *From Jim Crow to Jay Z: Race, Rap and the Performance of Masculinity* (University of Illinois Press, 2011). He lives in Central Europe where he is working on a literary novel about the drug wars.

Index

201